ISRAEL LAND

Elizabeth Hirsh Naftali

PublishAmerica
Baltimore

Scripture taken from the Holy Bible, King James Version.

Hardcover 978-1-4512-0466-7
Softcover 978-1-4512-0480-3
PUBLISHED BY PUBLISHAMERICA, LLLP
www.publishamerica.com
Baltimore

Printed in the United States of America

I am blessed to be part of a long line of strong, independent minded women who have helped to shape my life and support my passions; my great-grandmother Helen Leder, my grandmother Natalie Friedman, my mother Anita Hirsh, my mother-in-law Marcelle Breen and my sisters Jennifer Hirsh and Pam Hirsh.

I am thankful everyday for my dear friends all over the world whose love and support many times is the wind beneath my wings. A special debt of gratitude to my friends Kay Sides, Diane Levin, Vicky Stern and Lori Marshall who have encouraged me while writing this book.

I give endless thanks to my special friend and mentor Chuck Haas, whose patience and guidance were and are monumental and whose friendship, I treasure.

To my husband Yehuda and our children Noa, Aaron, Eden, Kobe and Talya — who never let a day pass without reminding me of what is most important in my life.

"I'm going to Disneyland" was an advertising slogan I fondly remember from years ago. Celebratory football players from the NFL's championship team were asked by an unseen reporter, "You've just won the Super Bowl—what are you going to do now?" and each player with a huge smile would look out into TV Land and with great excitement proclaim, "I'm going to Disneyland!" I was covetous that not only did they win the championship, but also they were off to Disneyland, the most beloved place to visit in my youth. This phrase and the exhilaration of that winning moment run through my mind as I prepare to travel across the world with my husband and four children for one year to one of my favorite magical lands where unknown adventures await me. As I embark on the ride of a lifetime, I say to myself excitedly, "I'm going to Israel Land!"

* * *

First I need to back up and tell you a little about me. I am the mother of four children, two girls and two boys. I have two teenagers, who think I am downright archaic and two little ones, who adore me and think I am rather smart—this offers great balance in my life. We live in Los Angeles, California and my husband, Yehuda works across the world where he builds shopping centers and sells bottled spring water, two essential life sustaining commodities for the Jews who live in the desert of the Middle East or actually anywhere in the world. Yehuda for years has been making the long commute from Los Angeles to Tel Aviv for his work, but this

9

year we decided to take our four children away from their comfortable lives in the City of Angels and move to Israel to share a far away adventure.

It was a rather impetuous decision to make this move, but as the months passed, I clearly saw the potential goals for my family other than simply supporting my husband's work. It is a tremendous job to move four children, close down a house, open a new house and start all over again especially in the middle of a life that is working just fine. One thing that keeps me motivated is the belief that we will all, especially the children, enjoy and benefit from this experience. As I prepared for our departure I began to compile a list of my goals for the year; personally to slow down, breathe and smell the roses; to have time to read and write; to offer my children interesting and challenging adventures and move away from materialism and many negative L.A.isms; to bring my children to live in a neighborhood where it is safe to walk down the street in the dark at night; for all of us to bond with our Israeli family; for Yehuda to focus on his work; and for Yehuda and me to spend quality time with our four children. As I consider my goals, I am aware that they will transform as we all change through the year, but I will use them as my guides as I weather the journey.

I spent the month leading up to our departure watching the Second Lebanon War on CNN with the rest of the world as the Israelis battled Hezbollah in Lebanon, hoping for the fighting to end before too many lives were lost and before the destruction and despair of war became insurmountable. Selfishly I watched the news coverage of the Second Lebanon War knowing full well that to make a move with four children while Katyusha Rockets fell not even fifty miles away from our rental house would have been crazy. As it was, concerned and desperate family and friends in Los Angeles were calling around the clock as I prepared and packed; "Why are you moving to Israel?"

"Are you crazy?"

"Aren't you scared?"

"Don't be stupid!"

"It's too dangerous—don't go."

Finally a hudna (ceasefire) between Israel and Hezbollah was declared for Monday, August 14th 2006. Sadly, I had to leave the blue eyed, silver haired swashbuckler CNN reporter Anderson Cooper, on whom I had developed quite a crush and dependency on over the last month. Anderson and I had spent many hours examining and exploring the Israeli's and the Hezbollah's positions, their artillery, their territories and their civilian populations. We analyzed what this war would mean for Lebanon, Israel, the region and the world. I already missed Anderson who would not be with me 'twenty-four seven' to pick up the pieces in the Holy Land. Then as we were about to depart for the year, Scotland Yard announced a terrorist plot in London intending to bring down a multitude of planes in mid air to and from the United States with liquid explosives. We were scheduled to be on one of these flights to Israel via Heathrow Airport. This caused another delay in our plans.

Ha At-hala (The Beginning)

Just after midnight, the jumbo EL AL plane with the blue Star of David proudly displayed on its tail gently touches down at Ben Gurion Airport. The plane erupts with passenger's howls and whistles accompanied by the sound of excited, clapping hands. Quietly, I let out a deep breath that has lain hidden in my nervous chest for six long months now. As the El Al plane slowly taxis to the terminal, I observe all four of my children silently looking out the plane's windows dazed and relieved that we have passed a long twenty-four hour travel with ease and officially commence our year abroad in Israel. Within seconds of touching the tarmac, I hear seat belt buckles snapping open and cell phones ringing in a symphony of sounds—the welcoming chaotic resonance of Eretz Israel. The flight supervisor unsuccessfully tells the passengers at least five times over the sound system to "remain seated with your seatbelts fastened until we have come to a complete stop." Once the doors open, a small group of Jews step off the airplane, kneel down and kiss the ground, while the other three hundred passengers hurry off the plane laden with large duty-free bags full of chocolates, alcohol and cigarettes.

At Passport Control we meet a young, pretty Israeli woman with pale skin, large green eyes and a small gold earring on the side of her nose. She looks carefully at our stack of dark blue American passports with Yehuda's brown Israeli passport on top and asks the obvious question, "Why don't your children have Israeli Passports?"

"They are Americans," I answer.

"But their father is an Israeli," she responds. She is correct and it is important for Israelis to be correct, but this still does not change the fact that the children only have American passports. Slowly and methodically she checks each passport. She looks up with her misty green eyes and stares at Kobe with a serious expression as if at four years old, my youngest son might be a security risk or perhaps an imposter. I know that this is the ritual for all who enter this country and a clear reminder that patience will be required over the next year in the Holy Land.

We push four carts piled high with our bags into the enormous brightly lit visitor's hall, where security guards hold back the large noisy crowds of people waiting to welcome their loved ones home from abroad. The arrival ceremony of Jews to Eretz Israel is a very profound and vital part of the country's culture. This country would not exist if people like us did not arrive over the years for a visit or to make A-li-yah (move to Israel). On the other hand, Israelis joke that even if an Israeli travels on a forty-five minute flight to Cyprus for a weekend of fun and sun, when he returns all of his friends and family gather in the visitor's hall to welcome him home.

Outside the cool air-conditioned terminal, we are smacked with the incredibly hot and humid midnight air mixed with the thick smell of cigarette smoke from cabbies and Israelis who light up the moment they leave the 'smoke free' terminal. Cars honk, people with piles of luggage are everywhere, groups of tourists wait for buses and a black hat religious couple passes with their identically dressed flock of children. A policeman unsuccessfully tries to move cars forward and amidst it all the boisterous sounds of the Hebrew language soar through the warm late night air.

We arrive at our new house to the warm embraces of Saba (Grandpa) Shabtai and Safta (Grandma) Marcelle. Safta has prepared a bountiful meal for her American grandchildren highlighted by three different forms of chicken; tender baked chicken with potatoes, flavorful brown rice with chicken and le-ve-vote (fried chicken patties). Safta appears convinced that I have not fed her grandchildren or Yehuda, her firstborn son, a decent meal in a very long time and as a result they all suffer from a serious poultry and carbohydrate deficiency. I am too exhausted from our travels to really eat, but manage to swallow a few bites of chopped salad so I do not insult Safta, which would be a huge fashla (mistake) in my first few hours here. Yehuda and the kids eat like ravenous pigs, which of course prove her point that they have not eaten adequately for months.

Quickly the four kids spread out to find their rooms. My little ones, Eden and Kobe are upstairs next to us and my teens, Noa and Aaron are down in the basement level of the house as far from their parents as possible, while still living under the same roof. I walk out of the kitchen past ten large duffle bags full of our clothes and items that we will need for this year. It amazes me that with all the things we collect in life, the essentials my large family really need all fit perfectly into these bags. I enter our hot and sticky bedroom and the walls begin to spin which is my cue to crawl into bed. I lie down, but the room continues to spin and the bed moves like a surfboard gliding over waves until I slip into a deep and yet very short sleep dreaming that I awake to discover the luggage unpacked, the house furnished and four happy and well-assimilated children.

* * *

The sun blazes early on a Friday morning spreading brilliant natural light through my new home. I open the sliding glass doors to the backyard and am met with great heat and even greater humidity. I immediately begin sweating. Within minutes of stepping out of a cool shower, I sweat once again. This is Israel, a desert by the sea at the height of summer I remind myself.

The children and I eat a quick and tense breakfast devoid of conversation, but full of anxiety, as we are about to head off to the American International School to become oriented. Noa already worries that the best colors of the uniform shirts will be gone by the time we arrive. At the school gate, two clean cut Israeli security guards sitting in a small kiosk (free-standing booth) welcome us. I need to leave my California driver's license in exchange for a plastic laminated AIS badge. The guard buzzes us in through the gate. This is not the most gracious welcome to a new school; however, under the circumstances I do not need friendly security guards. These important men have only one responsibility as far as I am concerned and that is to protect my three children, who do not appear fazed at all by the new academic security arrangements. Once we are safely in the school, my attention immediately focuses to the multitude of simple white paper signs decorating the walls with the words BOMB SHELTER printed in bold black letters and embellished with arrows that point in the direction of the intended 'bomb shelters'. My precious flesh and blood now attend a school with bomb shelter signage, let alone actual functioning bomb shelters, near to where Katyusha Rockets fell a few days earlier while protected by armed and good looking security guards. What the heck was I thinking moving my family to Israel?

The bell rings for the morning break and hundreds of children pour out of classrooms and converge around the food kiosk and picnic benches. Tiny elementary school children are mixed in with mature high school students and even with the uniform t-shirts and the school's common English language, the students are quite diverse in appearance and call out to each other in many different languages. My own teenagers keep their distance from me when all the other students appear and Eden clings even tighter to my side at this point. Looking around it strikes me that the children at this school are the real characters from the Small World attraction at Disneyland. They laugh and play in many different languages, yet they share the distinct rhyme and rhythm of all children throughout the world.

As we leave the school, I hold on to the image of excited children and hum to myself the theme song from the Small World ride while I try to distance from my mind the 'BOMB SHELTER' signs. We are all dripping wet when we arrive at the car, which is a sauna and I can actually see the heat escape as we open the doors. My offspring get in the car like zombies and do not speak a word on the drive home, which is daunting and does nothing to alleviate my own insecurity about how this move will affect them. I look in the rear view mirror and glance at my sweet little Eden, who at eight-years old is definitely anxious and my stoic, thoughtful Noa, who at fifteen-years old is nervous yet optimistic. Next to me is another story; my angry son Aaron who at thirteen years is opposed to this move and just sits expressionless and distant. Not even the happy words to the song in my head can ease the discomfort.

* * *

It is extremely hot outside; over 105 degrees at midday and most of the air-conditioning units are broken; an uncomfortable combination. I religiously spray sun block on fair skinned Kobe and brown skinned Eden as we spend most of the weekend in the naturally warm pool, offering some relief from the incredible heat. We have to wear flip-flops as the cement around the pool burns and the bright green Astroturf lawn can singe the tender foot. There is no chance to forget for a moment that we have arrived at the desert land of the Middle East.

After we decided to move to Israel for the year, the kids and I had one unanimous request of Yehuda; that the house we rent be within walking distance of the sea. Yehuda found this large creamy white house built a few years back, and then abandoned after an ugly divorce by a Swiss couple who made sure that neither side could actually reside in it. The funny part is that our new residence is too grand to simply be called a house and in light of Jewish Law that considers a man's home his castle, I quickly name our new home with palatial high ceilings and embellished with green marble and gold trim 'the creamy white castle'. The castle's living and dining rooms are enormous and the spacious kitchen is filled with two sets of brand new appliances making it possible to separate meat and dairy. I have never kept kosher, perhaps this is another change I shall institute this year? Upstairs each of the spacious bedrooms has a lovely balcony with a birds-eye view of the neighborhood and one can ride the shiny-mirrored elevator down two floors to the basement where the grandeur continues. In the basement, Aaron claims a pristine mahogany office with a polished Donald Trump desk; he should just do his work this year and I will look beyond the obnoxious nature of the room. Noa quickly moves into the guest suite with its own bathroom and kitchenette that will soon double as informal closet space. The basement also harbors a control room full of machinery and technology to operate the castle; a washroom that is large enough for a small hotel attached to an enormous storage room; and a clean white ma-mad (bomb shelter), which is a simple room with one window to the outside world that can be shut off air tight by a thick metal door in case of bombs or air raids. I know that the ma-mad is customary in homes throughout the country, but now that I have my very own, I get a stomachache as scary thoughts creep into my easily fearful mind.

The creamy white castle is technologically complicated; slick computer screens and touch pads along the walls control all of the electronic functions. In the beginning, I am thankful to find some old fashioned light switches that simply turn the lights on and off. Even with all this beauty, the castle feels sad; we have inherited a true victim of a bad divorce, a home with an elegant composition but a cheerless and wounded character. As I look around my Israeli castle, I can't help but think of my house back in Los Angeles. I left a comfortable, furnished and loving home and have arrived to an empty castle with all its 'bells and whistles' waiting for me to breath joyful life into its constitution.

* * *

The town we are living in is called Herzelia Pituah; it sits along the Mediterranean Sea with its wide sandy beaches, attractive villas and apartments, beachfront hotels, a modern marina full of yachts and sailboats and a fancy indoor shopping mall. Residing in Herzelia Pituah is an interesting mix of Sabras (native Israelis) and expatriates; international business people, United Nations staff, ambassadors and embassy workers. Embassy residences located amidst villas in this neighborhood have their country's official state emblems posted on their gates and their national flags hang from flagpoles in their front yards. The larger and more powerful nations also have armed guards in kiosks in front of their residences. Our new neighbors are the Egyptian, Spanish, Chilean, Colombian, Peruvian, Canadian, Ghana and Japanese Ambassadorial residences. A few blocks away on Galei Tchelet, the most prestigious street in town, the enormous well-guarded American Ambassador's residence towers over the cliffs of the Mediterranean with a large American flag blowing in the wind. Yehuda's office is nearby in Herzelia's

Industrial Zone, a district with large, modern office buildings, banks, restaurants, coffee shops and markets. Many international businesses and high tech companies that Israel is famous for are located in this area and Tel Aviv, the most cosmopolitan city in Israel, is fifteen minutes away.

* * *

I escape the creamy white castle on this beautiful Shabbat (Saturday) morning to visit my kha-ver (friend). I actually run down the street ensuring that no family member follows me with a question, a thought or most likely a complaint. As I descend the stairs to the sand, all the stress of packing a family of six for a year abroad amidst a war temporarily melts away in the summer heat. My dear khaver and I meet and silently say shalom (hello). Special khaver-eem (friends) reunited who have not visited in some time but pick up exactly where they left off the last time they were together. I smile and feel a wave of contentment fill and electrify my cells and my soul because I know that no matter the challenges I will face this year that the beach, my khaver will be here for me.

The entire depth of the beach is full of fresh tan sand awash with people escaping the intolerable heat that blankets the cities. I slip off my sandals and with each step feel the warm and soft sand fill up between my toes as I approach the water. I walk along the shore refreshed by the water as it rushes over my feet and splashes my legs. Everyone is at the beach; families with small children, groups of anorexic teenage girls admiring their pierced navels, life-guards parading their tan buff bodies in skimpy Speedos, naked little children playing in the sand and kids boogie boarding in the gentle waves among sea bathers. Ice cream vendors pass through the crowds with Styrofoam boxes yelling "glee-da" (ice cream) at the top of their lungs, people eat watermelon under umbrellas, and restaurants are full of lounging customers. My khaver is just as I left it on my last visit to the Holy Land and just as I expected to find it—alive with energy and celebration, as a beach should be in the summer especially within a week of being at war with the hostile Hezbollah neighbors to the north.

The hudna (ceasefire) between Hezbollah and the Israelis holds, which means two things. First, the large assaults on Israel have ended and daily life in most of the country is tranquil with some small isolated incidents still taking place along the border. Second, the nation has retreated to its familiar state of waiting for the next big attack to occur while the news is full of stories analyzing and criticizing the Second Lebanon War and the leadership. The news is one of the most prevalent and influential facets of this country where over twenty newspapers in Hebrew, Arabic, Russia and English circulate; each hour on the hour Israelis hear the latest news broadcast on the radio and by the evening, the television is full of more in-depth news. It is also a well-known fact that Israelis are pundits on most subjects; they are a population prepared to launch into a discussion, debate or speech about any topic at any time. Israelis inhale their news, as it is almost as plentiful as the air they breathe.

* * *

The children officially commence their studies at AIS (The American International School) this morning. Noa and Aaron disappear the moment I park the car without saying a word to me. Eden is terribly nervous and walks very close to me as we make our way to the third grade classroom. When we enter, two little girls, Niharika from Angola and Ricardina from Portugal greet us while the teacher busily prepares for the day and barely takes a break to welcome Eden. At this moment I desperately miss our small school back home where Eden was so comfortable and the teachers would stop their work and warmly greet a new student. The bell rings and I leave my usually upbeat daughter alone in a school where she has no friends with signs all over the walls that lead to active bomb shelters. What kind of a lunatic mother am I? Tears fill my eyes as I stand outside of the room reading the names of the kids in her class posted on the door. Amidst the tears I have to laugh—where else in the world would Eden be in a class with three kids named Asha, Dasha and Yasha?

I return home and find Kobe happily watching Bob Sfog (Sponge Bob) in Hebrew. These Hebrew language programs are Kobe's jumpstart for kindergarten still a couple of weeks off at a kibbutz (farming community) near our home. Before I can share Eden's painful start of school with Yehuda, he dashes off to work. I close all the windows and turn on the air-conditioning in the living room and the kitchen to escape the heat and the pounding from the construction at the next-door neighbor's house. The living room cools quickly, but the kitchen vents spew out warm and humid heat. Sitting next to Kobe who is entranced by Bob Sfog, I commence my first official 'To Do List' for the year. The first line item to take care of is the air-conditioning and easily the list grows until I decide that I have more than enough projects to focus on.

Later that morning, Kobe and I set off by foot to the ma-co-let (small neighborhood market) at the end of the street to buy the ingredients for chocolate chip cookies, the perfect comfort food for our transition. At home in my warm kitchen, I place the ingredients on the counter and realize that the measurements are all in grams and liters and I need to convert them to cups. After I do the math, I prepare the dough and start to bake the magical cookies; a panacea from America that I am sure will bring smiles to my children. Within minutes I can tell something is terribly wrong; the cookies look awful and taste even worse. Tears of frustration roll down my cheeks, as I realize I am incapable of quickly easing the discomfort of starting life here for my family. I toss three-dozen dreadful cookies into the trash resigned to the fact that assimilation is a learning process that does not happen over night.

While my family's transition is fraught with friction, I quickly see that there is rampant political strife within the country; government attacks itself for a war mismanaged and not won; families of fallen soldiers accuse the leadership of using their sons in vain; the enemy is holding three kidnapped Israeli soldiers, and political corruption is plentiful. And this is just the abridged list of troubles in Israel.

* * *

I force myself to leave the cool castle on yet another scorching hot morning and drive to the Super Sol Market. I am welcomed by a skinny, dark skinned Ethiopian Israeli security guard who opens the trunk of my car to check for explosives or weapons. He looks under the chassis and then he opens the door to the back seat and observes that a very un-dangerous almost five-year old with blond hair accompanies me. The guard who appears less bothered by the heat than the boredom of his job finally hands me a receipt, opens the gate and officially waves me into the underground parking lot. Another security guard at the market's entrance checks my purse as he lifts the bag from the bottom, peaks in and asks me in Hebrew "Ne-shek?" (Weapon) To which I answer "Lo!" (No) and with the nod of his head, he signals us to enter the market.

Super Sol is like any large and modern market we have back at home; the most obvious exception being that everything here is written in Hebrew. I start in the produce sections where two young Arab Israelis call out to each other in Arabic as they stock the aisles of fruit and vegetables. Holy Land produce is not as shiny and robust as it is in L.A., but here it is fresh and definitely tastes better. From the side of my eye, as I watch these gentlemen, I fill a bag with small green pickling cucumbers which are jewels in the world of Israeli vegetables and I realize that if I did not hear these men speaking Arabic, I would not know that they were Arabs Israelis as they show no distinguishable physical difference from Jewish Israelis.

At the detergent section I study the big and bright pictures on the shiny bottles for clues to determine the areas in the house that they clean. I speak Hebrew well enough to get along, but reading and comprehension are still a great challenge for me. I notice that Kobe had no problem identifying the chocolate yogurt, the chocolate and peanut butter cereal, the potato chips or the ice cream he wants, as it is all in the child friendly international junk food language highlighted with enticing pictures. Kobe, with his sincere sky blue eyes, earnestly tells me why he has to have every item as he adds each one to our overflowing basket. I make a mental note that once Kobe's school starts, I will never bring him back to the market.

At the check out counter, the Russian Israeli cashier begins to run my items through while she converses with the neighboring cashier in their native tongue. She does not look at me, but as the counter fills I interrupt their conversations with the one word I know will save me from schlepping the bags home myself, "mi-shlo-akh" (delivery). She halts her conversation and obviously annoyed by my interruption lets out a huge sigh. She places a few large yellow delivery cartons onto the end of the counter and motions for me to begin filling them. Suddenly she speeds up the conveyor belt and rushes the items through knowing full well that I cannot possibly load the cartons, run back to the basket to add more to her conveyor belt and keep an eye on Kobe, who is still shopping for gum and candy. I have learned that Israelis like to be in the position of shli-ta (control) and ko-akh (power) even if it is at a cash register in Super Sol.

In a maternal and commercial attempt to alleviate my children's pain and suffering, I stop at Max Brenner, the heavenly chocolate store across the street from the market to buy my children little boxes of chocolate. At home, I write each child a note expressing my love and pride in how they have navigated their adventure so far and place it with the chocolate on their desks to discover when they return home, I hope, from a good day of school.

* * *

Haam (hot) does not truthfully describe the intense heat and la-hoot (humid) does not accurately describe the moisture in the air. Today, it is simply a roasting sauna in the Holy Land. There are not enough fresh water showers to control the incredible and continual sweat dripping from my body in my kitchen and outside. I have been unsuccessful in getting the air-conditioning repairman to the house although he is rumored to be coming later this afternoon.

In front of the school, I park on the sidewalk behind other cars and wait as freezing air-conditioning blasts air into my face. In America, red and white painted curbs usually denote parking for emergency vehicles but I have learned in Israel that these markings are actually an invitation for me to park. At 3pm sharp, I watch the great exodus of kids in bright t-shirts leave the school. Six sad eyes approach and enter my car. "How was your day?" I ask with a happy air conditioned blown smile.

"I miss L.A.—I hate this school."

"My math teacher does not know how to teach."

"I ate lunch by myself."

"These kids are weird."

"Can we go back to L.A. now?" And all I can think as the smile melts from my face is that 'I am the worst mother in the whole world'.

I have prepared a meal for the kids. Slowly, the food resuscitates them and I start to recognize the children that I brought to Israel and not the miserable monsters I picked up at school an hour earlier. A little later, I pass Noa's room to find her sitting at her desk on the computer and Eric, her new German-Ecuadorian friend, is sprawled out on her bed. A handsome young man lies on my daughter's bed and I panic thinking that his lovely head of long puffy hair could have ki-neem (head lice), a problem of epidemic proportions in the Holy Land. If Noa's long thick hair becomes infested with ki-neem and spreads to the rest of us, I shall not survive this move.

Kobe and Eden play ball in the shallow end of our naturally warm pool and when Aaron surfaces from his room they plead with him to join them. Aaron acquiesces, jumps in and throws Kobe like a ball. He screams in delight thrilled to be the center of his big brother's attention. I cannot remember the last time Aaron played with his siblings for such an extended amount of time and with so much o-sher (happiness). He spent most of his thirteenth year with his pubescent friends and if he was not physically with them, his Sidekick or the Internet electronically connected him. Seventh grade was a year of countless Bar Mitzvah parties where he did not think about his siblings and barely tolerated his parents. I wonder what changes the new school and the new country will bring to my thirteen-year old son?

The doorbell rings. A young man from the company Bite Ha-ham (Wise House) arrives with a computer under his arm prepared to fix the air-conditioning that now spews hot air in the master bedroom, as well as the kitchen, for the third time in our first week of residence. As I have learned, it is the standard practice for each Israeli repairman before he enters the house to wipe his feet, kiss his fingers and touch the me-zu-zah that is affixed on the doorway. This gentleman is no different and performs this same ceremony before he enters. After he works for half an hour, he announces with great confidence, "Ha-kol-be-seder"

(Everything is fine); however, by the time I reach the cool kitchen, the small screen on the wall flashes incoherent numbers and letters and upstairs the master bedroom circulates warm air. The irony in the name 'Wise House' would make this whole situation humorous if it were not so uncomfortable.

I make the terrible mistake of asking my children what they want for dinner.

"California Pizza Kitchen."

"In And Out Burger."

"Benihanas,"—all restaurants from L.A. There is a Benihanas restaurant a few hours drive north in Beirut, Lebanon and if it were not for the border and the hostilities, I would get in my car at this very moment and drive my children all the way to Beirut for dinner. Instead, we drive to Eden Bar at the seashore for a dinner of rich and creamy humus and pita, schnitzel (thin, breaded and fried chicken breast), French fries, finely chopped salad and cold and crisp sweet watermelon with salty feta cheese. As we eat on the sand, the bright orange sun slowly disappears below the horizon turning the sky to brilliant shades of purple and yellow; on the sand, the beach volleyball courts are full of players; and on the plasma television screen, a soccer match is being played. The dramatic gold and purple sky and my children's company on the sand make me stop to realize that this is one of those perfect and unforgettable moments. For this brief instant, I am not the worst mother and none of us miss the restaurants back home.

* * *

Noa sits in front of me at the kitchen table with her long wavy brown hair covering most of her face. She energetically vents what did not go her way in journalism class today as she devours juicy wedges of watermelon. I cannot help but focus on her deep penetrating eyes as they dance around and remember like it was yesterday the intensity in her eyes minutes after she was born fifteen years earlier. After thirty-eight hours of labor, my firstborn daughter arrived angry, put off by the long wait and her screams in the delivery room let us all know it. From the moment I first held her,

I knew her name was Noa, a powerful female character in the Bible who led her sisters in a successful battle to inherit their father's land when he died. Prior to Noa, only male heirs could receive their father's inheritance.

Noa continues to live up to her name and be motivated for challenges; she enthusiastically volunteered to leave her life in L.A. for a year and take part in this crazy adventure to Israel armed with three important weapons; a cell phone, an iPod and a Mac Book Pro. In a short period, Noa for the most part likes school and has an active social life, but she is still a teenager who finds things to complain about to her mother and excels in rolling her eyes in disapproval. She goes crazy at the thought of missing a party, or even a chat at a coffee house.

I wish Eden's transition to third grade were going as smoothly. She still has no one to eat lunch with and has not made any friends. We attempt to bake chocolate chip cookies once again, but this time we add real butter and have all the measurements correct. As Eden mixes the creamy batter with her hands, I ask her if there is anyone with whom she would like to sit with at lunch. "No," she responds. I keep going over the same argument in my head—'this experience will strengthen my children'. I suggest that she needs to walk up to some kids, sit down and just join in. "I can't," she tells me. We add the eggs and the flour and I encourage her to take a chance and it will be fine. We are about to add the chocolate chips and Eden looks at me thoughtfully and says she will consider it. The cookies are in the oven and Eden seems to be in a good mood as she licks the remaining cookie dough from her fingers. The baked chocolate chip cookies taste fine and are wonderfully fragrant, but they still do not have the smooth texture or roundness of Toll House. The girl who delivers the sushi this evening removes her helmet and with a smile says, "It smells like my grandmother's house in America. I used to visit her every summer when I was a little girl."

Aaron appears the most miserable and most withdrawn. He walks around with his basketball, his teen version of a security blanket and is only happy when he is dribbling and shooting the ball. When we decided to move to Israel for a year, the promise of playing a lot of ball was the only selling point for Aaron who despite his height disadvantage is a quick and thoughtful player. He is well versed in NBA scores, players' statistics and has 'advice' for coaches and their teams. I am convinced that if my thirteen-year old son put enough energy toward his studies, he would be a great student. But Aaron has decided early on that he does not like school and he tells me that the other students are boring and not his 'style'. I am curious to learn exactly what his 'style' is, but I know that he misses his friends from L.A. with whom he communicates across the world on iChat daily. He has only one friend in Israel, Idan, whom he has known since they were four years old. Together they train each afternoon at Sport Tec, a local park with many basketball courts.

* * *

A cool blast of fresh air passes through the open bedroom window and gently wakes me. It is peaceful at this hour while the madness of daytime is still fast asleep with the family. I rush downstairs for my morning coffee alone with a newspaper before the pounding from our next-door neighbor's construction will awaken everyone to commence the morning commotion. I enter the kitchen and am smacked by the powerful scent of shoom (garlic) that has fermented and found its way into every pore of the downstairs during the night. I rush to open all of the windows before I faint from these obnoxious gases taking over my olfactory glands. Last night while I was at a school meeting with Noa, Safta cooked her kitch-re (a rice and lentils dish sautéed and cooked with tomato, butter and shoom), a favorite Iraqi meal for everyone in the family except me, the non–Iraqi shoom intolerant member. The power of the Iraqi Safta and her kitch-re survived in our house over night just as it has survived hundreds maybe thousands of years. After seventeen years as my mother-in-law, I also know that Marcelle reaps pleasure controlling the scents in my house with her cooking, while guaranteeing her four grandchildren's and her firstborn son's gastronomical happiness.

I escape outside to my Astroturf garden with a cappuccino and the Herald Tribune/Haaretz English newspapers, a perfect combination of international news and local news all in English. I am thankful for news that does not come in a Hebrew font and require tremendous effort and skill that I do not possess. I do not get far when Kobe in his bright yellow

Bob Sfog pajamas approaches rubbing his tired blue eyes. From this moment on, it is a mad dash to wake up two sleepy teenagers, push Eden along, help Kobe get dressed and make breakfast for four children.

By 10am, onions sizzle in the oil and Safta, who has already moved into the castle, cooks ti-beet (tasty Iraqi rice with chicken, onions, tomato paste and a special blend of very aromatic secret Iraqi seasonings that must be prepared and purchased in special Iraqi markets) for her grandchildren's dinner. Simultaneously, Marcelle makes her light and creamy cheesecake mainly for Aaron, her first-born son's first-born son, to eat when he returns home from school in the afternoon.

My mother-in-law, Marcelle, was born in Baghdad in 1922. Her marriage was arranged before she was twenty years old to a man thirty years her senior. In five years she produced three boys in a loveless marriage ending in divorce. Back then, many Jews were leaving Iraq and making Ali-yah to Israel. As a single young woman Marcelle could not bring her three sons out of Iraq alone so she sent Yehuda and his little brothers to Israel with her parents posing as the boys' mother and father. They were welcomed to their new country with a shower of chemicals to kill off any diseases they might be bringing with them. A few months later Marcelle joined the boys in an immigration camp on the sand dunes of Hadera where they were staying until they all moved to Kibbutz Hatzor, a farming community where as a single woman, she believed that she could successfully raise her boys. Life on the kibbutz required hard work from each of its members and the children lived separately from their parents. Each day Yehuda and his brothers visited Marcelle in the late afternoon after school, but returned to slumber with the other kids in dormitories. After some years on the kibbutz, Marcelle married Shabtai, a widower with a daughter who originally made Aliyah from Massachusetts.

* * *

I can't help but smile as I walk with my khaver on this stunning morning; the sky is crystal blue and the tanzanite sea is escorted in by the high tides overflowing on the sandy beaches. A lone lifeguard glides over the still water on a ha-si-kay (over-sized white surfboard) dragging the large two-sided paddle from side to side through the ocean water while standing balanced in the middle of the board. Once upon a time, Yehuda would borrow a ha-si-kay from the lifeguards and paddle me around the sea.

At Nof Yam Beach, the northernmost destination of my walk, I encounter an ancient white haired woman in a bright pink bathing suit sitting under a wooden canopy tossing breadcrumbs and joyfully singing out to a flock of gray pigeons with shiny emerald green and fuchsia neckbands. These flying rats scavenge for food daily along the beach and afford her the company and attention she appears to embrace and suddenly at this very moment, I gain an appreciation for these otherwise abhorrent creatures.

A few hours later, I open the door for Tali, the new Israeli housekeeper who walks in talking on her cell phone. She continues her conversation as she follows me to the kitchen where Yehuda and I sit quietly reading the newspaper and enjoying the air-conditioning that finally works. There are many rooms in the castle and yet she places her bags on the counter and carries on her loud conversation for another few minutes right next to us. Yehuda and I look up to each other and share a smile in disbelief. I should not be shocked. She is an Israeli Jewish housekeeper, which alone is a paradox and while her conversation is lively, shortly Tali's energy will be eclipsed by exhaustion as she slowly moves throughout the house selectively attending to those things 'she does clean' and ignoring the many things 'she does not clean'. It is crazy—most mornings in anticipation of her arrival, I find myself rising early to straighten up the house in preparation for her workday.

Israeli laws make it nearly impossible to hire foreign workers; many folks from the Philippines, India and South America reside here illegally and are eager for cleaning jobs, but can only receive work visas from diplomats, the elderly and handicapped persons. If I hire a foreigner cleaner and am caught by the police who patrol this neighborhood, the worker will be deported and I will receive a large fine and a criminal report. In the meantime, I try to abide by the law and as Yehuda say, "At least she shows up on time."

I find refuge in my office most of the day in front of the computer attending to work from L.A. and reading the latest world news while blocking out the vision of Tali's misery as she cleans. She may not clean well, but she is quite a talented sufferer. Today my first e-mail is from a friend who informs me with grave concern that the hudna between Hezbollah and the Israelis is shaky and she is concerned for my family's safety as from her vantage point sitting behind a computer eight thousand miles away; the whole country is under attack. Literally she is not wrong; the one thing I am very clear about is that Israel is always under attack. This country is truly my gee-bor-ah (hero). At 58-years old, Israel is a strong state that has not been left alone by neighboring enemies since its establishment as a nation in 1948 and its survival is based on the belief that not for a moment can the country assume that it is not under attack. While my gee-bor-ah protects its borders, it strives to achieve greatness as a country—the successes and the achievements of its people in the short period of life are unequaled by any of the neighboring nations.

* * *

This morning, I drive home still feeling guilty about our decision to take a year abroad. After years of dedicating myself to my children's happiness, I am now responsible for their misery. I remind myself that in L.A. I had gone over board. The abundance of artificial things made my children happy; I could not stop giving and overdoing and Yehuda was no better than I. Everywhere around us it seemed that parents overindulged and this craziness was spinning out of control in our lives as well. Leaving for a year was a great way to pull the plug on the endless abundance and give my children the opportunity to spend a year in a different country. I had hoped this experience would help them identify with change at an early age, but all I see are my children suffering from withdrawal like other addicts. Can they survive? Can I survive all of them?

Kobe and I return to the empty and cheerless creamy white castle. My family is here to breath life into its walls with laughter and happiness—when will this start? Darn, it is hot. Once again the air-conditioning does not work in the kitchen so we find cool refuge in the living room. Kobe beats me at a few rounds of the memory game, and then abandons me to plays with Pokémon figurines, his only friends in Israel. As I sip a refreshing ice cappuccino and stare out at the Astroturf garden, I say to myself, "We will make it work and the sad eyes will pass. Eden will eat lunch with kids from her class. Aaron will make new friends. Kobe will start school and play with live children his own age. The children will recover from their abundance addictions and this adventure will empower them later in life no matter in what land they live."

While my family's instability gnaws at me, Israel, my gi-bor-ah (hero) is truly in a worrisome state of flux; the three leaders of Israel during the Second Lebanon War, Prime Minister Ehud Olmert, Defense Minister Amir Peretz and Chief of Staff Dan Halutz are daily attacked, dissected and destroyed by five million people for their poor management of the Second Lebanon War and the deaths of soldiers in the final days of fighting; three kidnapped Israeli soldiers (hopefully alive) are held by terrorist enemies in Gaza and Lebanon; the President of Israel, Moshe Katsav is all over the news accused of rape and sexual harassment of female staffers; the husband of Israel's richest woman attempts to overturn a sexual harassment case in which he was sentenced to six months in jail; Chaim Ramon, the former Justice Minister faces trial for kissing a young female officer against her will; and Palestinian militants from Gaza daily send Qassam Rockets into the Negev cities. This is a heavy load for my strong and proud gi-bor-ah and does not even take into account the daily Palestinian strife in Gaza and the West Bank both very close geographically and psychologically and an important part of the news that affects the emotional welfare of the country. Currently the two Palestinian parties, Hamas and Fatah cannot agree on a unity government while people on the streets of Gaza fight and kill each other; city workers have gone unpaid for months; residents suffer as food and medicine cannot get into Gaza; and yet militants have the funds and energy simultaneously to kill each other and to send Qassam Rockets into Israel.

* * *

I drop my children off under the watchful eyes of Marsha, the school's superintendant and handsome Israeli security guards stationed around the school's front gate and venture on the crazy highway dodging multitudes of vehicles traveling rapidly up north. Even in my Land Cruiser, I have to be cautious of their slippery lane changes and their crazy speed. I get off at the Poleg Intersection in South Netanya where the majority of cars turn right, which I know means they will be joining me at IKEA, the mecca of furniture and household shopping in Israel.

At the store's entrance a very uninterested security guard peers in my purse as I walk through a metal detector with a long line of Israelis. While I am always happy to see guards when I shop, I do question how thorough a job they perform and how useful they will be if a real terrorist appears. The location where I stand at this very moment is the narrowest strip of Israel; the distance between Netanya on the coast and Tulkarm in the West Bank is twelve kilometers (seven miles) and many suicide bombers have traveled this land passage on their way to kill.

IKEA Land is a retail amusement park full of endless rooms and displays for Israelis to admire and enjoy and at 10:00 am, the place is packed. People are everywhere with their hands in everything speaking on their cell phones and blocking wide aisles with their shopping carts. Zealously I fill my cart, as everything I need for the creamy white castle is here. At one point I stop to look at a huge round clock and a cart strikes me hard from the rear. This clueless gentleman speaking on a cell phone says "sle-kha" (excuse me) and "be-e-met te-una" (a real accident) and returns to his conversation. I get a sudden urge to let him pass and then run him over with my cart. Have I become too Israeli in such a short time? Either way, I do not have time for revenge as I must rescue Keren, Yehuda's secretary from Kobe who I decided would make a visit to IKEA a true death mission. The Russian Israeli cashier does not look at me nor does she say a word to me as she runs the merchandise through and I simply accept that one of the characteristics ingrained in Israeli cashiers is to be annoyed by the customer. This is not an American IKEA and I remind myself not to take it personally.

Ten minutes later, as I pull into the exclusive parking lot to gather my items, a small white car darts in front of my SUV barely avoiding a crash.

As I load my bags, I watch the man who cut me off seconds before, back into a parking spot where an older woman with frizzy blond hair stands dead in the middle of the spot saving it for the car that is on its way to pick up her stuff. She shrieks and shakes her arms in the air as millimeter-by-millimeter he edges closer to her and like a tank, she does not budge. Finally this large man jumps out of the car and yells at her while his pregnant wife with a nose earring quickly brings bags to the car that he has left midway in the spot. No one appears startled by such aggressive behavior as Israelis are used to this craziness; I, on the other hand, am relieved when the large man screams his final words, gets in his car with his wife and drives away abruptly ending the dramatic battle. I finish loading my bags into my car and can't help but think, 'Yes Lizzy you are in Israel Land.'

* * *

September 1st arrives. This is the day Israeli children return to school and my Kobe starts gan (kindergarten) on Kibbutz Shfayim near our creamy white castle. I am excited to introduce Kibbutz World to Kobe, as a kibbutz is truly one of the happiest places on earth for children. We drop the big kids off and drive slowly along the country roads through Mo-shav (a collective farming community) Rishpon behind a yellow tractor with gigantic black wheels on its way to the fields. This tractor reminds me of my father's big yellow John Deere tractor that he had on our ranch in my childhood. When I was Kobe's age, he proudly gave us rides in the tractor's scoop raised high in the air as he drove through the ranch—these rides are legendary to this day.

Kobe nervously walks into Gan Rimon (Pomegranate Nursery School) grabbing tightly to my leg; he cautiously watches a group of little boys playing with dinosaurs and another group building with blocks. After about thirty seconds, his tiny fingers gently unwrap from their firm hold and he walks away from me to survey the room up close. The small children only speak Hebrew, but Kobe feels at home. In Hebrew, Nili, the head ga-nen-et (teacher) explains that each day he will be able to play with all the toys he wants. Kobe's crystal blue eyes sparkle. In circle time Nili introduces Kobe to the group. I watch as he carefully examines his new classmates with interesting names—Gal (a wave), Noga (a bright star), Iftakh (a promise), Shira (a song), Shirel (a song of God), Ayel (a deer), Eli (the final prophet), and Neta (a planet). Kobe has learned the names of countless Pokémon friends; these foreign names should be easy for him.

After the morning meeting, the children sit down on small chairs around small tables and eat a fresh and hot breakfast that reads like a restaurant menu prepared by Alona, another ga-nen-et. Kobe is assigned to sit at Gordon's table, the one male teacher who is a native of Australia and can speak to Kobe in English when the need arises. Gordon, a large teddy bear with a thick Aussie accent instantly becomes Kobe's buddy and after my young son takes a few bites of cereal, he looks up at me with confidence and tells me that I can now leave him at the gan. Nili looks at me as though I were a crackpot leaving my kid alone on the first day, but promises to call me on the cell phone if Kobe needs me. (I do not get a call from Nili and when I return for Kobe at lunchtime, he wants to stay longer.)

On my way out, I walk through the play yard which is truly a Junk World full of old and battered objects; a blue tractor put out to pasture, a used stove with old pots and pans, a steering wheel, a few mattresses for jumping, a small white washing machine, a large metal cash register, old manual telephones, and a broken computer screen to name only a few of the treasures that fit into this imaginative Gan Eden (Paradise) for five year olds. I admit that I am a mother from sterile L.A. and am not comfortable with rust, disarray and dirt. As I drive home, I smile to think that these are all things I would throw away and on the kibbutz they create Gan Eden. I know that my son will be thrilled to play and grow here, but I am also greatly relieved that Kobe is up to date on his latest tetanus shot.

* * *

We travel on a windy country road past farmlands, forests and Yehuda's brightly colored BIG Shopping Center in the city of Bet Shemesh on our drive to Yehuda's nephew Nimrod's wedding. I feel like a pioneer, albeit in a modern vehicle, as we slowly bounce up the dusty biblical hillside to the natural farm at the mountain's peak. Inside an open wooden barn structure, the wedding reception takes place full of our Israeli family. This is the first time since we arrived at Israel that we meet all of Yehuda's brothers, cousins, aunts and uncles and I helplessly watch Eden and Kobe suffer through a painful face pinching ceremony by Yehuda's Iraqi uncles.

The rolling hillsides around us are earthy shades of yellow and brown from the dry summer months creating enchanting vistas. A gentle breeze fills the air as the beautiful young couple walks hand in hand along the breath-taking rocky bluff overlooking the pastoral hillside to the simple hoo-pa with four poles and a loose flowing fabric that blows in the wind. The words of a female reform rabbi are refreshing as she joins these two young people in marriage with the sun setting in the West. A female rabbi in Israel is quite avant-garde; it is still more customary for a secular couple to be married by an orthodox black hat rabbi. This wedding is a celebration for numerous reasons. Ten years earlier, Nimrod was seriously wounded in Southern Lebanon when Hezbollah guerillas attacked his troop on patrol. Other comrades lost their lives in the same attack. Nimrod spent many months in the hospital undergoing life saving and reconstructive surgeries. Nimrod's wedding also celebrates the nes (miracle) of life for his family and friends who thought they might lose him to war—too familiar a story in this land.

In the dark and cool evening, we take food from huge metal pots serving Bedouin style rice, chicken and vegetables. Our Israeli relatives are curious to know how our adjustment period has passed. We smile and take pleasure in the celebration of hope and fresh beginnings with the newlyweds here this evening. After dinner I sit with Kobe and Eden on low cushions by the stage and we eat small tubs of Ben and Jerry's ice cream. Speeches are made. The dj keeps the dance floor full as celebrants dance to techno-Israeli music under a black desert sky abundant with stars. I barely finish a glass of wine, but the fresh air and lovely setting relax me. My mind wanders back to the night Yehuda asked my father for permission to marry me and my father's response to a nervous Yehuda was simply "You are not what I had in mind." That was seventeen years ago and tonight I have to believe my father is up in the stars looking down and thinking, 'He was not so bad after all.'

* * *

Friday night we eat Shabbat dinner together, a fete I never managed to achieve in L.A. with any consistency, but am determined to accomplish this year. Noa and Aaron eat dinner with us and then they are free to go out. I am thrilled that my kids have found friends to go out with, but now I have to deal with my panic about their safety. I secretly harbor a fear that suicide bombers lurk and will show their ugly faces where my kids might be. This condition is a result of the horror stories from past suicide bombings where deranged Palestinian terrorists showed up at clubs, malls and restaurants with the goal of killing as many civilians as possible and the promised glory that martyrdom would bring to them and their families. I know that I cannot stop my teenagers from going out and I continually have to remind myself that it is safer here for teens than in L.A. In their eyes it is bad enough that I impose curfews on them, "No kids in Israel have curfews!" Noa and Aaron tell me. It is a fact that in Israel, many kids do not go out until 11pm and they stay out all night long, which is completely foreign to me.

Tonight Aaron goes with the Jordanian Ambassador's son and the Angolan Ambassador's son to the Arena Mall. On Friday nights, the stores in the mall are closed, but movie theaters and some fast food restaurants are open making it primarily just an indoor hang out where teens run around and act crazy. Aaron, who usually has few words to offer about what he did, eagerly shares with me the details of the Jordanian Ambassador's car, a bullet proof Mercedez Benz built for the King of Jordan and outfitted like a tank with extra-thick metal to provide protection in case of attack.

* * *

A slight sea breeze welcomes me as I visit my khaver early in the morning under a thick layer of gray clouds. A family of wild kittens eats from the trash left by weekend visitors along the slanted lawns and walkway down to the beach. The tiny, wild tricolored cats are beautiful, yet they hiss and raise their tails when I approach.

Daily, my family's transition to life here improves, but I am still overly sensitive to the thought that bringing my children to Israel this year will mentally impair them. I have been following the story of Theodore Herzl, the great Zionist visionary, who helped found Israel at the expense of his children. Herzelia, the city we live in is named after Herzl. Was our move to Israel to support Yehuda's work at the expense of our children? In his passion, Herzl neglected the needs of his children, Paulina and Hans who both led unhappy lives. In 1930, Paulina died from a drug overdose after a morphine addiction and Hans committed suicide when he heard of his sister's death. Am I fooling myself and neglecting my children's needs? This week Hans and Paulina's bodies are being flown from Bordeaux, France to be buried next to their father in the Holy Land.

As I finish my walk, I see a beautiful baby girl who sits cross-legged on the sand staring out to the sea while her young father sits behind patiently watching and giving her space to take pleasure in this experience herself. I want my children to enjoy and benefit from this year's experiences and I remind myself that I cannot rush it. Rather, I must sit back and give all four of my children time and space.

* * *

In honor of Kobe's fifth birthday, Yehuda's whole family is invited to our creamy white castle for brunch at eleven on this Shabbat morning. No one arrives before noon, which for Israelis technically means they are still on time. I pass the morning in the kitchen watching Dror, the caterer chop, mash, mix and stir garbanzo beans, olive oil, lemon, and seasonings into creamy and yet chunky humus. I admire how a traditional chopped vegetable salad can be dressed with seasonings, chopped green olives and pomegranate and become a culinary indulgence. He turns an effortless omelet into tza-tziki (eggs with spices, cheeses and grilled vegetables gently cooked over a low heat for a long time). Fresh loaves of whole wheat, French and raisin breads are sliced and brought out to accent platters full of more Israeli salads.

Kobe does not care for the gastronomic part of his fifth birthday party. Instead, he eats a bag of Bamba (peanut puffs) dressed in his black and gray Batman costume with cape, a present he received a few days earlier and stands guard over the menagerie of brightly wrapped gifts piled up in the living room. Yehuda's relatives sit in our dining room around our new wood tables plates piled high with the meal I carefully observed Dror prepare earlier. Normally this Iraqi-Israeli clan is loud and energetic when meeting, but for a few moments a quiet hum passes through the room with clanking of silverware echoing the sounds of a perfect culinary success. A few minutes later, conversation resumes and the room is loud and alive with energetic family members. It is an afternoon of warm embraces, passionate political debate and lots of story sharing. I am thrilled that our year here affords my children the opportunity to share time with their Israeli family. I am also excited to have a room full of adults to speak with and listen to who are not in my home to repair anything. I probably sound god-awful as I break my tongue speaking Hebrew and by the end of the afternoon I am exhausted from the gratifying linguistic workout.

* * *

I steal an early morning walk with my khaver before anyone notices I am missing. A tinge of sound kindly fills the air from the small, orderly waves gently breaking along the shore. I quickly pass two young men standing on the sand, facing the sea and practicing yoga. I admire their clear focus on the water and the calm movement that comes from their chest as they inhale and exhale. This reminds me to breathe as I walk and live—remembering to breath will remain a valuable focus of mine this year.

During the day, I speak to very few adults other than the repairmen who fix the house. Yehuda is busy at work. He actually works longer hours than I imagined at the start of the year. I enjoy my quiet time, but sometimes scarily, I find myself carrying on a conversation with the kid's fish, Sponge Bob, Patrick, Mimi and Jack and Dr Pepper, who live in glass bowls on the kitchen's window ledge. I realize that I need to be with live friends; I ought to have coffee with my old friends Dominique and Tzipi and not depend on Tom Friedman's poignant editorials from the New York Times or my friend John Stewart from The Daily Show whom I download from iTunes to be part of my social life and make me think and laugh. I can visit with Anderson Cooper at five in the morning, but I am not desperate enough for his companionship at that hour. From my small office in the castle I work on my business, correspond with friends and inhale the constant flow of material from the kids' school. All the while I keep telling myself I will jump-start my social life a-ha-ray ha ha-geem (after the holidays); Rosh Hashana, Yom Kippur and Succot.

* * *

Noa and her friend Daniella awake late in the morning. As I prepare their brunch, I send the girls up the street for watermelon and milk. I love that my children can walk up the street to the market. Back home, this simple activity would require getting in the car and driving. While I chop cucumbers and tomatoes, I speak to Mimi, who stares at me from the round glass tank with her little mouth puckered open as she begs for more food. The girls return with three small melons. We cut one open and there is no crackle sound when the knife goes through and sadly we discover soft orange mush inside. The second and third watermelons fare no better. Chava, the fruit lady grabs the bags full of rotten watermelon. She is very annoyed. "Lama? Lama?" (Why, Why) she yells at me for cutting open all three melons that now she cannot sell to some other unsuspecting customer. I start with the fatal mistake of conversing with her in my Hebrew, which gives her the conversational advantage. Noa and Daniella disappear as to not be a part of this watermelon standoff leaving me alone with Chava who continues to fume; "Lama? Lama?" I apologize as I leave her small produce store and do not even ask for my money back, but she follows me outside insistent that I return for more discussion. I continue on my way dropping the girls off at school for a program in preparation for their upcoming trip to Poland.

I return home to find the air-conditioning man fixing units in the bomb shelter where I will need to stay in case of an emergency and, in the meantime, Noa's hang out with her posse of school friends. Aaron let the technician, a complete stranger in our home and went to shower. In the Holy Land we are much more trusting of strangers, but even this is a little too much. I find Aaron wrapped in a towel as he steps into the shower and say, "Aaron, there is stranger walking around our house. You are home alone with him. What are you doing?" Aaron, at thirteen years old, needs to take a shower and is completely perplexed and annoyed by my questions.

* * *

Three men in wet suits and black masks approach the sea armed with large underwater guns. Seeing these guns does not alarm me, as guns are simply a part of Israeli society. Male and female soldiers at eighteen years old walk the streets in their khaki uniforms with Uzis draped over their shoulders to protect their country; guards at entrances to malls, markets and restaurants have guns to defend the customers; and civilians with licenses have and carry guns. All these guns are legally administered and rarely do we hear of shootings or misuse of the weaponry. So even these sea warriors on the sand of Herzelia Pituah seem normal hunting for tender branzino (sea bass) that hide under rocks. On my return walk south, I see the aqua men swimming out in the distance and my mind wanders to Yehuda and his reunion later with his troop and commander, the men who he fought with in the 6-Day War (1967) and the Yom Kippur War (1973) when he jumped out of planes, fought battles with the enemy, climbed the Golan Heights, conquered the Suez Canal and worked together to survive while fighting for Israel's right to exist. Yehuda is hesitant to attend. He has not seen these men in many years and this painful part of his life he has honestly tried to erase from his memory. "I will not recognize any of them, I have not seen them in thirty years," he says. I still encourage him to attend.

We leave the kids at home and drive to a mo-shav in the center of the country where the reunion takes place at the home of Yehuda's former comrade. Noa and Aaron baby-sit Eden and Kobe. I decide if Yehuda survived the 6-Day War and The Yom Kippur War, my four children can survive each other for this one evening. It is Thursday at four in the afternoon and the traffic crawling out of Herzelia Pituah is already heavy, as we make our way north along the bright blue sparkling sea. We drive though fields of cotton plants in the midst of harvest, white and bountiful countryside as far as I can see in every direction. At the end of the cotton fields, we arrive at a major intersection where the large Arab city of Fureidis sprawls out in many directions. We continue to drive between mountains until we arrive at Yoknaam, a city built in the hills east of Haifa full of large housing developments clustered together by design and colors. We stop at an empty lot in the middle of Yoknaam where a single tractor sits motionless on a flat dirt field, the future home of one of Yehuda's BIG Shopping Centers.

Finally, we arrive a little late at a small house on a mo-shav surrounded by dairy farms and agricultural fields where Yehuda's army reunion is underway. Yehuda's army mates are simply a bunch of older men; some are bald, some are gray and most are round in the belly. It is hard to imagine that these men were once young and fierce warriors. Yehuda is actually in high spirits seeing their faces and hearing old wartime stories that shake him to remember the past. Speeches are made and a young man who currently serves as a reserve fighter pilot speaks to this crowd of veterans about the missions he flew during the Second Lebanon War— the same ones Anderson Cooper and I watched and evaluated from CNN footage. He describes the newer technology, the missiles he dropped and their damage and accuracy. I am intrigued and try hard to understand all that he says, but he speaks very fast in technical Hebrew. We eat dinner at round tables under the stars in the simple farmyard. After many bottles of wine and re-bonding, Yehuda and his old army buddies slowly transform into the soldiers they once were; they laugh, recount episodes, put their arms around each other's shoulders and the familiarity of long ago both in time and circumstance creeps back into their beings. As the evening progresses, I feel more and more like an outsider. It was another time and life for Yehuda and all these men that I simply am not a part of, being an American who never served in any army to defend my nation's existence.

* * *

I relish the fact that Kobe loves to go to gan, be on the kibbutz and speak Hebrew with his new buddies. This morning he enters the gan's small house and runs to the table where the children shape their khallah (sweet bread) dough. His friend Eli yells, "Koooo-be" from another table where he draws on white papers that will be folded and used to envelop the freshly baked khallah. I leave my young baker and joyfully walk to my car along the same path I take each day. The smell of fresh cut grass fills the air like a natural perfume and the sight of the large bright red and pink bougainvilleas enlivens me. Everything about this place feels so right for my young son, my one child who is experiencing an authentic Israeli life.

In the middle of the day, Noa sends me an SMS on the phone, 'I need a razor.' As I am still insecure about the fragile mental well being of my older children, I am not sure if she is having a rotten day or if she is sitting in Spanish class, wearing a very short mini-jean skirt and notices a patch of unshaven hair on her tan legs. A few hours later, Noa and I meet in the kitchen to share watermelon and no mention of the razor takes place. I slice through the hard green rind and once we hear the wonderful crackling sound the cut makes, we know this is a choice watermelon. I cherish each moment as we sit at the kitchen table talking while the sweet red liquid drips down our chins. Noa tells me of her plans to go out with her friends after our Shabbat family dinner. She knows that I have a great fear of pee-go-eem (suicide bomb attacks)—I actually experience sheer panic, when I think too much about pee-go-eem and my teenagers out and about at night. There will be a guard at the entrance to the restaurants I tell myself, but this does not really allay any of my worries. I have devised a 'list of requirements' for her to follow that artificially subdue some of my fears which she recites to placate me before she goes out, "I will not stand in a line to get in anywhere, I will not sit by the entrance to a restaurant or coffee house, I will not wait around in crowds, I will keep my eyes open and look around for anyone approaching with a trench coat." I know very well if her friends congregate outside a club, Noa will be right there with them oblivious to her surroundings. I remember being fifteen when I too basked in a state of feeling invulnerable, but it was a safer time in America in 1979.

* * *

By the Nof Yam lifeguard station a chubby old woman wearing a green paisley bathing suit stands with perfect posture; her arms are flanked by the sides of her body with her eyes closed and her wavy red hair blows in the wind. Her entire body and bathing suit are caked with dry brown clay-mud. She seriously attempts to be at one with nature and her meditation is earnest, yet she comically earns a good look from the multitude of walkers this morning. When I return down the beach, she is still covered with the dry mud but now moves around, stretches her limbs out and performs a form of TaiChi.

"A-har-ay Ha Ha-geem" (after the holidays) is a commonly heard phrase that easily and conveniently leaves the tongue expressing why people do not start any new activities at this time of the year. While the public elementary and high schools start like clockwork on the first day of September, the universities wait until "A-har-ey Ha Ha-geem" to begin which depending on the Jewish calendar falls as late as the end of October. These days I also find myself saying "A-har-ey Ha Ha-geem" to just about everything that I want to push off. I have successfully started four children at new schools, found a housekeeper who does not like to clean, made new friends with a school of fish, have become immersed in local and international news and repaired and furnished my large creamy white castle. But soon I want to start exploring and living adventures outside of my home or this year will pass too swiftly and I will have few of my own stories to tell.

Just this morning, I spent three hours with four different repairmen fixing the leaking pipe in the basement. Each of these very nice gentlemen kissed the mezzuza on the doorframe when he walked in with the promise of solving the problem. After each unsuccessful visit, the repairmen blamed someone, left the broken pipes and with a sincere, "Hag sa-may-akh" departed. I celebrate my defeat with a delicious cappuccino and an Italian sandwich alone at Arcafe Coffee Shop. I have no one to call and share this frustrating domestic saga with in Israel. These friends are far away where it is three o'clock in the morning. "Ha kol yi-he-yay be-seder," I say laughing to myself as I sit alone amongst young people in the high tech business on their lunch break. 'Everything will be okay' as long as I am very patient and have few expectations.

* * *

The turquoise seawater is placid this morning; it feels more like a resort in Cancun than the Middle East. I stop along the northern beach where I discover hundreds of beautiful gray, brown and white concave and spinning seashells; jewels amongst the common half circle seashells and sea rocks lying on the beach. I fill my pockets with as many treasures as I can to take home. Each one of the shells is part of collection I am creating, not unlike the imperfect pieces of our family's puzzle I am putting together this year in Israel. Some how with all the imperfections I will succeed and the finished creation will be beautiful.

Noa and I continue to improve our chocolate chip cookies by adjusting the amount of flour and the temperature of the oven. The cookies are rounder and tastier and Aaron, the ultimate cookie and food critic gives his approval but adds they could still be better. Charming chocoholic Kobe loves the cookies and tells us that they are fabulous. Eden comes home from school and happily reports that she sat with a group of girls at lunch. I feel a great sense of relief knowing that she has found friends. Yehuda is buried in his work; he is in meetings all day long and exhausted when he comes home in the evening. He sits with us at dinner still dreaming of his empire and digesting the last meetings of the day. At seven o'clock each evening an orange business paper arrives to our doorstep, which is the businessman's bible that he must scour before he can go to sleep at night. Our lives, like the chocolate chip cookies, are improving and little by little, I start to relax and enjoy my new surroundings.

* * *

The sea smells deliciously salty. I am tempted to jump into the warm inviting waters fully clothed, but time is my opponent this morning. I still have to run to the kikar and then return home to pack for a weekend on the Island of Cyprus to celebrate Rosh Ha-sha-na.

As always in the middle of the morning, the kikar is full of shoppers. First I stop at Sporty, a tiny store stuffed with enough merchandise to fill a store ten times the size. It is a great ba-la-gan (mess) of sportswear; only the owner knows where everything is located and miraculously the place has everything one needs. I pay for a black leotard I had ordered the week before. "Sha-na To-va" (Happy New Year) and "Hag Sa-may-akh" (Happy Holiday) we recite to one another with warm smiles and I depart. As I pass to the other side of the kikar I dodge a yellow Hummer, the vehicle used by the Israeli Army for years, and now the bright and shiny commercial Hummers grow in popularity here. My phone beeps with an instant message that wishes me, "Sha-na To-va" from the cell phone company. I have never received a message like this on my L.A. cell phone. I step into the pharmacy to visit Oren, my friendly pharmacist to get an inhaler for Noa. Before I walk out, Oren says with a smile, "Sha-na To-va" and "Hag Sa-may-akh", which I happily answer with the same script. I love this part of being in Israel before a holiday. These phrases automatically roll off everyone's tongue with great ease and sincerity. Even from a complete stranger, these words feel warm and genuine.

I arrive home dripping with sweat. I smell awful and look terrible, but I am happy. I spent time with my calm and beautiful khaver; I ran my morning errand by foot in my little town; and I have become more comfortable with the choice to shake up my kids' lives with the move. I have also concluded that this experience will strengthen and enrich all my children and I must cease to compare my parenting skills to those of Theodore Herzl.

* * *

Seven hundred and fifty was the monthly quota of Jews allowed to enter Palestine after World War II by the British Mandate. My father-in-law Shabtai was a young, American Jew who served four years in the US Army in the South Pacific. After the war, he pursued his dream to make Ali-yah to Palestine to help create the Jewish State of Israel. He arrived in France and was immediately offered one of the seven hundred and fifty positions that were allotted each month to refugees, the concentration camp survivors, desperate to make their way to the Holy Land. He refused to take the spot of one of these survivors. Instead he volunteered with the Jewish Underground in France and worked to get Jewish refugees out of Europe and on their way to Palestine. After a few months in Southern France, Shabtai was asked to escort a group of survivors across the Mediterranean Sea. He boarded an old run-down boat and sailed with minimal means and supplies out of Bordeaux, France and on to Palestine. These beaten Jews sang, prayed and dreamt of a better life together under rotten, horrid conditions on the sea, yet they were free and not under Nazi control. Upon their arrival to the port of Haifa they were refused entry by the British, sent back out to sea and escorted to the Island of Cyprus where they were detained in more camps. In the camp along the beautiful coast of Cyprus, Shabtai was a liaison between the Jews who waited to be granted permission to go to Palestine, the British Military and the World Zionist Organization. The camps became a temporary home, where residents set up shop with pre-holocaust expertise, sang songs from the Jewish homeland and waited. After six months, Shabtai left to Palestine. When he finally arrived in the Jewish homeland, he moved to Kibbutz Hatzor near the southern city of Ashdod. Sixty years later he is still a resident.

* * *

The first thing I think about when we land in Larnaca, Cyprus is the obvious and unique juxtaposition of Shabtai's arrival sixty years ago to his arrival today. Just shy of his eighty-ninth birthday, Shabtai, a proud Jew, Israeli and American grandfather of sixteen, great grandfather of four and citizen of Israel, arrives a free man to celebrate the Jewish New Year.

At the baggage claim, the monitor above the carrousel next to us notes that the bags arrive from a recent Beirut, Lebanon flight. The Beirut Airport has only been open for a short time since being bombed by the Israelis during the Second Lebanon War this summer and now we stand side by side with these Lebanese travelers waiting patiently for our luggage. It should be this easy living side by side in our two countries if it were not for religious fundamentalism, which infects the vital organs of a country and makes democracy impotent, while glorifying hate and difference. I want to share this moment and my thoughts with Anderson Cooper, but I know he is far away.

We drive for two and a half hours on narrow highways, through low mountain passages, past cities, towns, farms, groves of olive trees and vineyards. Christos, our driver mostly drives on the left side of the road, a remainder from the days when the British ruled this Mediterranean island, but he also drives in the middle of the road and on the right side as he speeds along comfortable with the surroundings. Cyprus is a beautiful island republic controlled by the Greek Cypriot majority and the Turkish Cypriot minority. There are two languages spoken here, two forms of currency, and strong cultural identities of both Greece and Turkey on this small Mediterranean island with less than one million inhabitants. Cyprus is well known for fancy resorts and castles, pristine beaches, casinos and cruise ships as well as for the fighting between the Greeks and the Turks, border disputes and policy arguments.

We arrive to a slice of heaven. The resort's large white Mediterranean buildings accented with ceramic roof tiles and blue doors and windows sit on a beautiful bluff over looking the vast dark blue sea. From the balcony of my light and simple room, small paths full of lush greenery framed by millions of tiny white, pink and orange flowers make their way to the pool and the beach. For three days, we eat fresh fish and tomato and cucumber salads adorned with authentic Greek feta and rich olive oil. We devour mou-saka (baked vegetables covered in a white sauce), small pita and Greek humus and tza-diki (a thick white, yogurt full of cucumbers and seasoning), grilled blackened shrimp topped with olive oil fermented with sage, lots of chilled, local dry wine and plenty of ice cream. We swim, boat, jet ski, talk, laugh, play cards, watch videos on Macs and soak in the fresh air together, three generations of family from five to eighty-eight years old. For the first time, I am truly calm about the move to Israel and hopeful that I am doing well by my children. The strip of beach where we walk and play has just finished hosting the birth of small sea turtles and the remnants of tiny peach colored eggshells lie in and around holes where the mother turtles laid their eggs. Like a proud uncle, the beach boy tells me that this beach is free of human poachers and not many fish swim close to the shore providing a safe environment for a turtle to hatch, enter the seawater and survive.

"When you are on vacation, you are not in a hurry," a British woman says as she passes me, Kobe and Eden as we slowly meander down the flower-lined path. These words play in my head over and over the rest of the day. I covet the thought of not being in a hurry and hope that a year in Israel will give us all a chance to slow down and appreciate what goes on around us. Life back in L.A. had become a big, blurry hurry. We always seemed to be in a rush to get through each day as we packed so much in with school, family and friends. I was so busy that I could seldom recall what I did the day before without referring to my calendar. I feel like my family is those baby turtles; we have hatched and made our way down the sand and now we enter the seawater to start our swim. I do question if we can survive…

The final afternoon we take a speedboat around the Island. As Aaron happily pilots the boat, he tells a very content Kobe at his side all about the pirates in the sea that we escaped from. At one place, he points in the direction where the pirates hide off in the distance and Kobe spellbound squints to make out this locale. We pass the Bath of Aphrodite and Noa educates Eden on the importance of Aphrodite and at the same time, she explains to Eden that Jews have only one God and the Greeks have many Gods like Zeus, the king of all Greek Gods and Aphrodite, the Goddess of Love. This brief moment in time speeding along the Mediterranean with the wet wind in our faces is a precious treasure I will always embrace.

Shabtai eats more than all of us over the weekend—perhaps making up for his last stay on the island sixty years earlier. Shabtai swims, walks, and he even wades through the surf to get hoisted on the speed boat by two workers after he nearly topples over on the thick, rocky sand while staring at a young, tan woman sunbathing topless. He illustrates for his grandchildren what it means to live life to the fullest and the value of sharing and enjoying time with family. Every minute, every hour, he has a smile on his face, a thank you on his tongue and a kiss for all. Shabtai brings in the Jewish New Year with a glass of wine and a toast to his family about a-ha-va (love) and the value and beauty of being together this year and in the future.

* * *

The sweltering heat is back. The beach offers little relief from the thick warm air hovering over Israel. At Sharon Beach in front of the lifeguard station, hundreds of seniors with speckled gray and white hair blissfully flavor the calm blue sea. Two lifeguards sit motionless on the balcony of their lifeguard station as they reserve their energy and watch the older generation commune in the shallow water. Looking north, a herd of young bare breasted runners make their way under bright blue skies toward me at a rapid pace through the shallow sea like a tight pack of wild gazelle. Young men just shy of their eighteenth birthdays, physically strong with shaven heads, train for their upcoming army service, when they will proudly take their turn to protect and serve their country. Quickly on the beautiful beach, I share a moment with these two distant generations.

These young men cause me to think of my oldest son, who quicker than I like it, approaches this age and may one day choose to join the IDF (the Israel Defense Force) like his father. For the time being, Aaron plays in a neighborhood basketball league and spends most of his free time at the Sport Tech where he plays more basketball. I see very little of him and when he is around, he is cranky and snaps answers at me when I try to talk to him. He has no patience for me and barely tolerates any of his family. The congenial kid who piloted the speedboat seems to have stayed in Cyprus. Noa happily settles into her new life, meeting a group of kids from school each afternoon and on the weekends at the kikar or the beach to just 'hang out'. Eden slowly makes friends and ceases to complain about lunch companions or partners to walk around the track. Kobe loves the gan and speaks a lovely form of Hebrish with his new friends.

Eldad Regev and Ehud Goldwasser, the soldiers kidnapped by Hezbollah terrorists from Israeli territory along the border of Lebanon on July 11, 2006 still remain captives. Israel is small territorially and tightly connected emotionally. These men represent every Israeli's son, brother, boyfriend and husband. The nature of 'six-degrees of separation' ensures that everyone knows Eldad and Ehud either through a personal network or by way of the very personal and intense nature of news in this country. Just a couple of weeks before Eldad and Ehud were ambushed and kidnapped, a young soldier, Gilad Shalit was kidnapped by Palestinian terrorists who dug tunnels from the Gaza Strip into Israel with the clear goal of kidnapping soldiers to hold and exchange for Palestinian prisoners who sit in Israeli jails. These vibrant and dedicated young men running past me are just like Eldad, Ehud and Gilad, as they commence their service to their country, which can span more than thirty years.

* * *

I walk to visit my khaver. The waves are deep and robust this morning, yet the tide is quite low and many scattered seashells and rocks are exposed along the shore. I walk mindful that each step I take is normally covered with water and feel at this very moment a huge smile take over my face. I have rediscovered my smile muscles that I did not exercise much during the first month here and it feels good celebrating the New Year with my smile's return. This morning Noa, my least athletic child actually set her alarm clock and took an early morning walk along the sea with her friend Ruth. I hope that this year Noa will discover what she has passions for other than shopping and going out to eat. Perhaps drastic is an understatement bringing a fifteen year old around the world to help her discover fervor for life but now I feel the wheels are in motion. In a rare conversation, Aaron tells me that the son of the Jordanian Ambassador fasts and refrains from PE for the month of Ramadan. Aaron is impressed; he knows it would be very hard for him to miss even one meal.

He contemplates fasting on Yom Kippur, something he never has even conceptualized.

We are in the middle of the Yo-meem No-ra-eem (Days of Awe or Days of Repentance) between Rosh Ha-shana and Yom Kippur; ten days where Jews pray, consider the sins of the previous year and repent before the start of the New Year and then pray some more. The Muslims in Israel and all over the world commence Ramadan, the holy ninth month of the Muslim calendar when the Angel Gabriel sent the Koran from Heaven to the prophet Muhammad. Ramadan is also a time for worship, personal reflection and contemplation when Muslims refrain from eating, smoking and sex during daylight. These religious cousins, Jews and Muslims, celebrate two different holidays that share parallel significance. I just wish they could also share understanding and tolerance.

* * *

At Nof Yam, the most northern beach, I realize that the large stones I have seen protruding from the seawater are really pieces of ruins that fell from the Apollonia Park just above. From the sand I look up and see the fortress' broken wall along the palisades once built as protection from the enemy. The missing pieces are those that have tumbled to the sea and are part of my daily walk. I make a note that one day I must visit the park and learn more about the Phoenicians who first settled in my neighborhood and also must have enjoyed the beautiful Mediterranean locale as I do 2000 years later.

"Hag sa-mey-akh," two young repairmen say to me after they fix the front gate lock for the fifth time in two weeks. Each time they come to fix the lock they announce that the gate is perfect and I should sign the work order. Last week, I asked one of them to show me how the front gate worked 'perfectly'. When he shut the door it popped open and with his head hanging low, he exclaimed, 'sheeet'. Now a week later, he is back but I have a more urgent matter; water sprays from a large crack in the gray plastic pipes in the supply room next to the garage and floods the floor with half a foot of water. I call Shmulik, the gentleman whom we pay to help us navigate the problems of this castle. "Al-ti-da-gee" (Don't worry),

"Ha kol yi-he-yay be-seder"' (Everything will be okay), he says in his slow drawn out voice. I have learned that when an Israeli says either 'Al-ti-da-gee' or 'Ha kol yi-he-yay be-seder' it is actually an ideal time to start to worry. Shmulik informs me that it is hard to get a plumber during the holidays and it will be expensive. Perhaps my screams in Hebrish that I cannot live this way for an entire weekend snap him into shape and he miraculously finds a plumber who arrives at my house an hour later.

The plumber and I wade through the small indoor lake. He surveys the problem and with a serious expression, he begins to explain in Hebrew what needs to be done. I ask him to speak in English as I have come to understand when I deal with Israeli service people, I need to speak English to have the conversational advantage and not leave anything to independent interpretations. This gentleman in his broken English explains how the piping system is American and the Israelis have glued it all wrong. He plays with a few nozzles, drains the flooded floor and places a bucket under the subdued leak, which he tells me to dump every few hours until he can come back and fix it. "Hag Sa-may-akh" and he leaves me.

Life for the family continues on an upward spiral. Aaron plays basketball every night and complains less about school. When he is willing to speak to me, he assures me that he is doing his schoolwork at his Trump desk while his display of empty Dr Pepper cans grows on the shelf behind him. Dr Pepper is a precious commodity in Israel; I can only find it in certain markets and go out of my way to make sure he has it hoping like a cock-eyed optimist that this will make him happy. Kobe is happy at the kibbutz; he plays with the kids and now speaks Hebrew in the "I" form, which means no matter what he says or with whom he speaks, he changes the verb and the subject of the sentence to be for and about him. Noa has a group of friends (mostly boys) who come in and out, eat dinner over, swim and just hang. Eden makes more friends at school, loves her hip-hop classes and has returned to being happy. I breathe much easier each day.

* * *

I am astonished by the number of people walking before seven on Shabbat morning, and even more remarkable is the high percentage of people with rainbow-colored rubber Croc sandals on their feet. Crocs have reached epidemic proportions taking over the feet of Israelis from small children to seniors. Israelis love trends; they are bold people who can make even bright rubber footwear a perfect fashion statement for all ages in a record amount of time. Later in the morning, I see a family walking in front of the creamy white castle on their way to the synagogue and the three little girls in long white lace dresses all wear shocking pink Crocs.

Today, as part of my commitment to change in the New Year, I put away my Blackberry and valiantly go cold turkey. This is my brave attempt to escape from being the constantly connected and available woman, technology junky, who from the moment I awake until I fall asleep at night, gets high from the vibrating and gonging of all incoming messages.

While I refuse to wear Crocs and distance myself from the addictive world of Blackberry connectivity, Eden literally joins the circus. My eight-year old daughter discovers a new passion for flying though the air and hanging from a thin rope. She embraces the feeling of leaving the secure floor for the unknown. I am unfamiliar with this part of her character, but am thrilled that she takes chances and challenges herself even if it means I must close my eyes and hold my breathe when she is dangling upside down in mid air on the trapeze. Noa also embarks on a frightening yet powerful adventure as she prepares to travel to Poland and immerses herself in the tragic story of the Holocaust. Each Sunday, her group meets with a representative of the Israeli Education Ministry to learn the facts, hear the stories and absorb the tragedies of the Holocaust, before they face the locales where the atrocities transpired. Noa is a student hungry for information and her character is greatly inspired by what is fair. I know this trip will deeply affect her and I will not be there to support her. This is another important step for me as a mother accepting that I cannot control everything my children are exposed to and that they must go through some tough experiences without me.

* * *

The light blue seawater is clear and serene like a swimming pool that appears motionless as far as my eyes can see. Yehuda and I walk the stretch of beach under the cliffs just below the United States Embassy Estate sharing stories back and forth. We returned from the weekend in Cyprus rested and relaxed. We have passed the challenging acclimation of our family to Israel where we snapped at each other over many little and unimportant things. Today we laugh and Yehuda helps me look for the funny odd shaped seashells. Slowing down is a challenge for my husband, an international businessman who does not generally make the time to enjoy the beauty in silly things such as seashells.

In the afternoon, while Kobe and Eden are in the pool, my teenage son appears. The little ones attempt to coax him into joining them. He is not eager to jump in, so I dare him to ride the old bike lying by the side of the pool into the water. And to all of our delight, he takes off his shirt and happily pedals the bike into the pool. He flashes a smile when he surfaces and for a brief moment, I am reminded that my sweet son still exists under that cranky teen exterior.

Tali, the Israeli housekeeper quits. I am too demanding, she tells me. Truthfully, she does not want to work hard, but I gracefully accept her criticism. Julie, a petit young woman arrives at my door. She is a gift sent from the G-d of Cleaning who I believe has taken pity on me. Jews have only one G-d, but for this situation I make a small exception. I will harbor Julie, an illegal Philippine worker, and protect her from the politicians and the police, who in my opinion, have larger problems in the Holy Land than domestic help in Herzelia Pituah. If caught, Julie will be deported and I will be fined thousands of shekels and have a police report written on me, a chance I am willing to take at this point to free me of my Israeli household servitude.

* * *

At the North beach on the narrow sandy shore, a beautiful and eccentric beachfront home exists built into the rough jagged cliffs. It is a true masterpiece built in the style of the Spanish architect Antoni Gaudi on the most ideal beach real estate. An eight-foot wall surrounds the front artistically constructed with boulders and stones of all different shapes and sizes placed tightly next to one another. Inside, there is a small courtyard and I have heard that the owner opens up an informal beach café and serves pita and humus from time to time in the summer. Up along the cliffs, a combination of tunnels and structures jut out forming rooms and hallways and throughout the property, roof tops and open spaces are adorned with a menagerie of hand crafted art pieces featuring a multi-colored Star of David mosaic, a cement Buddha head with large mirror eyes, brown and green beer bottle monuments, large cement fingers and a faded blue and white Israeli Flag blows in the wind. It is a spectacle and no matter how many times I pass, I am entertained by new details that appear. I have never seen a home as personal as this one.

Noa leaves early for a trip to Yad Vashem, the Holocaust Memorial Museum in Jerusalem. Today she will be immersed in the history and the memories of the Jews who were murdered by the Nazis. She will walk through the rows and rows of information and remaining personal articles; clothing, bags, shoes, badges, dolls, toys, armbands, books and journals. She will hear stories, watch movies and spend a day immersed in the tragic and terrifying Holocaust, all commemorated so profoundly at Yad Vashem.

Meanwhile, in a land not far away, Iranian President Mahmoud Ahmadinejad uses his public appearances to call for the destruction of our nation while arguing that the Holocaust did not happen. His premise being that if there were no Holocaust, then it was a mistake for the United Nations to give Israel to the Jews. He also discounts that this land has been the Jewish Homeland for thousands of years. The Iranian government is the main financier of the Hezbollah spiritual leader, Hassan Nasrallah who has attacked Israel from Hezbollah strongholds in Southern Lebanon long before the Second Lebanon War last summer. At the same time in Gaza, President Ahmadinejad finances the Hamas party which daily calls for the destruction of Israel, authorizes text books for children that urge for the destruction of the Jewish Nation and supports the daily Qassam Rockets sent into Israel by Palestinian terrorists.

* * *

"Yom Kippur is the most fun day of the year," Kobe excitedly exclaims as he rides his bicycle down the street on Kol Nidre, the eve of Yom Kippur. I am a bit uneasy as my five-year old proclaims with pure delight that on the holiest day of the year for the Jewish people where we are supposed to atone for sins, reflect on bad deeds, ask forgiveness and fast to show honor to G-d, he feels this way. But my son is absolutely correct—it is pure joy to bike down the public streets in the heart of our town void of cars, buses and trucks amidst other bicycles. A whole nation stops; life as we are familiar with it, ceases for 24 hours and the air is fresh, free from auto exhaust.

"It's a school tradition," Noa says with one foot out the door as she convinces me to let her spend the whole night out on the dark streets with the high school kids. Aaron rides with us for a short time and then he too disappears on his bike. We continue on our adventure passing through streets we are only accustomed to driving through in our cars. Late into the night, we pass hundreds of well-dressed young religious families congregating by the synagogue as their children also ride around on tricycles and bikes. Our neighborhood synagogue is open to anyone who wants to attend a service or pray at any time during the 24 hours of Yom Kippur, but as far as I can see in our neighborhood the emphasis is on freedom and not religion.

The next day under sunny skies, more people and children fill the streets riding and running in all directions. Aaron rides with his friend Idan and returns by 2pm famished and exhausted, but does not yield to food. Noa sleeps most of the day as she tries to avoid food, but at 4:30pm, I receive a tearful call that she does not feel good. She also does not yield to food. Back in L.A., Yom Kippur means dressing up, sitting in a hot synagogue (as there always seemed to be a heat wave), looking around at all the other Jews making their bi-annual visit to shul (temple), listening to the Rabbis and of course praying. I may not be in shul, but I am in the Holy Land, which is the ultimate temple. Later in the day, Aaron who usually is a cotz (prickle) to Eden offers to take her out for a ride. Perhaps his day on the bike with no food has caused him to reflect on his behavior toward his sister?

After sunset, three generations; my mother who is visiting, my husband and me and our children sit down to eat the most delicious dinner to break our day long fasting. I continue to be amazed by the different ways Jews celebrate the same holiday. While we were biking, religious Jews spent the day deep in prayer. Many religious also performed the pre-Yom Kippur kaparah ritual where slaughtered roosters and hens representing men and women were swung over the heads of sinners and prayers were made to symbolize that the chickens died freeing the sinners up so they could have a good and long life. I am not sure I have been freed of any or all of my sin, but my Yom Kippur bike riding experience exhilarates me. Today we celebrated the most holy day in the Holy Land in a meaningful and memorable manner and I appreciated it more than praying with strangers in shul. I do wonder if there is anywhere else in the world where a whole nation simply stops operating for 24 hours?

* * *

I am definitely getting old. One day after riding a bike and a scooter through Herzelia Pituah and fasting for twenty-four hours my rear is in pain, my knees ache, my head spins and I am physically and mentally exhausted. I muster up all the energy I have for an Iyengar Yoga session this morning focusing on my breath; taking air in and letting it out slowly through my nose while in triangle pose. I ponder the message written on my yoga guru's t-shirt, 'Yoga is a mirror to look at ourselves from within. BKS Iyengar'. In Israel, I appreciate the need for yoga where the focus is on positions rather than pace and reflects one of my personal goal this year, to slow down and take care of myself, which is proving to be more illusive than I had thought.

The cleansing process continues after yoga; I open the kitchen cabinets and start throwing out the many cereal boxes full of sugar, chocolate and peanut butter. I am shocked that in a few months, Kobe has successfully convinced me to buy all this crappy breakfast food. As I fasted on Yom Kippur, Kobe consumed Peanut Butter Crunch cereal for breakfast, Coco Puffs for brunch and Nestle's Crunch for lunch. I can no longer say "Lo" all the time to my five-year old chocoholic. The just solution is to remove the tempting items from the house for the New Year.

* * *

A small man with a blue pirate bandana on his head is sculpting the figure of a naked woman sunbathing on the moist sand. The woman has a beautiful body; large luscious breasts, an ample stomach, round and sexy hips and solid muscular legs. Many walkers in bright colored Crocs slow as they pass the sculpture but do not stop, not trusting the unusual occurrence. This year I focus on the need to make the time to stop and observe everything I can and this show is a real treat. Near the end of my walk, I enjoy the Mediterranean beauty one last time making a mental picture of her thinking that the only thing she is missing is a pair of Crocs.

We are invited to Shabbat family breakfast at Yehuda's Aunt Shula and Uncle Yacov's apartment on the top story of an old building along the Yarkon River in Tel Aviv. Yacov and Shula have lived in Israel for over half a century, yet they remain very much Iraqi in their customs and the majority of their friends are Iraqi and speak Arabic. Shula is without a doubt, the finest chef I have encountered in all of Israel. Her breakfast buffet is a feast for the senses; tender grilled eggplant and squash, soft, brown hard boiled eggs, finely chopped salad perfectly seasoned, sautéed yellow and red bell peppers, lightly scrambled eggs with tomatoes, peppers and cheese, vegetarian egg rolls, thinly fried vegetable patties, salads and Arab flat bread. On top of this, Shula prepares in my honor, her world famous Ti-beat that she cooks many hours on the stove creating a crispy crust at the bottom that is then served upside down featuring the crunchy divine outer layer. The feast does not end here; platters of cheeses, small warm phyllo turnovers filled with salty cheese and bowls of fruit served with bread and preserves that Shula makes herself follow served with piping hot, strong tea in dainty, gold trimmed glasses. Shula has placed out two extra tables to fit Yehuda's large family, which is gathered in honor of my mother's visit to Israel.

As we eat breakfast, Eden, Kobe and the other small children run around and play. These meals have the same flavor as those at my grandparent's small apartment when I was a little girl. Memories send me back to a time when my brother, sister and I would happily run around and play with the many toys my grandmother kept neatly in her closet while the adults sat at the table eating and speaking mostly in Russian long after we finished our food. At one point, Kobe invites me to join him for a visit with Jacko, the green parrot who lives in a large cage in Shula's enchanting kitchen. Boldly Jacko calls out in Hebrish to anyone who might listen while standing ready to nip at the fingers of any little children who dare to stick them through the gaps in his cage.

Yehuda's family sits around the table enthusiastically discussing politics and politicians, each member with a different opinion on what to do with Hezbollah, Hamas, Iranian President Ahmadinejad, and Prime Minister Olmert. Passion and frustration dominate the unharmonious conversation where everyone freely expresses his or her opinion and others loudly disagree, but in the end, no feelings are hurt—I love this about Israelis. Years earlier Uncle Yacov, who grew up in Baghdad living among Arabs, made the point to me that Arabs only understood ko-akh (power) and not words; he personally witnessed the dislike many Muslims had for the Jews in Iraq. I have wanted Yacov to be wrong so many times. Prime Minister Itzhak Rabin used words to disprove Yacov's theory of ko-akh and make a peace with the Palestinians during Oslo Accord but did not succeed before his assassination.

I daydream back to the beautiful sand sculpture this morning as I sit in a room admiring the very strong and intelligent women in Yehuda's family. The Midrash says that man was created from the dust of the earth and woman was created from the bone of Adam with bone being stronger than earth and not easily broken. In the Knesset we have strong and intelligent women like Foreign Minister Tzipi Livni and Speaker of the Knesset Dalia Itzhik, who offer a wonderful combination of strength and sensitivity in the struggle for a comprehensive peace that their male associates cannot. We need female Israeli leaders to find their counterparts on the Arab side, intelligent Palestinian women, to initiate dialogues and work alongside men to find a real and long lasting solutions to bring about co-existence and shalom.

* * *

I lie in my bed in the middle of the night staring at the ceiling frustrated by the climate of hate around me here in the Middle East. The fear and distrust that I experience places me unconditionally on the side of the Israelis who I know are not always right, but I am aware that if we behave naively and let our defenses down, we will be attacked either by rockets, missiles, pee-go-eem or far worse. There are six million Jews living in Israel and sometimes it feels like there are equally as many Arabs surrounding the nation who are eager and ready to die for Israel's destruction. How do I find the strength to be a pacifist when I am aware that these killers are eager to annihilate my children? Six million Jews on one land surrounded by hate makes the pacifist in me go AWOL at times. Intellectually, I know that war is not the answer, but emotionally under the circumstances war feels like the only option. In May of 2000, the IDF (Israel Defense Force) pulled out of Southern Lebanon giving up the buffer zone between the two nations and there has not been peace or security along the border since. In the summer of 2005, the Israelis pulled out of Gaza and since then there has neither been peace nor security along this border. Occupation was not the right answer; pulling out from these two lands was not the solution. How can Israel exist with hostile neighbors who do not respect the nature of national borders?

After some time, I go outside on the balcony to the cool air to admire the millions of stars densely packed in the clear dark sky. This experience is not possible back in L.A. where too many city lights obstruct this view. I am tiny in this enormous universe, but the multitude of stars that fill the clear skies empower me to think that anything is possible even in the crazy Middle East.

* * *

The mayor leans over and whispers, "At least we can sing about shalom," as a young woman, sings passionately in Hebrew on the small stage. We sit under a white canopy on a hot sunny morning at the dedication ceremony of a pedestrian passage and playground my mother donated the funds to construct in the ancient city of Jaffa. Nearby the blue Mediterranean Sea glistens and the Muezzin's beautiful call to prayer from a neighboring mosque fills the air. Jaffa is home to many Arab Israelis as well as many Jewish Israelis who live side by side in old stone buildings on dark narrow streets. Jaffa with all its character is very poor and run down from years of neglect, but in small pockets, urban renewal projects like this one take place. During the ceremony, a group of Arab mothers in dark colored dresses and head covering watch their young children swing in the playground. I wonder how these women manage in the heat covered from head to toe; I am wearing a summer dress and am sweating. We visit two remodeled nursery schools in a poor area of Southern Tel Aviv attended by a diverse group of Israeli children, the children of African refugees and a few Palestinian children whose fathers worked for the Israeli police in the territories and for fear of being murdered, as traitors cannot return. In each classroom, the children sing in appreciation of my mother, whose desire is to help children in the Holy Land regardless of race or religion.

* * *

Powerful waves crash upon the shore, rushing fast and furious up the sand. The usually bright blue water is now murky brown from the churning seawater. In the North, the sand passage is quite narrow and I find myself very close to the rusted barbed wire fence that prevents visitors from walking too close to the eroding cliffs. I am tempted to cross over through an opening, but am respectful and truthfully fearful of the message on the signs in Hebrew, Arabic and English that warns of landslides. It is evident by the piles of fallen rocks and sand that the layers of sandstone are sensitive, but this does not stop the fearless Israelis who ignore the warning signs and enter the forbidden zone.

The creamy white castle continues to fall apart; there is no water pressure; the front gate does not lock; the front door pops open; the air passing through the vents in Eden's room emits a pungent burning plastic smell; the washing machine stops working; the fax machine freezes; and the pipe in the garage still leaks. I escape the barrage of problems finding refuge at the Seven Star Mall. I know that many of the technicians I am waiting for do not work over the Sukkot holiday as they sit taking time off under their sukkah (Sukkot holiday structure).

The friendly Ethiopian security guard at the parking lot greets me with "hag sa-may-akh" and then he looks in my trunk and waves me through. The cool mall is active with children on vacation and people celebrating Sukkot. The lobby's passage is full of tables with different vendors selling enticing Sukkot foods and beverages; I stop to sample some cheese and crackers and then dip a piece of bread into divine green olive oil wishing that the bottles of wine on display were also being offered to sample. I move on to the final section and watch with pleasure as an Arab woman traditionally dressed lays open a flat pita bread and pours over it a ladle full of leben (creamy white sheep's milk yogurt), fresh olive oil and za-tar (a Middle Eastern herb mixture of sesame seeds, oregano, thyme and sumac). Then she wraps it in a napkin and hands it to me. Even before I pay, I take a bite into this delightful Arab burrito; warm, creamy and a bit tart from the leben and the zatar. "At o-he-vet?" (You like) She asks me in Hebrew, and my smile is enough of an answer to please her. I do not leave before she convinces me to buy bak-la-va (a Middle Eastern dessert of phyllo dough filled with honey and nuts) that I know Yehuda will enjoy. I also smile happily thinking that Jewish mothers and Palestinian mothers enjoy serving food to their children and their guests, a common thread with women and motherhood that cannot be overlooked and should be uniting and celebrated.

* * *

Yehuda and I walk along the sand in the late afternoon to bid farewell to the Eden Beach Bar on its closing day. It is a warm afternoon; still plenty of swimmers, sand castle architects, matcot players, Frisbee tossers and sunbathers along the beach while in the sea a large group of kayakers paddle by and groups of patient surfers wait for decent waves to ride to the shore. The sun hits the blue water making a bright path that glows as it rushes far off in the horizon decorated on either side by an array of sailboats. We walk barefoot enjoying the unseasonable warmth. Kobe trails behind us as he delights in seashells and young couples kissing along the sand.

Eden Beach bustles with energy. Techno music blares from large speakers; young people fill the deck by the bar and dance celebrating life and nature here on the sand and in the background the final games of beach volleyball are played. This celebration marks an end to the summer and an end to Eden Beach. Today is also Simkhat Torah, the final day of Sukkot, which also marks a culmination; it is the final reading of the Torah where the religious dance with and honor the Torah Scroll.

Yehuda and I sit on the used plastic chairs with our toes in the warm sand and eat heaping bowls of chopped salads with basil, a plate full of humus covered with delightful olive oil and of course, doughy and warm pita and very cold beer. While we eat our 'last supper' on Eden Beach, Kobe quickly devours a Nestles Crunch Ice Cream. Out of the house, I have less control over his terrible eating habits. He then plays in the sand with the tiny plastic lion he found along the walk and crawls around so that every nook and cranny of him is layered and filled with sand. We enjoy the fresh air and the sunset over the water, the beat of the techno music and Kobe in his own imaginary world—another perfect moment.

A-ha-ray Ha-ha-geem (After the Holidays)

It is still early when I take a cappuccino and the Herald Tribune outside to read. Before I sit down on my lounge chair, I am overcome by the putrid smell of someone burning trash nearby. This, coupled with the mornings when the shower water briefly runs a light brown color or arrives with the strong stench of Chlorine, reminds me that Israel with all of its growth and splendor in fifty-eight years is still a partial blend of the Third World and these are all normal growing pains for a developing nation.

Kobe and I laugh as we watch the goldfish Sponge Bob and Patrick Star eat like gluttons, lurching toward the flakes and sucking them in with round open mouths. Sponge Bob actually eats too much and a few seconds later the food flies out of his mouth back into the water. I glance out to the yard and see a small humming bird circle the tree branches. Mimi, Eden's last remaining fish after three passed away in less than two weeks, has developed a passion for playing with a string that has fallen in the tank. Eden is delighted as her fish shows talent unknown to goldfish, which is a pleasure after the tears that fell each time we flushed the other ones down the toilet. Aaron's Siamese fighting fish, Dr Pepper is listless along the edge of his bowl next to the knives on the counter. Lunches are made. Breakfasts are eaten. No one yells and no one pisses anyone off. It is a pretty good day and not yet eight in the morning. Yehuda drives the kids to school this morning. As they drive off, it occurs to me that we are now coasting thought the year; our lives have taken on the form of comfort and acceptance that this is now our home.

The Knesset marks the winter session's opening ceremonies and yet my gee-bor-ah continues to suffer; President Katsav is due to be charged with rape; Qassam Rockets land in the city of Sderot daily; Eldad and Ehud, the two Israeli soldiers kidnapped by Hezbollah are still missing; Hamas and Fatah still battle each other in Gaza; the IAF (Israeli Air Force) attacks locales in Gaza where it believes Qassam Rockets are being launched; the kidnapped soldier, Gilad Shilat is still a prisoner in Gaza and for him, the Palestinians demand a thousand prisoners be released.

* * *

The sea is stunning. The waves are huge and wonderful and the wind is alive and brisk. A team of men on surfboards attached to large brightly colored parachutes fly across the water while their chutes dance around the sky above them like gigantic butterflies drunk with color and rhythm. I bundle up with sweaters to stop the cold air from entering under my skin. As I walk north the wind pushes me from behind aiding my journey to Nof Yam. On my return the wind opposes each step I take, and while my body moves forward, my skin and my hair are constantly forced back in the direction from which I come. Thankfully they are a part of me and must journey on. Before I ascend to the street, I once more delight in these wild surfers and their manmade bright and excited butterflies flying through the air. I feel a bit jealous of their power and their 'joie de vivre'.

I spend the rest of the morning with a very good-looking man wearing a dark green shirt with the letters FOREPLAY written across his chest. Mr. Foreplay is the latest specialist deployed to help me with problems in the creamy white castle. Yorumthe gardener arrives for his bi-monthly visit to trim the hedges and blow the dust and leaves around—ironically supplemented by the strong winds today. He has no grass to maintain, as the Astroturf is indestructible. In the afternoon, I throw out the trash and see that Yorum cut down one of the kumquat trees in the front yard along the fence producing a gaping hole. I was home all day and we spoke, but he never mentioned that he was cutting down a tree. I call Yehuda at the office to voice my anger and hear complete distance in his voice. I realize that in his work, he has larger battles to wage than the gardener who cut down the kumquat tree, but in my small world it is a personal affront.

***

The beach is empty in the early morning as I walk alone sharing quiet time with my khaver and enjoying my solitude. As I approach the Gaudi house, I see a group of people congregating on the beach. In the middle, a cameraman is filming a man in jeans and a t-shirt holding a beer bottle who wades through the water while being hit by crashing waves. The air is cool and I imagine that the water is quite cold, but he appears to enjoy his attention from the camera and the crowd of spectators.

At the Arena Mall in the Herzelia Marina, Noa and I shop for a warm jacket for her trip to Poland where she will find freezing temperatures. The mall is not busy on this Sunday morning, as the whole country has commenced the workweek. We pass large windows overlooking the marina packed with sailboats. The usually crowded restaurants and coffee shops surrounding the marina are empty. My attention returns to the sparkling mall and my mission to buy a warm jacket—it is freezing cold and very wet all over Poland. My daughter Noa's goal is simply fashion. I am fully aware that if I battle this and make her take an ugly warm jacket she will be miserable. The freezing cold she can handle, bad fashion will not be so easy to overcome. In the end she wins and buys a long, black jacket that is lined with a tiny bit of warm fake fur. I have already waterproofed her Uggs four times, and each time I recommend that she blow-dry them daily so that she will start her mornings with dry feet, I am met with rolling incredulous eyes. Underneath this ceremonial teenage behavior, I can only hope she listens to me.

We walk through the market to buy snacks as she has heard the food on the trip is horrible. I am not sure what she expects—Sushi in Warsaw? We buy boxes of health bars, rice crackers, instant cup-a-soups, hot cereal, peanut butter, whole wheat bread and Special K Cereal. I am painfully cognizant of the irony here; I send Noa off to Poland with warm clothing and extra food rations so she will not feel cold or hunger, while she visits camps, villages and towns where kids her age froze and starved and there was not a single thing their mothers could do to control their situation.

Later in the evening, Noa and I sit outside on the stairs in the fresh air next to the broken step staring at the hole in the hedge where the gardener cut down the kumquat tree. We wait for her friend Ben to pick her up as I am 'the only mom who will not let her daughter walk around at night alone' in addition to being 'the only mom who requires that her daughter adhere to a curfew'. When Ben arrives, she pecks me on the cheek and says, "I love you mom" and rushes out the gate. I stare at the opening in the wall where my tree was chopped down. I smile and realize that the abyss I worried so terribly I was creating in my dramatic fifteen-year old daughter's life does not really exist. She is happy and I consider this a success.

* * *

I arrive with Noa at Kikar Sharon at two in the morning where it is dark and desolate with the exception of the brightly lit all night snack store and Pizza Domino. A group of students already sits on the ground and waits with their luggage, but there are no parents, no teachers and no bus. Noa pops out of the car and takes her bag, kisses me goodbye and joins her friends. I drive around to the other side of the kikar where I park and wait. No matter how liberal a mother I want to be, there is not a chance that I am leaving my kid with no teacher and no bus in the middle of the night in the kikar and assuming that she will make it to Poland. After about ten minutes, the enormous tour bus arrives followed by one of the teacher escorts. Noa walks over and invites me to wait with the other parents who have gathered by the bus. It is 2:30am and I find myself with a group of strangers, parents whom I do not know, sharing these insecure moments. I am acutely aware of my plastic smile as I attempt to cover my melancholy feelings. Noa gives me a final kiss and then disappears into the dark innards of the bus. I realize that this is the last time I will see my daughter for eight days as she embarks on her journey to learn about the horrors and tragedies of the Holocaust in freezing cold weather with bad food. I have waterproofed her Uggs so many times that they stand at attention and dav-ka (of course) the last thing she tells me is that she wants to fold them over for a more fashionable appearance.

I have written two letters to my oldest daughter expressing my love and respect for her on this difficult trip to Poland as well as my pride in how she has navigated the journey so far in her short fifteen years. She will receive these letters with my words of love and consolation along her painful travels learning about the Holocaust and seeing where the atrocities took place. This is a difficult experience for me as her mother; I have always yearned to make things bearable for my child and now I cannot.

* * *

The almost full white moon makes its way through the dark sky on Halloween night. Kobe in his gold and purple Kobe Bryant jersey and Eden in her bright orange pumpkin costume enthusiastically join witches, pirates, skeletons, vampires, princesses and an IPod for 'trick or treating' and collecting candy to place in their plastic Halloween bags on the designated street in Herzelia Pituah. While Halloween is not an Israeli holiday, the Americans from the embassy have designed an evening just for the students to experience the festivity. Many of the children have never celebrated this holiday in their homeland and are not even familiar with the phrase 'trick or treat', but with ease they dress in costume and collect candy.

The final house on the map is the American Ambassador's residence set behind a white wall and guarded by the same team of Israelis that protect the children at school. For an hour, we watch our children on a sugar high run around the resident's enormous park-like backyard with its rolling grass lawns. The Ambassador and his wife serve Eden Water, coffee and more candy. Before I know it, I am stuffing my purse with mini-tootsie rolls and realize that I have become like my crazy old Aunt Jean whom as a child I watched pocket food and dessert to take home when she had dinner at our house.

Eden and Kobe dump their full bags of delectable American candy all over the white kitchen table when we arrive home—Skittles, Tootsie Rolls, M&Ms plain and peanut, Reese's Peanut Butter Pieces, Milk Duds, Tootsie Pops, Snickers Bars, Milky Way Bars, and Starbursts—a major caloric score supplied by the American Embassy community that simply does not exist in Israel. In L.A. after a night of 'trick or treating' I check everything in my children's bags, but tonight I know where the candy comes from and am confident that no one has tampered with it.

* * *

At 3:45am the brightly lit welcoming hall at Ben Gurion Airport is packed full of enthusiastic and excited Israelis welcoming their loved ones home. All eyes focus on the non-transparent sliding glass doors opening and releasing arrivals into the hall. This is my first time on this side of the arrival ceremony to Israel. I stand by a group of energetic Ethiopian religious kids who carry signs and balloons waiting to greet their friends also returning from Poland. The boys have pretty embroidered kipot on their heads and the girls wear oversized sweaters with long denim skirts. Noa and her friends also wear denim skirts, just mini ones that cover very little of the legs. When the sliding glass doors open and a friend appears, they all scream and cheer and a few of the girls charge past the guards for a huge embrace as though they are meeting long lost siblings arriving from Addis Ababa, Ethiopia after years of separation. Their pure joy in these reunions is truly contagious and tears well up in my eyes as I share these special moments with complete strangers. As each door slides open, I become more and more excited and eager to be reunited with my daughter. Noa called when the plane landed so it is only a matter of time until she is discharged from the sliding glass doors and returned to me.

For eight days, Noa called me complaining about the lack of bathroom stops, the minimal food and the poor hotel conditions—typical teen complaints. She also acknowledged the amazing journey she was on; the towns, cities and concentration camps she visited; the stories she heard from a survivor, who joined her group daily; the memorials where they lit candles; and the synagogues where they had Friday night services. Noa's complaints were all superficial; a sensitive girl needing to vent and express her pain for more than room and board by what she faced when she looked at a pile of human ashes, gas chambers or entire villages where the Jewish people were exterminated by the Nazis. For eight days she witnessed the annihilation of six million people, the effects of this journey to be carried throughout her lifetime. In the back of my mind, I kept thinking about the teens during the Holocaust who lived in horrid conditions with no food, no warmth and no family and these teens had no parents to call. Noa's journey will give her a voice to answer the likes of Iranian president Ahmadinejad who publicly questions the Holocaust and calls for the destruction of the Jewish homeland. My offspring now lives and breathes the words 'never again'.

$* * *$

Tan and faded gold tones paint the sand and the sky only to be broken by the cool blue seawater. It is very peaceful to walk along the cool deserted beach so early in the day before the sun's light touches the water. The chain link fences around the lifeguard stations have been removed for the winter and the tall stations stand alone on the sand. The only signs of life are large flocks of black birds busily searching the sand for culinary treats. The bird's intensity of purpose in their quest for food reminds me of my son Kobe's determined pursuit of Kinder Chocolate Eggs; shiny red and white tin foil wrapped around hollow chocolate eggs surrounding smaller plastic eggs with a mini-surprises inside. These eggs are a bona fide 5-year old delicacy and incite great excitement in my young son. If he gets his hand on 5 shekels, he is eager to indulge in his passion to eat chocolate and collect small treasures to line the shelves of his room.

Stav (Fall)

We have been here for almost four months and finally the cold weather begins; harsh rains pound the country with intense hammering thunder while incredible lightening shows shock the skyline. At times the forceful rain strikes against the shutters and we feel like we are being physically attacked. The Astroturf floods with water and creates a shallow lake in our backyard. The days are short now—it is dark by 4:45 in the afternoon.

Our creamy white castle is an oasis. We sit together in the family room playing Scrabble and the Memory Game, reading books and sharing time together. Noa and I polish off the first season of the Weeds television show. Kobe crayons Pokémon characters and tells us fantastic stories with his large blue eyes shining. Eden dances hip-hop all around the house preparing shows for us to watch and Aaron hides in his Trump dungeon room. Yehuda reads his orange business newspaper and fields business calls on his cell phone 24—7. I do not miss the fact that my cell phone or house phone does not ring frequently like in L.A. and I have happily learned to live without my Blackberry as well. I receive few calls now, but I actually remember with whom I spoke and what we spoke about. I enjoy the tranquility that this has brought to my life.

The state of my ge-bor-ah like the weather is tumultuous. The military tirelessly attempts to halt the shipment of weapons from Egypt into Gaza via tunnels; the IAF flies over Beirut and declares that Lebanon does not observe UN Resolution 1701 (the cease fire that ended the Second Lebanon War in August), while Lebanon insists that it is not required to do so; the Egyptians have a plan to release Gilad Shilat in exchange for twelve hundred Palestinian prisoners; Avigdor Lieberman and his Yisrael Beit-enu Party (Israel Our Home), a vocally anti-Arab party, join Prime Minister Ehud Olmert's ruling coalition and Qassam Rockets still land in the South. All of this creates great frustration throughout the nation. Israel has flourished since her creation 58 years earlier, yet there are so many struggles to alleviate the difficulties she faces internally and with her neighbors, struggles that prevent a calm existence.

* * *

I admire one of the large fancy yachts leaving the marina this morning. We only have a few of these cruisers in the Marina representing the few billionaires who reside in Israel. I would love to be on the ship, alone for a week, where I would not hear anyone refer to me as "but mom". The idea of being alone used to frighten me, but now I welcome and desire it. The yacht along with my brief dream slowly becomes tinier until it disappears on the horizon.

I receive a text message from Noa at 11am, "I need mouse ears." Tomorrow she will be celebrating a delayed Halloween as she was in Poland on October 31st. I drop everything and run around like a crazy mom to the kikar and the mall looking for mouse ears. At every store, the sales people look at me like I am a complete fool requesting mouse ears in November and lecture me in Israeli style that they will stock them only in February closer to the Purim holiday. It is the equivalent of Christmas tree shopping in August. At times like this I think of the endless catalogues arriving at my L.A. house where I can order anything in minutes to arrive immediately. For now, I have to let the mouse ears go and celebrate that I cannot instantly fix every need of my children. Without mouse ears, Noa cannot come up with an alternative costume and gives up on the festivities.

* * *

Aaron turns 14. We celebrate with a wonderful seafood dinner at Mol Ha Yam Restaurant (which literally means 'in front of the sea') in the Namal Tel Aviv with Saba and Safta and his one friend, Idan. Mol Ha Yam serves the finest shellfish in all of the Holy Land; it is not kosher and any guilt I feel for this diversion is completely absolved by the fact that it is a world-class culinary experience and for a few short hours my miserable son is in gastronomic heaven and tolerant of his parents. Aaron finally invites us to attend his basketball game at the kibbutz, which of course makes me very happy and optimistic that my son may be turning a corner and becoming a mensch.

Israel honors the eleven-year anniversary of the death of Itzhak Rabin. On November 4, 1995, then Prime Minister Rabin was assassinated in Tel Aviv as he left a peace rally at Kikar Ha Medina. Even after all these years, the pain and the loss is fresh and each year a public memorial is planned in his honor in the same kikar, renamed since his death Kikar Rabin. The assassin, a radical Jew named Yigal Amir, was opposed to Rabin's work and progress on shalom with the Palestinians. Eleven years later we are not any closer to shalom with the Palestinians. Yasser Arafat, the Palestinian leader is dead and Shimon Peres now in his eighties is a leader in the centrist Kadima Party. The wife of Yigal Amir has been granted conjugal visits because Israeli Law supports a man's right to have children and populate the nation, regardless of committing the most heinous crime.

* * *

Kobe appears at my bed at 6:30am. "Mommy I have a small emergency. Sponge Bob is dead. I found him on his side. He is just dead." Shit. I am so tired after a late night out with Yehuda and two bottles of wine. I hug Kobe and we snuggle for a few minutes hoping that I can grab a few more precious moments of sleep. All week I had to wake him up for gan at 7:15am and now at 6:30am on my Shabbat, he has a dead goldfish, let alone his cherished Sponge Bob. "Kobe, fish go to fish heaven when they are flushed down the toilet." He looks at me incredulously not buying my explanation. I repeat this statement with more clarity and offer the added comfort that this is the 'express route' for fish to get to heaven. He likes this version much better; we flush Sponge Bob with a few kind and parting words and Kobe is off to another adventure. I dive into a cappuccino.

* * *

Scores of pine needles and pinecones litter the small path from my car to the gan. Kobe holds my hand as he walks proudly to the door; as he enters his soft little hand slides out from my grip and he disappears into a room where a bunch of little boys play with large plastic dinosaurs. He is too busy at this point to say good-bye or to give me a kiss. He has entered into Kibbutz Land with Nili and Gordon, his friends and the wild dogs he meets on his daily foot travels through the kibbutz. Kobe has started to eat food like goulash, corn and couscous. If they can encourage him to eat fruit other than apple juice and vegetables other than canned corn and ketchup on top of speaking Hebrew, I will consider this year a spectacular success. I walk back through the pine needles to my car and admire the yards full of trash items. I used to see a burning need for a tetanus shot; now all I see is a magical paradise for the imagination of young souls in Kibbutz Land.

I need to start my social life. For a few months I told myself 'A-ha-ree Ha-Hag-eem' and the holidays are now over. I make plans to have coffee with my old friend Dominique, a Belgian who made Aliyah to Israel many years ago, but she cancels at the last minute as her dog was hit by a car and cannot be left home alone. She spent the night at an emergency animal hospital where the veterinary was the son of the Vice Premier, Shimon Peres. I continue to be reminded just how small this country is and that six degrees of separation exists everywhere. We make plans to meet the following week. I have waited this long to be social, a few more days at home with Mimi and Dr Pepper, my aquatic friends, will have to suffice.

Aaron returns home from school with a document showing that he has made Honor Roll. I am pleasantly shocked. He plays basketball around the clock and still manages to get good grades. I can tell by the shimmer in his sea blue eyes that he is proud of himself, despite his tough exterior and critical analysis of the educational level at the school. He still makes little effort socially, but he seems happier in general. Eden, on the other hand, is now very social–having made friends and found her place, which is the answer to her osher (happiness) this year. She spends all of her free time with her new best friend Shiraz, a Swiss Israeli girl and is passionate about the circus and hip-hop. She only stops bouncing long enough to sleep at night. And Noa has blossomed into a very active social engineer organizing after school get-togethers, weekend dinners and clubbing with her friends. I am in awe of her management skills as she runs this business from her cell phone with the personalized ring tones and sends text messages at a record pace.

* * *

Noa and I leave for a meeting in South Tel Aviv on a dark gray Sunday morning with dense cumulous nimbus clouds lurking in the sky above us. We depart along Wingate Street, a well-groomed, perfectly manicured street lined with trees and large homes hidden behind strong walls. The street is wet and shiny from the rain that poured all night. Once on the highway we pass the Ramat Aviv neighborhood, a playground for gargantuan red and yellow cranes that move up and down without taking a break to build more apartment buildings in the remaining vacant lots between the already dense apartment buildings. This activity is symbolic of the rapid growth in Israel where apartments are built and occupied at a record pace. We pass the old domestic Dov Airport and a white and blue Arkia airplane takes off above us probably on its way to the Red Sea resort city of Eilat, a fifty-minute flight south. Next to the airport, Reading Power Station's huge cement tower stands tall in the gray sky with flickering bright lights warning planes not to get too close. After a few more turns, we pass the Yarkon River and enter into Tel Aviv. The road is lined with dilapidated two and three story buildings with filthy facades contrasted by clear glass storefronts and pretty signs for designer retailers, fancy apartments and five star hotels. All along the Mediterranean Sea is a large boardwalk bordering the sand, which in the summer is packed with people but chillingly empty this stormy morning as the turbulent black clouds and the huge steel gray waves dance passionately in unison.

We pass the Dolphinarium, a dilapidated large building on the coast that once housed the Dolphi Disco Nightclub where, back on June 1, 2001, a suicide bomber from Hamas came from the territories and blew himself up killing twenty-one teens and injuring hundreds of others who waited in line to enter the club that night. Boys and girls fourteen, fifteen and sixteen years-old like my Noa and Aaron all killed by a suicide bomber, a man who came with the desire to kill as many innocent children as he could with the promise of martyrdom. Across the street stands a small mosque where after the suicide bombing, angry crowds of Jews threatened the lives of the innocent Muslims, citizens of Israel who were inside. The police had to step in to offer protection.

We arrive in downtown Jaffa, South Tel Aviv near to where I had attended the dedication ceremony with my mother a couple of months earlier. Jaffa is home to a heterogeneous population of Israelis where everyone is represented on the streets; Muslims in traditional head cover and dress, Orthodox Jews in black suits and black hats and secular Jews and Arabs (biblical cousins) who dress and look alike in contemporary clothing. The ancient streets are full of produce vendors, fish stores (uncle Yacov buys his fish in Jaffa), fresh bread stands (Abulafia Bread Bakery on Yeffeth Street is world renowned for long lines of people waiting on the sidewalk to buy fresh baked breads all day and all night), shoe stores, toy stores and jewelers with store signs in both Hebrew and Arabic. Many storeowners congregate on the sidewalk smoking and talking while waiting for customers to enter their stores. As I drive through the dark narrow streets, I return briefly to the 10th Century B.C.E. when the cedars for the 1st Temple in Jerusalem arrived at the bustling Mediterranean Port of Jaffa from Tyre, Lebanon.

Noa and I arrive at Friendship's Way, a unique non-profit organization that offers after-school care and educational programs for both Arab and Jewish children from very poor families while stressing and working for religious tolerance. Friendship's Way has been in operation for over twenty years and is housed in one of Jaffa's ancient buildings, dark and dirty from the outside pronounced by this dismal day, the offices and classrooms inside are clean and colorful, a world away from the exterior. Noa volunteered here a couple of summers ago and was inspired by their work and the dynamic conversations that she shared with the Jewish and Arab workers, particularly the stories of two young Arab women who were helped by the program. This year, she is eager to find a way to assist Friendship's Way. I am pleased that she has some awareness outside her busy teen social world and does not sit back and accept the status quo.

The holy month of Ramadan is observed world wide, yet devout Muslims in Iraq and Gaza continue to fight and kill each other and their local and worldwide brethren do not appear to condemn this behavior. President Ahmadinejad of Iran continues his calls to wipe Israel off the map and no world leaders condemn his statements. But in Israel freedom of speech is well exercised—some may say too well. Many Jews publicly condemn their government for failing to speak with the Palestinians; many Jews publicly condemn the words of Avigdor Lieberman, the leader of Yisrael Beitenu who calls for the separation of all Jews and Arabs declaring, "I think separation between two nations is the best solution. Cyprus is the best model"; and many Jews publicly condemn the Orthodoxy for their attempts to prevent the Gay Pride Parade from taking place in Jerusalem. The list goes on.

* * *

The powerful moonlight glistens and creates a shimmer over the otherwise hidden ripples in the dark water. Rocca Restaurant set on the beach cliffs is light and bright full of customers dining inside and outside. We are having dinner with our rabbi from L.A., who is visiting Israel. Rabbi Harvey has been a part of our family for many years; he presided over our wedding, our children's bar and bat mitzvah and for many years was the head rabbi at our synagogue in L.A.. He is a wise and kind man who lives passionately for Judaism and equality for all mankind. He is also very personable and approachable, markedly different from the orthodox rabbis I see in Israel dressed in black suits and black hats who are quite daunting. We sit and eat reclining as Harvey passionately shares with us his work to bring the Reform Jewish Movement more power and access in Israel where Orthodoxy has for years controlled religion. He believes that in the Jewish state, many Jews simply do not participate in religion, as they are not given a choice. This may sound a bit ironic, but there is an overriding sense for many secular Jews that living in Israel is like living in the ultimate temple. In the middle of dinner I look over to the kitchen and a group of men in dark suites enter the restaurant surrounding Shimon Peres, the Vice Premier of Israel. He walks by our table and we all just stop in the middle of chewing to admire this dapper and well-groomed octogenarian. He must have just returned from Bulgaria where he is rumored to receive youth treatments. They appear to be working quite well. The traveling tribe follows Peres as he walks over to a table and greets the occupants. A minute later the tightly packed clan moves once again to a long corner table where the first woman Speaker of the Knesset, Dalia Itzik, joins them. I really want to join them as well and hear their plans and then of course share some of my own ideas. I am also curious to know if Peres will be running for President. Seven years ago, Israel's current President, Moshe Katsav beat out Peres for the job and now Peres is the lead candidate to replace Katsav, who is being indicted for rape.

* * *

The weather turns cold so daily I make soup; tender chicken soup, the traditional Jewish health remedy with carrots, potatoes and squash and minestrone full of fresh garden vegetables. Some days we eat the soup thick and chunky and other days I blend it and we eat it thick and smooth as a puree. In my family's perfect fashion there is no consensus; two kids like it pureed, one kid likes it chunky and one kids tries to convince me that he is allergic to vegetables. I tell myself that if we eat soup during the cold months, everyone will stay healthy. I would like to find a soup to serve my gee-bo-rah. She is a sick and tired nation and I wish I could find the right ingredients to help nurse her back to health. I am an American, but as I live here I feel the pride and the passion of the Sabras, yet am helpless like so many people.

Daily Hamas terrorists in the Gaza Strip shoot Qassam Rockets into Southern Israel. The residents in the city of Sderot live in fear; men, women and children are traumatized by a lifestyle, which is centered on sirens and bomb shelters. The IAF sends fighter planes over Gaza to attack Palestinian gunmen and by land, IDF troops and tanks move in to sweep houses, arrest suspected militants and locate their weapon caches. This does not thwart the terrorists; their bombing, which has gone on for years, continues. The international news is quick to cover the Israeli's defensive incursion, but has not been diligent in portraying the continual bombs landing in Israel or the continued fighting on the streets of Gaza as Palestinians kill Palestinians and the number of human casualties rises. Iran's continual calls for Israel's destruction are not met with any worldwide condemnation. The icing on the cake is the growing political corruption that my gee-bo-rah faces, which trumps so much that is wonderful in this amazing nation.

* * *

Last night the memorial rally for Itzhak Rabin took place with one hundred thousand people in attendance. The keynote speaker was novelist David Grossman, whose young son, a soldier, was killed in the final days of fighting in Southern Lebanon last summer. Grossman spoke to the large crowd about Israel's deficiencies, the terrible waste of young people dying, and the opportunities for the democratic nation to grow and prosper. He even went so far as to encourage the Prime Minister to keep working and negotiate with the Palestinains.

* * *

The sound of the crashing waves comforts me as I walk to energize myself and sweat off the frustration of a fourteen-year old son who won't speak to me for any apparent reason. In a few moments I move into autopilot and before I know it, I am at the northern beach and am shaken by a strong chemical smell and look to the seawater, which is a fluorescent yellow-green color. Obviously someone is dumping chemicals into the water, which should not be such a shock to me, as this is a First World Nation battling with Third World ills.

Marcelle and Shabtai come to stay with us, which I know means at least a week of interesting smells and full stomachs. The minute Marcelle walks into the house, she is planning what Middle Eastern caloric extravaganza to cook for her grandchildren and Shabtai is standing at her side ready to assist her. The first order of business however, is to appease the daughter-in-law and Marcelle begins by peeling a couple of pomelite (large sweet citrus fruit) and removing the seeds from a few pomegranates to place in the refrigerator for my snacks. I am very happy with this gracious gesture.

* * *

I drive to a Tel Aviv art gallery listening to the latest news on the radio; sixty armed Palestinian fighters believed to be sending rockets into Israel were hiding out in the Al-Nasser Mosque in Beit Hanun, Gaza exchanging gunfire with IDF soldiers. The Israelis sent bulldozers in to knock down the walls and part of the mosque collapsed. In the meantime, hundreds of women from the Hamas party traditionally dressed with burkas marched to the mosque to act as human shields for the gunmen and escorted the men dressed in the women's clothing out of the building. As they escaped, Israeli soldiers shot at men they identified regardless of the dress and head cover. This story takes place in Gaza, a short drive from where I am now and with this news, I am tempted to go home and hold myself up in the creamy white castle and call it a day, but I know I cannot give in to this fear and keep driving. This is how it works in this country—even amidst fighting and war, life continues and many of us play out our roles as passive observers.

I escape into an art gallery full of Israeli artists' work highlighted by the paintings of Menashe Kadishma, who in the 1990s started painting sheep heads in bright bold colors and shapes. While the subject is the same in each painting, the colors, textures, and feeling of each sheep is exceptionally beautiful and the expression in each animal's eyes in unique. Kadishman like Yehuda spent his early years as a shepherd on a kibbutz and his work reflects this period in his life. I hope to buy a Kadishman painting to bring back to America and mark this happy and memorable period in Yehuda's life. Paradoxically, Yehuda does not look at the personal or aesthetic value of most art rather the financial value; the Kadishman sheep head, which is very popular in Israel, is not a smart financial investment for him. I encourage Yehuda to stop and admire beauty with no relation to dollar or shekel. This is another interesting challenge in our lives.

Even after all of the attempts by the Israeli military to end the attacks from Gaza, Qassam Rockets still arrive in Israel. Support for Hamas grows while hundreds of thousands of Palestinians, many of whom are children live hungry amidst trash surrounded by the smell of raw sewage. Hamas refuses to recognize Israel's right to exist and calls for its destruction. As a result, western foreign aid is shut off, but Iranian leadership sends money to fuel the hate and terror. No Arab nations including Iran work to help the people of Gaza attain food and medicine, or develop education and infrastructure for a better quality of life. Their goal appears to be keeping the populace poor, uneducated and angry as soldiers in their war of hate. Palestinians who speak out against the Hamas regime in Gaza know that their publicized beliefs will endanger their lives and those of their families.

* * *

It is freezing this morning. Pounding Middle East rain and wind enter deep in my body and fingertips, my nose is red and my back aches. When the sun escapes from the clouds, it shines down with pleasure and gently warms anyone and anything its path, but only for a brief period of time. Days like this, Kobe leaves for the kibbutz in galoshes, long pants and a sweater and he returns in the afternoon barefoot, with the same long pants and a Lakers sleeveless jersey. It is unpredictable. It is full of extremes. So is life in this country in so many ways.

I head off to the American School for the shook mor-eem (the teachers' market) where all the teachers sit in the school gym and meet with parents. I have three children's teachers to meet, which means over ten teachers and Yehuda has flown to Turkey for the weekend to sail on his brother's new boat. I am panicked. How will I handle all of the information? What will they say about my children? Can I be nice to so many people in such a short amount of time? In L.A. there are three different schools and three different dates for these types of meetings. Here it is all at one time and overwhelming.

Noa and Eden are predictable; great students, who try hard, do well and are lovely to have in class. Aaron is anything but predictable. I keep reminding myself; Aaron made 'Honor Roll'. The Spanish teacher tells me that Aaron argues with her about the curriculum. I mentally prepare to take Aaron's iPod away for six months. The humanities teacher speaks of a smart kid, who enjoys arguing points in class even when he is wrong. I recognize this characteristic and am now taking away the computer as well as the iPod. Then he tells me about an autistic boy who has joined their class and sits next to Aaron. At first he could see from Aaron's expressions that he did not understand this boy, but he explained to Aaron what was going on and from that point on my son helped the boy patiently and kindly. I give him back the damn iPod and computer as tears well in my eyes. Then Aaron's science teacher and advisor tells of missing assignments, tired morning eyes and game playing with money owed for school activities, where he makes partial payments for things I have already given him all the money to buy. I mentally take the computer away for a second time. From the math teacher, I learn that Aaron is neither social, nor motivated, but he has great potential. I am now losing track of what more I can take away or what I can do to motivate the kid.

I am amused to think of the parallel between teenagers and Israel. My son, like Israel is both unpredictable and full of extremes. My gee-bo-rah has been the Jewish homeland for thousands of years, but has only been a modern country for 58 years and is growing up in a hostile neighborhood. They are both almost adults and yet still impatient and childish as a result of their youth and inexperience. As a parent, I am mixed emotionally in my disappointment and my love for my troubled son. I feel this way about this beautiful country as well. I do not have much influence on Israel but I certainly need to try harder with my son.

I return to the creamy white castle exhausted. I make a cup of green tea and collapse under a blanket on the couch with my newspaper. We royally messed up again. Nineteen members of one family in a house asleep on mattresses were killed in Beit Hanun by a stray Israeli bomb—another tragedy born out of hate and war. Just yesterday the paper said that Operation Autumn, the attempt by the IDF to clean out Qassam Rockets and other weaponry from Gaza was over. Now the head of Hamas, Khaled Meshal sits in Damascus calling for united Palestinian revenge against us. My great fear of pee-go-eem returns. For a moment I consider packing everyone up and returning to L.A.

The tragedy in Beit Hanun unites the Palestinians for the weekend and the world condemns my gi-bor-ah. Yehuda sails the Turkish Islands and I am alone with four kids in sick and scary Israel. I keep reminding myself that I did sign up for this and feel more confident in my belief that more dialogue needs to occur and less bombing. In the killing no one is winning, but who on the Palestinian side is there for dialogue to bring change?

Not even my desperate attempts to scare Noa about Hamas suicide bombers can stop her from going out with friends tonight. I cannot believe that I have resorted to scaring my child while attempting to keep her safe. It feels so unnatural and so necessary at the same time. In typical teen style, she ignores my blatant pleas to stay home; she is invulnerable as only a fifteen-year old can be and probably should be. She promises that she will be on the lookout for suicide bombers, but her words do little to reassure me. Aaron leaves to ride his bike and I remind him to wear his helmet to which he responds, "No Israeli kids wear helmets." He is correct, as I rarely see Israeli kids wearing helmets, but I remind him that he does not have an Israeli passport and ask him to wear his helmet. Begrudgingly, Aaron leaves the house with the helmet, unfastened and hanging off his head. Kobe and Eden—the only two children I have any control over are asleep. I open a bottle of Italian red wine and drink by myself.

* * *

The seawater appears as an enormous gray sheet jutting out from the light sand to the dark cloud infested horizon. The vast sky is one shade of gray lighter than the water as no sun has arrived from the East to introduce orange or yellow to the picture. A tinge of sound from the breaking sea ripples shatters the vacant quietness of this cool morning. I am exhausted, but I have to make the walk before the clouds arrive at the shore and dump the latest buckets of rain on Israel.

I woke painfully early in a panic after dreaming that my wallet, my iPod, my phone and my blackberry all were stolen. All of my stimulants and connections to the world were gone. I was feeling quite vulnerable and stripped down to the bare basics, back to a state of being that technology had long done away with. My dream was a clear message about my dependency on connectivity—actually all of our dependency on technology. I remember that before I left L.A., a friend asked me how I packed up four children and left for a year. Lap top computers, cell phones and iPods were the answer, as these items could artificially sustain me and my children anywhere in the world with the possible exception of Noa, who would also need a closet full of jeans. While I joke about my teenagers and connectivity, I also realize that teenagers with computers, cell phones and iPods are less likely to throw stones—they have too much to lose. How amazing would it be if I could go to world leaders like Steve Jobs and Bill Gates to enlist their support in arming the Palestinian youth with technology?

* * *

The garden is cool and refreshing in the early morning light. I savor my cappuccino and enjoy the few small gray birds quietly singing while my newspaper sits unwrapped and unread. Eden approaches me ready for school, proudly singing the Latvian National Anthem. Her elementary school chorus has been invited to perform at the Latvia Day reception in Tel Aviv later in the week. Eden's arrival is my cue to go down to the bowels of the house and wake my teens from their deep sleep in their pitch-black rooms. Noa and Aaron love the electric metal window shutters that close tight and do not let an ounce of light into their rooms. Each morning, I partially open the shutters to prove to my teenagers that it is indeed daylight and to encourage them to wake up. Their entitled sense of independence is dashed by their inability to take responsibility to awaken by themselves in the morning. They do have alarm clocks, but they are impervious to their rings, chimes and music.

As I pass the bomb shelter, I cannot help but think about the Palestinians who continue to send rockets into the cities of Ashkelon and Sderot and neighboring communities from portable field locations in Gaza. The terrorists still do not have great accuracy, but when enough Qassams manage to reach Israel, they explode, destroy and kill producing great fear and panic in all the effected communities. Residents live nervously around warning sirens and bomb shelters as they wait out each bombing—young children in these communities know no other life style. My sister-in-law, Shlomit's kibbutz along the border with Gaza is in constant danger of falling Qassam Rockets.

I hear the words of the writer David Grossman who calls on Prime Minister Olmert to talk to the Palestinians about their suffering. Can Israelis and the Israeli politicians find empathy for the Palestinians even when rockets land, wound and kill Israelis? Who is Olmert supposed to speak to? What can we do for these people? Palestinians are divided; Hamas in Gaza opposes negotiations with the Israelis and Fatah in the West Bank supports negotiations with Israelis. Olmert and his government speak with the Fatah leadership, but it is Hamas who condones sending Qassams Rockets into Israel. Palestinians who are opposed to the Hamas leadership are branded as traitors and collaborators with Israel, America and the West and fear for their lives.

I see a need for new leadership and a new style to the peace talks—we need intelligent Israeli and Palestinian women who give birth and create life to speak and find a dialogue that can start to break the system of hate and distrust. This notion may be naïve, but the belief that the men alone after all this time will bring change and end the conflict is more naïve. Men start wars and therefore men fight wars to win, while women do not as easily send their men and their sons to war. Women find solutions, balance needs and understand compromise; I do this almost every day in my warring home. If tomorrow borders are drawn with public policy, but we fail to pay attention to the hearts and souls of the people, the hate and distrust will continue to erode the process.

* * *

Fresh westerly winds have blown the blue skies sparkling clean and the early sun highlights the massive groups of surfers who paddle crazily for the perfect rides on the large round waves. The number of young men and women in black suits congregating in the frigid water who make such an effort early in their day impresses me. Their passion and pleasure is self-evident. I wish I could take some home to share with my teenagers.

Noa manages to come upstairs a few minutes before we leave this morning; she makes coffee in a sluggish motion, pours cereal into a bowl and eats painfully unhurried in a haze. Aaron gets up only when I scream as we are leaving at the last minute. In record pace, he jumps out of bed, puts on his sweats, washes his face, dabs some stinky teen cologne on himself and gets in the car with shoes and sweatshirt in hand. He knows that even if I yell, we all sit in the car and wait for him. Lately after school we wait for him and after basketball practice we wait for him. I am bothered by the fact that I cannot just leave him one time. Maybe this would teach him a lesson? No matter what I do lately with my teens, I feel that I am a cranky screaming mother. I desperately want to change this. I send Aaron and Noa an e-mail highlighting important information that is tricky for teens like when they need to get up and what time we depart for school. I feel like a deficient mother resorting to technology for communication, but I hope this method will avoid too many creative teen interpretations. I am tired of hearing, "You never said that" or "You never told me."

Kobe asks me everyday to make a 'play-date' for him, but I do not know the parents of his classmates and most of the children live on the kibbutz within walking distance from each other so 'play-dates' are a natural phenomenon. I seek advice from Gordon. He tells me Kobe plays with a little boy whose mother is fluent in English and lives off the kibbutz. This afternoon I approach her. She is a pretty dark skinned woman with long flowing ringlets of black hair and a warm, friendly smile. I simply say, "Hi. I'm Kobe's mom and Kobe would like a play-date with your son."

And in perfect New York English, she says, "Great, what is a play-date?" We are off to a marvelous start.

* * *

The brilliant yellow sun hovers low along the cloudy blue horizon. I take pleasure in the final moments of light and warmth from the sun as it disappears early and rapidly this time of year. I pass fifty young boys with shaved heads who train in a boot camp paired off with their elbows locked behind their backs wrestling each other backwards on the soft sand. Two young women walk amongst the trainees critiquing their efforts while these future soldiers yell out sweating and digging down deep into the soft sand and their souls.

There are many mat-cote players on the beach this afternoon. Mat-cote is a popular game at the beach where a small black rubber ball is hit very hard between two players each armed with a round wooden paddle standing about twenty feet apart. Players go at it intensely for hours along the water's edge while runners and walkers dodge their scary and deadly swings. There is no real point to mat-cote other than hitting the ball back and forth, harder and harder and not letting it drop. This bares frightening resemblance to what goes on in Israel daily. We have battles of mat-cote with the Palestinians and our hits are harder but we drop the ball, then Hamas sends over rockets from Gaza and we respond with even harder hits. Hamas kidnapped an Israeli soldier from our land in June 2006 and we retaliated by air and land to eradicate the rockets and terrorists from Gaza. In this battle, we are still not victorious; our soldier is still a captive, bombs land in Israel every day and the cycle of hate rolls on.

The sun continues its descent through the clouds along the horizon. Once the round fireball departs a beautiful silhouette of orange light shines neatly and frames the light gray clouds. Is there hope for shalom? Can the mat-cote players ever yield to the outnumbered peaceful walkers? Most are intensely focused and cannot even stop to say to-dah (thank you) if you retrieve a ball gone astray and toss it to them. They just start the game again.

* * *

Latvia day finally arrives. Eden still has no idea where Latvia is located on the map, but she knows that the Vice Premier of Israel will be at the event. She also has no idea who the Vice Premier is, but she has heard that he is quite special. I tag along as a chaperone as I have to get out and mingle with adults who do not fix my house or work in supermarkets. Attending Latvia Day is also a great opportunity to see the mix of dignitaries from all over the world sent to represent their countries in the Holy Land. I embrace the hope that these people may hold the key to making good things happen.

We enter the hotel's ballroom full of these potentially magical diplomats socializing and eating Latvian food and desserts. Back in L.A. it would be a beautiful costume party; the wife of the Latvian Ambassador, a pretty blond woman wears a traditional white Latvian dress trimmed in gold; Indian women wear bright colored saris with bindis on their foreheads; Muslim women wear formal dresses and burkas; Greek Orthodox Priests appear in white robes with gold trim and large, thick gold and bejeweled crosses hanging from their necks; and other women and men are in business suites. Everyone mingles while the Small World singers sit on the stage waiting patiently for Vice Premier Shimon Peres to arrive.

Shimon enters the hall like he is the grand Premier, not just the Vice Premier, with a bright aura around him, surrounded by Knesset Speaker Dalia Itzik and a team of clean cut, serious looking bodyguards. Shimon appears in mint condition. He is truly a remarkable eighty-three-year old man, who slowly and graciously weaves through the crowd of important dignitaries. Shimon and Dalia finally make their way to the stage and speak with the children. The room is quiet as the Latvian Ambassador briefly welcomes the distinguished guests and then Shimon speaks for what feels like an eternity. The children on the stage begin to yawn and a few boys squirm; slowly a low conversation hums throughout the room.

Finally, the children proudly rise to sing for this distinguished international assembly that is now quiet and gives respect to the small singers on the stage. Children from all over the world dressed alike in black pants and collared white shirts stand on risers and sing the Latvian National Anthem. These lovely children's voices sing a song whose country none are from. Then they sing the beautiful Israeli National Anthem Ha-tikva in Hebrew, 'As long as the Jewish spirit is yearning deep in the heart, with eyes turned toward the East, looking toward Zion, Then our hope—the two-thousand-year-old hope—will not be lost: To be a free people in our land, The land of Zion and Jerusalem'. Eden stands front and center, the upside of always being one of the shorter kids. I am thrilled that my daughter sings these powerful words and feels a loving connection to Israel. Most of these children are not Israeli and are not Jewish, but they too sing with great pride. I am reminded that for children love or hate is innate and fostered by their family and their community as they grow; these young students develop a love and a respect for the foreign land they live in and for distant lands whose place on the map is still unknown to them.

After the performance, Eden and I leave the waiting room to find her teacher so we can return to the bus. Hand in hand, Eden and I enter the party room just as Vice Premier Peres walks out with a group of his bodyguards. I ask him to please take a picture with Eden. He graciously takes Eden under his arm and I capture Eden's proud face with the octogenarian politician who looks extremely good even close up. I will put this photo next to the one I have with President Clinton on the wall of our home in L.A.

* * *

Plenty of walkers comb the beach this Friday morning. At the north end under the cliffs, I find the Russian fishing group 'weekend regulars' in their usual spot; four round women dressed in muted colors sitting on red coolers and engrossed in a lively Russian conversation. In the middle, sits my favorite woman whose short brown hair is accented with bright red dyed bangs. Three short men with round bellies and pointy mustaches, stand by their fishing poles at the water's edge discussing strategy and even in Russian the subject matter is apparent.

The school gym is full of cheering students sporting red and blue shirts; music blares and hip-hop dancers perform while machines send out white plumes of smoke. This is all part of the opening ceremonies for the middle school Hockey Marathon, an all day event. At the end of the opening ceremony, parents join with teachers and students for the international fight song, Queen's 'We Are The Champions'. I observe that no matter what country the kids are from and no matter their race or religion, thirteen or fourteen year olds really do not want to hang out on campus with their classmates and their parents even if we are invited guests. Aaron completely ignores me when he walks by with his blue team. Eden on the other hand sees me across the gym and waves with a huge smile. All day long, the teens battle in the hot smelly gym. Yehuda and I return at night to see Aaron make the final goal of the tournament. He actually previews a smile, which his math teacher tells me it is the first one he has seen Aaron reveal this year.

* * *

This morning I encounter a sweet couple of funny zebra colored birds with long thin needle beaks enjoying their time together on the hillside park that borders the beach. Unfazed by my intrusion, they are busy in search of breakfast on the steep lawn that snake its way to the sand. In the summer this grass is full of Israelis who barbeque at a slant by the sea, but today the few visitors are the zebra birds and other young lovers who lie arm in arm enjoying the sea air and panorama.

The court date arrives for former Justice Minister Chaim Ramon, accused of kissing a young soldier against her will. Ramon is a dark and handsome politician in his mid-fifties who has been in the Knesset for many years and is currently a member of the Kadima Party. The young woman who accuses him of the forced kiss is an unidentified young blond soldier whose face we have not seen. The press has been alive with stories, photos and opinions about 'The Kiss' for months now offering the news as a brief respites from the Palestinians and the failed Second Lebanon War reports. This entertainment precludes me from the need to watch the Argentinean soap operas, which are very popular television programs here, as life in this country is a live daily soap opera. While Israel is populated with seven million residents, the whole nation feels like an extended family that lives in one large neighborhood. We all watch and discuss the same television programs and have an abundance of details about the political and military leadership making these individuals personally close to all of us.

* * *

Early in the morning I drive with Eden, Noa and my stepdaughter Talya visiting from New York along Highway 6 to Jerusalem. At one point, we drive along the border with West Bank towns. It is eerie to be so close to the barren high walls separating us from Palestinian Land—a place that we cannot physically visit, but is so closely connected geographically and emotionally. I look at the stark high walls as security against my greatest fear—suicide bombers, who too easily enter the country. The fear of terrorism paralyzes me at times and yet I would like to look past the walls to the innocent faces of children or the warm and gentle expressions of mothers and grandmothers. I would like the opportunity to meet and acknowledge our differences; and once we did this, then we could forge on to discuss tolerance and coexistence. I know we all love our children; we want them to be happy, healthy and educated and mostly we want them to return at the end of the day to have dinner with us and sleep under our roofs.

We continue to drive through vast agricultural fields, gloomy and listless in the faint morning light. As the sun rises, the patchwork farmland becomes green and brown and shoots out as far as the eye can see until broken by the construction of new highways and bridges. Shortly after, we arrive at patches of forests with pine trees as the road starts to wind up to Jerusalem. The Jewish National Fund has planted enormous and impressive pine forests for over one hundred years by generous philanthropic gifts to help beautify and make green the small desert land of the Jewish people. My grandfather traveled to Israel thirty years ago in search of the trees he paid for. Whenever I pass fertile green pine forests on trips, I see my old grandpa as he shook his head in disbelief that he could not find the exact location of the trees that his donations supported. As we ascend higher, the dense and beautiful forest creeps close to the highway. Speckled amongst the pines, the boulders and the shrubs are the remains of machinery that memorializes the Jews who struggled to reach Jerusalem sixty years ago when Arabs surrounded the city and the paved roads were blocked. These Jewish warriors made their way up the hills with unsophisticated machinery, sheer will power and an undying belief that motivated them to save Jerusalem. A kosher McDonalds appears at a hillside exit and small white Jewish and Arab villages fill the Judean landscape, as we get closer to the city. I start to feel the excitement of arriving in this magical land; Jerusalem is a powerful city packed with history, religion and culture and after many visits, I am still in awe and amazed at being in the Holy City.

A couple of miles from the city's entrance, we find ourselves stuck in bumper-to-bumper traffic; cars full of people entering to the Holy City for a day of work crawling along and blue and white Israeli flags on lampposts, blowing strongly and proudly lining the road. Slowly we follow the signs in Hebrew, Arabic and English to the Old City, another world altogether where all the buildings whether modern or ancient are constructed with Jerusalem Stone creating the perfect facade for the menagerie of colorful and diverse people on the streets. We enter the Old City on foot through a security checkpoint designated for females; men and women have their own metal detectors and their own guards to check bodies and bags before being permitted to enter the Kotel (Western Wall) Plaza.

The Kotel, the only remains of the Second Temple constructed over two thousand years ago is tremendous and powerful—each time I stand in front of the enormous stones wall, I have a personal religious experience. The Kotel stands over sixty feet tall and this is just what is seen above the ground—the Wall goes deep underground as well. Thousands of tiny little notes with handwritten prayers are tucked into the many cracks between the large stones. Men and women rock back and forth as they pray separately at the Kotel; the larger side is full of men who pray dressed in black with ki-pote or black hats and ta-leet (prayer shawls) and the much smaller side is full of women in bright dresses and many colorful hats and head covers. In the background of the Kotel Plaza; a yellow tractor works to excavate close to where groups of tourists congregate; religious gentlemen walk to and from the many yeshivas (religious schools) housed in the stone architecture; and a homeless man sleeps wrapped in a white floral comforter in a corner spot in the winter sun.

We arrive to the entrance of the dark and cavernous Min-he-ret Ha-Kotel (The Tunnels of the Western Wall) for a tour. A thin path surrounded by damp cool stones leads us along the Wall just below where hundreds of people pray in the sunlight above us. We see the water channels from the time of Herod and we stop at The Cave where Jews believe is the closest anyone can get to the Holy of Holies. I believe this is the closest to G-d I have ever been in my life and emotionally place my hand written prayers in the cracks between these divine under ground boulders. With each step in this narrow, dark and claustrophobic area, I think about the people who thousands of years ago built the tunnel— many of the stones weigh over two tons and the whole wall is 1600 feet in length. At the end of the Min-he-ret Ha-Kotel we arrive at a small door and exit the dark tunnel. It takes a few moments to refocus as we are hit with the bright sun in the Old City. This exit was the site of a major riot back in 1996 when seventy Palestinians and sixteen Israeli soldiers were killed after Prime Minister Bibi Netanyahu ordered it opened and the Palestinian leader, Yasser Arafat told his people that the opening would cause their religious buildings on the Temple Mount to collapse. Riots broke out. People were killed. Nothing collapsed.

On Via Dolorosa, we follow a group of very serious Irish tourists carrying a large wooden cross as they retrace Jesus' steps along the Stations of the Cross on the ancient stone streets making their way to the Church of the Holy Sepulchre. The beauty of the narrow stone streets of the Old City, the charming doors, the nooks and crannies and the local people whom we pass enamors me. Eden places her hand on the indented section of a stonewall where Jesus is said to have placed his hand to prevent himself from falling as he dragged the cross through the streets. We are amazed that one man's force could dent a rock, but then again we are talking about Jesus' powerful hand. We continue our bonding with

Jesus at the Church of the Holy Sepulcher, which is packed with religious tourists. Eden is a faithful participant; she touches the oil in the Stone of the Anointment where Jesus was prepared for burial and upstairs she touches Jesus' tomb with the zeal of touching a famous hip-hop star.

After the religious experience we stroll through the Muslim Quarter of the Old City, a fascinating land full of intrigue with a tinge of danger. Today it is calm and open, but over the years has been closed due to violence. I feel safe with my daughters as we walk the narrow Old City roads in the Arab Quarter where everyone is an Arab, the signs are in Arabic and the sounds of Arabic fly through the narrow market place. We stop at a cave-like room where a small man prepares unusually thin dough wrapped around a special cheese that he bakes in a large oven and sprinkles with powdered sugar. We are told that this profession has been passed down from generation to generation and he is the only person left in Jerusalem to prepare this delicacy. A few shops further, a toothless Arab gentleman grabs a few bright red pomegranates from a large carefully designed pile and squeezes a cup of fresh juice for us. It is the best pomegranate juice I have ever tasted. We buy khaki green t-shirts with the army symbol for the tzam-ha-neem (parachute division), which was Yehuda's division in the army and gray t-shirts that say peace in English, Hebrew and Arabic. I would like to give all the residents of Israel, Gaza and the West Bank one of these shirts to wear with the simple words for peace in these three languages. We eat humus from a tiny world famous stand that only sells humus in pita and with one bite I know why—it is divine. Noa convinces me she needs a nargila (Arab smoke pipe) to make her Israeli experience a true one for a teenager. In the spirit of the moment I enter the small cavern where on both walls hundreds of nargilas are lined up. I feel as though I am at Disneyland where souvenirs are smartly marketed everywhere in the park and call out to my children that I need to buy them these items before we leave. It is part of the spell in a foreign land; there is instant gratification with no thought of actually needing or using the expensive items once you leave the magic land. Noa chooses a silver rimmed nargila that costs 150 shekels. I start to bargain with the proprietor saying that I only have 100 shekels and before I can stare the gentleman down, Noa, who does not pick up on my fine bargaining skills offers out loud to give me more of her own money to help pay. We end up paying 150 shekels. On the walk back to the car, we stop in an ancient building to see the cramped stage where we are to believe that the Last Supper took place.

We depart Jerusalem on Highway 443 to avoid the traffic that we met when we entered in the morning. As we descend the mountain fast and free of traffic, Yehuda calls and asks where we are. I tell him, "Highway 443." He then warns me that this highway passes through West Bank Palestinian land and I need to be careful. As I speed down the open highway, I am not sure how I can be careful. A few moments later, we slow down and pull up to an IDF security checkpoint where a group of young army officers in khakis congregate with their Uzis. One young fellow looks at us and then waves us on. Enormous cement blocks are placed at points where West Bank residents are prevented from passing on to the highway. These cement barriers were put in place after the Second Intifada in 2001 along the 9-kilometer section of the highway that crosses through the West Bank near the capital city of Ramallah. While I enjoy the ease of the road and beauty of the landscape, I know that these blockages cause great difficulties for the Palestinian residents to get from place to place. Can Israelis and Palestinians ever share this road again? Can crazy people from both sides be controlled so that normal good and honest people can live and thrive side by side? Can the Israelis and the Palestinians cooperate to ensure safe passage for all residents? We exit the West Bank and are back in Israel proper—the immediate danger I felt only when Yehuda advised me to feel it, is now behind us.

* * *

Parents park their cars on any vacant sidewalk space; between trees and in front of driveways waiting for their daughters to finish dance class. I park up the road and on the sidewalk, a sign that I am inherently Israeli. As Eden and I walk back to the car in the dark, we strategically dodge the tight ba-la-gan (mess) of bumpers and rear view mirrors. I carefully drive off the sidewalk and a black Volkswagen Toureg, driven by a ballet student's father, rushes towards me, breaking and smiling only when he realizes I am a ballet mom. He recognizes me and therefore can yield to me. So it goes in Israel and especially with driving—you cannot be a freyer (sucker) and yield to a stranger, but for someone you recognize you can acquiesce and show good manners.

After Eden's ballet pick up, I continue my job as the family driver and retrieve Aaron from basketball practice. I drop Aaron off to get pizza at one kikar and drive quickly to another kikar, to the pharmacy to get a medicine for cold sores in Eden's mouth. I have to hurry, as a plumber is due at the creamy white castle to fix the main plumbing line that broke off and flooded the basement and the street for a second time in less than a month. While I waded in the six inches of water in my Ugg boots, Yehuda on the cell phone from Mumbai, India directed me to shut off all the water to stop the flooding.

Oren, the pharmacist sees Eden's mouth full of cold sores and immediately dials his kids' pediatrician, on his cell phone and hands it to me. I explain the problem to the doctor who invites us to come right over. I scoop up Aaron and two wonderfully fragrant pizzas, drop him in front of our house and drive quickly with Eden to the doctor's small home office a few blocks away. He checks Eden, prescribes some medicine and tells me to watch her mouth. If there is no improvement in a week, we will do blood tests. By the time I return home there is still no water and no plumber. Once again, I call to Shmulik and he assures me that the plumber is on his way. "Al ti-da-gee!" (Don't worry) easily runs off his tongue instantly causing me to worry. I comfort myself with a piece of doughy pizza margarita seasoned with basil and oregano from Pizza Domino and a glass of Italian red wine. At 8:30pm the plumber finally arrives. I ask him what he thinks happened. He looks at me with a blank expression and shrugs his shoulders as he connects the old black hose to the broken pipes once again.

Perhaps in my frustration, I will join the current strike of six hundred thousand unhappy civil workers—almost ten percent of Israel's population. The airports are closed, government offices are shut down and the country's trash is not picked up. The strike is quite a common response by Israelis that can last for long periods of time severely crippling the nation.

* * *

A thin older man roams the beach this morning with a medal detector that he moves slowly back and forth along the rough sand in front of the empty beach cafe. When the detector beeps, he stops and digs through the sand looking for the possible treasure to stuff in the pouch tied to his belts. He resumes his routine and continues to glide the medal detector over the sand. How I wish for him to discover a great jewel to celebrate his laborious and mundane activity on this cool winter morning.

Today what began as a routine police transfer of a convicted serial rapist from his cell to a hearing near Tel Aviv turned into a big fa-shla (stupid mistake) as the prisoner escaped from police custody. And to make matters worse, the news reveals that the police transferred him on the wrong day and with minimum security. Now the rapist is free.

I am constantly reminded that there is nothing routine about life in Israel or the Middle East for what it is worth. A fragile cease-fire between the Israelis and Palestinians is in place but rockets sent from Gaza still fall on the city of Sderot every day and at the same time, the Palestinians are not able to agree on a unity government. The news tells us that the Palestinian workers have not been paid for months, children go hungry and there is no money for doctors and hospitals. I bring my daughter to a fine Israeli doctor in minutes of wanting an appointment for a minor problem while seriously sick and injured Palestinians are left to fight for minimal medical attention in less than decent facilities. No matter which side one is on, this situation is cruel and inhumane and I feel immense frustration. But I am clear that if we let down our guard, Hamas will take it as a sign of vulnerability and attack our people. How do we keep a dialogue alive with the Palestinians who want to talk and not let the voices of hate be the final ones heard? The solution is simply confusing. If the Palestinians can form a government that is not led by Hamas, foreign/ western governments will resume sending funds to the Palestinians for humanitarian needs. This is all tricky as Hamas was voted in by the Palestinian people in the last election that the Americans encouraged them to hold. Like a cock-eyed optimist, I look for Palestinians to stand up and tell their leadership; "We want to live in shalom. We need to stop killing each other. We need to recognize Israel even if we don't like it. The Jews are not leaving. We need to negotiate a just two state solution and get on with living our lives, get back to work, celebrate and thrive as a society and as a country. Enough is enough and we will no longer be pawns in a game that we do not win."

The Israelis also bear responsibility in this war with the Palestinians—one obstacle is the ever-growing settlements in West Bank territories, which are offensive in the battle against a two state solution supported by the majority of Israelis. In Israel, I admire that speaking against the country's leaders and policy is a norm and is expected; citizens continually speak out against the government with no fears of retribution and this is a huge difference from Arab areas.

* * *

I edge along the highway in a traffic jam on my way to pick up Kobe at the kibbutz; a usually short highway jaunt turns into a forty-minute crawl. I keep myself occupied gazing out along the far-reaching barren fields bordering the highway and listening on my iPod to the beautiful music of Achinoam Nini, who is the mother of Kobe's new friend Ayehli and a well known singer in Israel. Finally I arrive at the kibbutz, where Kobe stands alone looking dejected and holding his homemade Shabbat khallah wrapped in a white paper that he has personally decorated with colorful dinosaur stick figures. After a he-book (hug) and a ne-she-ka (kiss), Kobe is miraculously revived and runs to say goodbye to his friend Eli. Within seconds, two little boys, one with large blue eyes and the other with sharp black eyes, run over to me and request in Hebrew that Kobe come over for a 'play-date'. I cannot say "Lo", even if it is ridiculous that I drove for forty-minutes to send him off to a friend who lives on the kibbutz—such is the beauty of motherhood. My only request of my young kibbutz-nik is another he-book and a ne-she-ka before I get back on the highway.

We have been in Israel since mid-August and I feel that the time flies by quickly. We have had our rough share of occasions, but we now seem to thrive in our new environment. The children are busy with the lives that they have created here. Yehuda is buried in his work. Living in Israel full time has allowed him to entrench himself even further and work even longer hours than I could have imagined. I constantly think about the three soldiers; Gilad, Ehud and Eldad who were kidnapped before we arrived. For their families the last few months have not flown by and their days are painfully slow until the release of their loved ones. These opposing realities are markedly appropriate for life in Israel.

* * *

"Peace will come to the Middle East when the Arabs love their children more than they hate us." Golda Meir

A large black and white stork floats alone in the sea; she holds her large head and slender long beak proudly as the tide carries her in a southerly direction along the shore. The few Israelis hanging out on beach chairs in front of the Sha-blool Beach Café rise and walk to the water to shoot photos of the beautiful lone stork with their cell phones and yell to each other "Ma zeh? Ma zeh?" ("What is it? What is it?") The stork and I travel down the coast in solidarity both on our own journeys, she alone on the seawater and I alone on the sand. I relish this silent time together. Many storks migrate through Israel each year on their way to Africa; birds have migrated through the Holy Land as far back as Biblical Times.

Hanukah quickly approaches; menorahs of all shapes and sizes decorate shopping centers, store windows and even some large menorahs appear on top of cars. Eden has two Christmas-Hanukah choral productions; Noa organizes a toy drive at school for the children of Friendship's Way while she prepares for midterms; Kobe sings Hanukah songs and lands the part of a looter in the Hanukah show; and Aaron plays basketball on the high school team, which I think he likes, but true to his nature, he does not share much information. He walks around mad, though at times he reverts to the Aaron who is loving, funny and kind. I patiently and painfully wait for these times, aware in the meantime that I have to be the recipient of his anger and frustration—he is fourteen and I am his mother.

Hanukah also means that markets and bakeries begin to sell suv-gan-iot (Hanukah doughnuts), fried bread balls light and doughy on the inside, properly crispy on the outside and then dusted with powdered sugar. The standard suv-gan-iot are plain or filed with jam. Fancier suv-ga-niot are also available in small and large sizes, filled with chocolate, toffee and cream. Suv-gan-iot are a caloric festival and nightmare all at once. It is truly miraculous how rapidly one enters my mouth and I feel it arrive to my rear end. However, it is a custom to eat suv-gan-iot at Hanukah and I am a firm believer in observing traditions especially while living in the Holy Land.

While the festivities are under way, there is a great deal of terrible news—Prime Minister Olmert leaks classified military information that Ehud Goldwasser and Eldad Regev, the two reservists who were kidnapped from the border of Lebanon in July are most likely dead. Large yellow wanted posters with the deranged escaped rapist's face are plastered all over the country. For a few days this small ghoulish character from a dark fairy tale was thought to be around Tel Aviv and then the Sharon area where we live. One rumor spread that he hid within an ultra orthodox religious community offering him anonymity as these people do not see news and billboard announcements. Wherever he is hiding, women all over the country are afraid that he may be lurking nearby. We are also involved in prisoner swapping negotiations with the Palestinians; the plan calls for over one thousand Palestinian prisoners to be released in a few stages for the return of one kidnapped Israeli soldier, Gilad Shalit, and this includes some Palestinian members of terrorist organizations with "blood on their hands".

* * *

Citrus trees are in full bloom producing the primary winter fruits; bright yellow lemons, pink grapefruits and orange oranges joyfully decorate the dull winter yards of my neighborhood; I am tempted to stop and pick as much fruit as I can to squeeze fresh juice for my family to fight off colds. The castle's yard is full of tiny orange kumquats; the fruit itself is not tasty but its color warms the garden.

I return home with the kids and we see Safta Marcelle's car is in front of the house. The moment I open the door, the divine sweet smell of Safta's cheesecake greets us. The kids all exclaim with excitement "Safta" as they run upstairs to find their Saba and Safta on the couch reading newspapers and a beautiful creamy cheesecake still warm from the oven, tanned on the top waiting for them on the kitchen counter. It is the perfect moment to eat the cake. When the light sweet cheese melts in my mouth, I look around at my children who with great pleasure devour Safta's cheesecake and the memory of my grandmother's cheesecake returns to me. It had a completely different texture and taste, but I looked forward to special occasions growing up when she baked it with the same love for her grandchildren that Safta has today. I feel her absence profoundly at this moment; she died five years ago but the taste of her cheesecake is still fresh.

* * *

I join Eden's class on a field trip to the Soreq Caves outside the city of Bet Shemesh; the mountain terrain in the Judean Hills is rough with magnificent views of distant hillsides and valleys below and the dry air is a refreshing change from the humid air by the sea. We enter a magical door in the mountain side to discover a brilliant old world; an enormous moist cave full of 300,000 year-old stalactites—thick, orange and gooey that hang everywhere from the cave's ceiling like solid long dripping icicles. The stalactites meet their counter parts the stalagmites rising from the ground like huge sand drip castles children make at the beach by taking very wet sand and letting it drip down out of their hands. Some of these stalactites and stalagmites still actively grow. I follow the children along narrow man made paths in and around the natural formations enjoying the children's wonder and awe in the size and shapes of these natural treasures in this magical underground world that existed in the Holy Land long before the Jews, the Romans, the Turks or the Arabs.

After the journey through the underground world, we eat our lunch with Shiraz and Joanna on large boulders in the shade of old trees and enjoy the fresh mountain air. Eden eats quickly and then jumps into action with Shiraz and Katie, flirts with Austin and Javier, talks a mile a minute with Niharika and Ricardina and dances around everyone. With it all, she enjoys my company in stark contrast to my older children. I continue to take pleasure in the dynamic personalities of Eden's diverse international classmates and admire that they all have great symbiosis, regardless of their very different nationalities, religions, languages or cultures.

* * *

The sun shines brilliantly on the dark blue water while the large waves crash shooting white wash in all directions. I watch a lone female surfer paddle like crazy, rise to her feet and ride the wave in as the wind blows her long blond hair in the air. For a moment I imagine myself in her place and then quickly recall the surf lesson I took a couple of years back and the difficulty I had simply hoisting my body up and standing on the moving surf board. It was a short-lived endeavor and a clear reminder that I was not twenty anymore.

At night, Yehuda and I drive on a very narrow one-way street lined with three and four story stucco apartment buildings, quite common in the older neighborhoods of Tel Aviv where cars are parked tightly on either side of the road. Crowds of people ooze out on to the sidewalk from the art gallery where our friend Killy's art is being exhibited. The only parking spot I see is a red and white zone on the curb, and I feel like an Israeli, so I indulge and drive up on the curb and park. Tonight Killy exhibits a small group of large canvasses; her art is generally bold and lively, but this period of painting is sad and full of darkness, devils and anger. Upstairs other Israeli artists are featured; portraits, landscapes, house parts and one painting of a raw brisket that sits in a pan of oil. The third small exhibit contains images of people incarcerated in their homes looking at the outside world. The most poignant painting has two young and soft hands on a windowsill as though a child looks out across the hilly terrain to a beautiful white village obscured by a barbed wire fence; the painting is framed with Hebrew and Arabic words. All of the art exhibited this evening exposes the melancholy that permeates throughout my ge-bor-ah and affects so many of her citizens these days.

We return home and find Aaron and Safta watching Maccabi Tel Aviv play a Greek team for a European basketball title. Aaron has not figured out how to watch NBA Lakers games on the Internet, which is one of the many things that currently anger him. Tonight he watches this game like an Israeli fan with his safta, who has moved in for a few weeks. Aaron lies on the couch like a prince as she serves him potato wedges and a hamburger—we ate a full dinner just a few hours earlier. I listen appreciating Aaron's dissection of the game in his unused Hebrew. She is truly thrilled by the attention and respect her grandson, the young prince bestows upon her.

* * *

I walk briskly as it is very cold this morning. I am alone with my khaver until I discover two men wearing skimpy Speedos walking toward the sea. I slow down to watch them enter the water while gray waves crash at their legs, their hips and finally when the water reaches their chests, they dive into larger breaking waves and begin their swim. From my perspective all bundled in a sweater, scarf and hat and walking fast to keep my body warm, these men are lunatics.

Noa calls me from school in tears. She approached a group of friends and reminded them to bring a new toy for her Friendship's Way Toy Drive to benefit the children of Yaffo and one boy told her point blank in front of the others that he would not help her Arab children. She was devastated by this boy's animosity and pride in sharing his negative sentiment among his peers. This followed an episode a few days earlier when she asked another male friend to prepare the artwork for her Holiday Toy Drive flyer and he produced a well designed flyer full of guns and military toys–not exactly the message for any children's charity let alone one that works to heal the disparity between Arabs and Jew.

* * *

'First they came for the Jews and I did not speak out because I was not a Jew. Then they came for the Communists and I did not speak out because I was not a Communist. Then they came for the trade unionists and I did not speak out because I was not a trade unionist. Then they came for me and there was no one left to speak out for me.' Pastor Martin Niemöller

Drizzle falls from the cloudy gloomy sky; my large floor to ceiling windows in the living room are coated with thick water drops. I lie on the couch, my body aches and my head is heavy. Yehuda is abroad for business again. I do not plan to move until the moment I have to bundle up with a warm fleece and Uggs to pick up the kids from school. I lie for hours admiring the kumquat trees bordering the backyard bountiful with small round orange fruit. Many of these bright fruits also lie unattended on the Astroturf reminding me of the miniature golf course I used to play on in my youth. I dream of filling a basket with kumquats and preparing preserves until I return from delirium and remember that I do not cook let alone prepare preserves. I should bring them to Aunt Shula, who would consider them culinary gems from which to make divine creations.

Last week at Shabbat brunch Shula served two homemade preserves and in my spirit of adventure, I tried both. One was reddish brown, thick and chunky made from ha-boosh, an apple like fruit that is never eaten raw and tastes like a mix between an apple and a berry, both sweet and tart. The second preserve was yellow and full of triangular shaped chunky pieces of rind from a hoosh hash, a thick skinned relative of the lemon that is not available in markets but found in people's backyards. This preserve tasted sour like a lemon and at the same time was well sweetened with sugar. I love that I ate food called ha-boosh and hoosh hash.

Lying around bestows on me the opportunity to read books, but it also affords me too much time to follow the news and actually absorb its terrible severity. I am terrified as I watch Iranian President Ahmadinejad, a modern day Hitler prepare for and finance the intended destruction of Israel. Iran sponsored Hassan Nasrallah and Hezbollah in Lebanon as they worked for the destruction of Israel, made very apparent in the Second Lebanon War. Iranian President Ahmadinejad also courts Palestinian Prime Minister Ismail Haniyeh. In a large stadium Haniyeh stands side by side with Ahmadinejad and denounces shalom with Israel, promising never to recognize Israel's right to exist, never to accept previous Israeli—Palestinian agreements and never to condemn violence. The reward for this speech is over $250 million for Hamas in the territories—a record payment for any political speech, which would be greatly welcomed if it paid for humanitarian needs and national infrastructure, rather than its obvious intent to pay for waging war on their Zionist enemy. In Gaza, a Palestinian gunman opens fire on a car killing the three young sons of a Fatah leader as they drive to school in the morning, Internet cafes are destroyed, a young girl found in jeans is beaten up and the streets are not safe. Radical Islam imported from Iran arrives rapidly in the streets of Gaza.

Within the same period of time, the Iranian government sponsors a conference in Tehran that denies the Holocaust occurred. President Ahmadinejad knows this forum will incite hatred and establish doubt that the Holocaust existed in the minds of the Arab masses. His goal is to prove that the United Nations should not have used the Holocaust as a reason to establish the Jewish state to make his call for the destruction of Israel and the right of the Palestinians to inhabit all of the country valid. I personally feel Ahmadinejad's hate for my children, my husband and myself because we are Jewish, we are American and we live in Israel. In this country, I may not see the hate but I eat, drink and breathe it daily— it is not something than can be isolated or disregarded.

Ho-ref (Winter)

Purple, orange and yellow strokes of color fill the sky's canvas as the sun meets the horizon early in the evening. Other colors emerge less bold and less defined, but equally mesmerizing and intriguing. Rapidly the sun disappears and the sky is sullen and dark with no hint of the circus of colors that just entertained me on my late afternoon walk.

Tonight, Yehuda and I are invited to a party hosted by the bank in the Namal Tel Aviv (Tel Aviv Port). As we prepare to leave, Eden and Kobe look at me incredulously. Kobe stops arranging his collection of rubber Pokémon finger puppets, runs over to give me a hug and tells me how much he loves me and will miss me. Eden pouts because I am going out and she is not. Noa takes over and we leave into the dark, drizzly night.

The Namal Tel Aviv has been revived from a slummy old port into a trendy district full of restaurants, bars and clubs along the water. It is not crowded when we arrive at 8:30pm, a ridiculously early hour by Israeli standards. We pass the kids' favorite chocolate shop Max Brenner and the aroma of rich chocolate wafts through the air, tempting me to stop and indulge. For a moment I seriously consider a mad dash for the comfort of hot chocolate, forgoing a large party full of Hebrew speaking strangers.

A photographer snaps our photo as we enter the large hanger space. It is an evening for the bank's best customers who wine and dine on salads and soup served in bread rolls, sautéed salmon, grilled mini meats and rice dishes. Bank executives welcome Yehuda enthusiastically, and I am greeted as the trophy wife who simply needs to smile and stand by her husband's side. I am in the Middle East I quickly remind myself. It is also odd to be in a room with hundreds of people and not to recognize anyone.

After listening to speeches thanking the distinguished bank customers, servers dressed in black walk around with trays of mini chocolate mousses and miniature Crème Brule, while others carry long wooden canoes full of fresh fruit. Roses are presented to us at the door when we leave. We walk to our car in the slight drizzle past the chocolate shop crowded with customers at this late hour.

The enormous parking lot is also packed and we are unable to move as some creatively parked cars have choked up the small entrance-exit. It is typical Israeli gridlock and no one wants to be the first to yield and be a freyer (sucker) to free up the blockage. We sit motionless for five minutes before Yehuda gets out of the car and goes over to the impasse to help negotiate the opening of a safe passage for all of us who need to get out and free up parking spaces for the long line of cars waiting to enter. We finally exit through the gate where the attendant oblivious to the blockage continues to give out tickets to cars waiting to enter. In Israel nightlife commences around 11pm and these cars are full of people ready to start their late night fun. The mess of cars bothers Yehuda, my modern day Moses, but I, unfazed, simply acknowledge that this is part of life in Israel.

We drive home in the drizzle and I think maybe Yehuda's basic ability to problem solve could be used to help free kidnapped Israeli soldiers from Hamas and Hezbollah. For many months these men have been held and I have watched the government battle unsuccessfully for their release. If Yehuda had not stepped out of the car and gone to the heart of the problem, we would have remained at a standstill indefinitely and tempers would have flared. Rarely do I see Israeli or Arab politicians 'get out of the car' and go to the root of the problem to alleviate the pressure or worse be cast as a freyer, instead they quarrel from a distance without getting wet.

* * *

Angry and harsh waves this morning spray salt water through the air as they announce the latest storm to arrive in Israel. I look at the incredible abundance of sea foam and recall that Aphrodite, the Greek Goddess of Love was created by sea foam off the coast of the Island of Cyprus where we boated on Rosh Hashana. How I wish that a Mediterranean Goddess of Shalom could rise from the sea foam on the shores of Israel and Gaza to help heal these two peoples. This would be a wonderful Hanukah gift.

Me-nor-ahs and draddles (spinning toys) decorate the Seven Star Mall that is packed this afternoon with holiday shoppers. I roam through the stores looking for Hanukah gifts, but find myself watching and listening to the enthusiastic shoppers around me instead. While I know almost everyone is Jewish, the faces and the native languages of many Israelis are beautifully diverse. Yet everyone is unified in their excitement for the upcoming holiday. Gifts are bought, parties are planned and children's shows crop up at local theaters and community centers. Life in Israel is a great dichotomy; Israelis enjoy large and festive celebrations, while the harsh realities of stubbornness and mistrust, war and hate take up so much of the big picture. It is surreal. I happily shop for holiday gifts in the mall, while bombs fall in my sister—in—laws kibbutz along the border with Gaza and three soldiers remain in enemy hands.

* * *

I spend quality time in the morning with my Mac Book Pro answering e-mails and reviewing work projects back in L.A. The Internet enables me comfortably to run my small business from 9,000 miles away with a ten-hour time difference, which is my personal proof that The World Is Flat. In the background, the rain pounds against the windows producing a steady noise. This outdoor water pressure is a stark contrast to the fact that we have had no water pressure in the castle for a couple of days now. By noon, the rain miraculously stops and the sun bursts out drying the Astroturf lake that filled my back yard all morning. I open the sliding glass doors and fresh clean air dashes inside the castle. It feels wonderful.

Saba and Safta join me for Kobe's Hanukah show. He is a Greek warrior dressed in a white tunic who proudly bares a large wooden sword. When asked about his role, Kobe simplifies it by saying he is a 'bad guy'. We all sit on mini chairs intended for little behinds and watch happy children sing and dance as they present the story of Hanukah. Kobe and the other soldiers destroy the temple and Yehuda Maccabi and his followers discover the ransacked temple and the small amount of oil left which miraculously burns for eight days. After the show, Kobe is very proud of his performance and runs around excitedly with all the other performers. I am beaming with pride as I watch my son playing with his friends and confidently performing in his new language and enjoying himself along the way.

The celebration of oil continues with a suv-gan-iot picnic outside in the cool air with the winter sun's warming rays. As I eat my 'one' suv-gan-ia, a wild green and yellow parakeet watches me from the bare tree branch over my head. I am sure that she is a live incarnation of my conscience questioning why I am eating fried bread filled with sweet jam. Kobe devours his third doughnut and before he can obtain a forth, we escape the fried bread reception. Yehuda is out of the country, this time in Greece and Macedonia looking for real estate opportunities. This year we had intended to spend time together, but Yehuda is out of the country more and more and on special occasions like Kobe's Hanukah show, I greatly feel his absence.

While Israelis celebrate Hanukah, the Palestinians prepare for Christmas celebrations and decorate Bethlehem, the birthplace of Jesus Christ. The Christian Arabs are currently the minority in the city—many Christians have left over the years to avoid the continuing West Bank violence where there are very few opportunities to make a living. Christmas time is a perfect opportunity for the Muslim leadership to showcase to Christians all over the world that they are taking good care of Jesus' birthplace. Now in addition to fighting on the streets of Gaza, Fatah and Hamas battle in Bethlehem to provide funding and seek favor in the Christian world.

* * *

Doron, the taxi driver takes me to Ashdod, the port city south of Tel Aviv for my nephew, Ilad's engagement party at his fiancé parents' apartment. Ilad and his fiancé, Avigail are studying in London and have returned for a weekend of engagement celebrations in Israel. Tonight marks the first time that all the Georgian Jews from Avigail's family will meet all the Iraqi Jews from Ilad's family. Yehuda is still in Greece for business.

I am welcomed at the door by Avigail's father, Avraham a small gray haired man and her mother Nina, a pretty blond woman with a great smile who looks like she could be Avigail's sister. Avigail's safta, a round babushka dressed in black proudly corners me at the desert buffet and explains that many of the fried breads and syrupy twisted deserts on the table are from a local Georgian bakery, and are similar to the ones she ate back in Georgia. Everyone gathers around the dining room table just below a shiny plank filled with bright and flickering candles for a toast. Avraham introduces the Georgians and then Roni, Ilad's father introduces the Iraqis—two very proud tribes joining together for a future generation. This union is like so many in the Holy Land, a nation created by bringing together Jewish people from all over the world to live united in one country.

I cannot believe how fast the years have passed. I remember meeting Ilad when he was a little boy and Yehuda's entire family, his parents and all his brothers and their kids traveled to L.A. shortly after we started dating. I was overwhelmed by the intensity of their tribal gathering and the Hebrew language, as back then, the extent of my Hebrew was the word 'shalom'. As I watch this lovely engagement ceremony, I am struck with the notion that Ilad is older today than I was when we were married and now I take my place as part of the older generation by watching the young begin their cycle of marriage and babies.

* * *

My dear friend Hedda and her teenage sons arrive from Melbourne and stay with us in the creamy white castle. During the day, we play endless games of Scrabble, practice yoga, drink cappuccino and simply enjoy each other's company. I realize how much I miss having a good friend around and enjoy speaking English with someone who is not a child, a repairman or a fish.

Tonight I join Hedda and a few other women for a late dinner at my second kitchen, Rocca Restaurant. We drink wine, we laugh and bond as women do so well when sharing time together without men and without children. I look around the table and admire six strong, thoughtful and independent domestic executives with years of practical conciliatory experience in a wide array of relationships and whose talent is desperately needed in the war between the Israelis and the Palestinians. Women bring sa-vla-noot (patience), se-khel (wisdom) and ko-akh (strength) to the playing field—qualities that appear to be missing from both sides of current negotiations.

* * *

Forty screaming children and a few outnumbered adults sit in a large purple bus stuck in traffic in the middle of Tel Aviv on the way to the Knesset in Jerusalem where they have been invited by the Speaker of the Knesset Dalia Itzik to perform at the New Year's reception for foreign dignitaries and religious leaders. For this choral performance, I had to invite myself and then push hard to be included; only at the final moment did I succeed in receiving my pass.

At dusk, we arrive at the Knesset's guard gate and are immediately welcomed by very cold and crisp Jerusalem air as we disembark the purple bus. The security is tight as we pass guard stations, have our bags x-rayed and show our passports to gain access. We walk through the very large open plaza to the impressive Knesset building made of beautiful Jerusalem Stone and surrounded by strong high columns. We enter the Chagall Hall, named for and dedicated by the artist Marc Chagall, where state receptions are held and the performance will take place in a couple of hours.

The children rehearse, but no sound comes out of the speakers. Frannie, the music teacher unsuccessfully attempts to get the soundman to work with her. I stand at the back of the room and yell over to the technician in Hebrew. He listens and raises the volume. I have truly become an Israeli. The soundman's equipment is in front of an amazing Chagall wall mosaic the 'Angel of Redemption' who spreads out his arms to the Jewish people and calls for them to return home to Israel. "A-nee po," (I am here) I answer to the mosaic.

The hall is full of dignitaries and religious leaders. I run into an old acquaintance Nadia Hilo, an Arab Christian Knesset member from Jaffa who is speaking with Ali, the Jordanian Ambassador who I know from the kid's school—once again 'six degrees of separation' prevails in this small country. Dalia Itzik welcomes this large gathering of influential leaders from all over the world and talks about the need to work together to bring shalom to the region. Her words are followed by the real splendor of the evening; the beautiful and fresh voices of children representing nations, religions and races from all over the world sharing a message of tolerance and appreciation for diversity in the Jewish Homeland. The children perform on a stage in front of three enormous Chagall tapestries with bright colors of the rainbow moving from one color scheme to the next relating the history of the Jewish people, stories from the bible, the connection between the Israelites and G-d, the Holocaust, the Jews return to Zion, the building of modern Israel and the holidays that the Jewish People celebrate. I snap a few pictures with my cell phone attempting to hold on to the sight of forty kids from all over the world singing about children, love and shalom in front of these monumental pieces of art at the Knesset and noting the prophecy of Isaiah embedded in the tapestries, "The wolf also shall dwell with the lamb, and the leopard shall lie down with the kid; and the calf and the young lion and the fatling together; and a little child shall lead them" (Isaiah, 11:6)

* * *

Posters plastered on the freeway underpasses and bus stops display the faces of Army Chief of Staff Dan Halutz, Prime Minister Ehud Olmert and Foreign Minister Amir Peretz with the words 'Mem-shala Ha-loo-zer-eem Ha-bite-a' ('Government of Losers Go Home'). They replace the face of a gray haired black hat rabbi who very seriously tells viewers that the 'Mesiah is coming'—two very different posters that both equally portray the feelings of this nation.

I am invited to prepare khallah with Kobe as part of the weekly Shabbat tradition. Kobe, my five-year old pastry chef insists that he knows how to prepare the khallah and I should follow his direction. We roll the dough out on the table, cut it into strips and then clumsily Kobe spreads Nutella (chocolate/hazelnut spread) on to the sticky raw dough. We round off each strip and then braid the three pieces together. By the end, more of the brown chocolaty Nutella covers his fingers than the dough. Kobe is thrilled to bring home his khallah and share it with Aaron who each week relishes its sweet taste.

* * *

From the bluff above the sea, I watch a class of young students windsurfing along the energetic seawater like a school of fish skimming the dark surface. Noa and I are sitting at Rocca with my old friend Kati and her adult daughters, Maya and Dana. Kati is a pretty petite French woman with a 'super-sized' character always adorned with gold and diamonds on her ears, neck and hands. She came to Israel thirty years ago from Provence, a Jewish convert with more passion and love for Judaism and Israel then most Sabras I know. Kati knows everyone in Herzelia Pituah and she knows 'everything about everything' in Israel and proudly shares this absolute knowledge in her perfect English or Hebrew flavored with her thick and rich French accent. We drink cappuccino, eat chocolate mousse, laugh and enjoy the moments together as the beautiful orange sun ball is perfectly suspended over the clear blue horizon.

* * *

I recognize the loud and heavy pounding sound of an army helicopter in the distance traveling down the coastline. Within seconds the powerful camouflage helicopter flies overhead producing a penetrating vibration through my body that only leaves me as the huge flying machine continues down the coast. My first thought is that there is an incursion somewhere in Israel, although I have not read anything about any altercations these days.

Kobe stays home from gan with a runny nose. He is not too sick to send off to the kibbutz, but I am happy to share a day with my little son alone in the quiet castle. We spend the entire day indulging in his great passion—Pokémon. We discuss, draw, color and breathe Pokémon for hours; I delight in his exciting stories and adorable facial expressions, but mostly in the closeness and hugs that we share this day. I watch Kobe, who strongly resembles his older brother and fondly remember time alone with Aaron when he was little and stayed home frequently with sore throats and earaches. Aaron's passion was Power Rangers and I recall the many conversations where he earnestly tried to explain to me the talents and adventures of the different colored Power Ranger. I miss those days.

My gi-bor-ah continues to face great internal strife. Israel's President Katsav looks desperate and guilty as he delivers a ballistic speech yelling and accusing journalists of persecuting him and of course claiming his innocence in the rape charges against him. Chief of Staff, Dan Halutz resigns after the Army's internal investigation found failure with his command during the Second Lebanon War last summer. Prime Minister Olmert and Defense Minister Peretz do not show any signs of departure from the political stage, instead they are embroiled in a public feud while not speaking to one another, and each one publically attempts to choose the next Chief of Staff. Prime Minister Olmert is also the subject of a formal investigation of illegal private real estate transactions, and improper help to a friend when Bank Leumi turned private in 2005. The head of the Israeli Tax Authority, Jacky Matza, is in the middle of a corruption scandal and former Justice Minister Chaim Ramon's kissing trial awaits a verdict providing the Israelis with a great deal to discuss and argue about. All of this takes place as the former Prime Minister Ariel Sharon lies in coma for almost a year now. Israel is a young country that has grown very fast in fifty-eight years, and difficult 'growing pains' are to be expected—but so many at one time? While the Arab nations around us forgo democracy, the Israelis realize the difficulties in developing an open democratic government. Raising a nation is a bumpy process not unlike the experiences I have of raising my children. I am sure that all of these experiences will strengthen and develop this country for its successful adulthood. Likewise, I am really beginning to believe that the experiences this year will strengthen my children.

* * *

This morning I stumble upon a cache of beautiful seashells by the Gaudi house and stop to gather as many as my pockets and hands will hold. This is my therapy freeing me from the crazy problems in the creamy white castle, the coordination of my family's busy lives and helping me escape the troubles that my gi-bor-ah faces. I have two large glass jars full of these shells on the mantle in the family room representing many hours of this therapy, which is much less expensive than my therapist in L.A. A third large glass jar is already half filled and I still have another half a year here. I consider starting a business packaging shells in small glass containers and selling them world wide as Holy Shells from the Holy Land.

Noa and Aaron sit in the family room with the shades closed and watch the television series The O.C. about teenagers and their complicated social lives in Orange County, California. They love the stories and the characters. At this point, The O.C. is Aaron's substitute social life, because he still does not like the kids at school. Noa, on the other hand, is out of the house every Friday and Saturday night. Her social life is not a casual activity but has become a serious and full time pursuit. The television shows may have the glamour of Hollywood, but the endless teenage frolics here in Israel are extreme compared to L.A. I have never seen a society where teenagers are so free and spend so much time just 'hanging out', which is a nice way of saying partying, drinking and smoking. I recognize this is the Israeli youth's time to be 'free' before the responsibility of joining the army at eighteen years old—all offering a balance in the long run.

* * *

The ocean is stunning; each depth of seawater is a different blue hue from pale to almost black. I walk rapidly north along the hard wet sand as the wind behind propels and pushes me forward and I feel as though I can run a marathon, but when I turn around at the most northern tip of sand

and oppose the strong wind, I am kindly reminded that I am a terrible runner who lacks stamina and I must labor hard to return.

I have locked myself in the little office to work. Yes, I live in a huge castle, but this week, Julie the housekeeper is fighting with her Israeli boyfriend as she cleans and I can hear her screaming at him on the cell phone. I do not want to get in the middle of her war and I live in fear that she will leave and I will be forced to clean the whole castle by myself. In between all the work and e-mails, Yehuda's secretary Keren calls me at least a dozen times to go over his travel schedule for the next few months. Each time she calls, she commences the conversation with, "Ma shlo-mekh?" (How are you) Calls separated by five minutes or forty-five minutes start with the same phrase and I give the same answer, "Be-se-der, ma nee-shma" (Good, what's going on) and "Ma shlo-mekh?" (How are you?). Then we proceed with the conversation. While Israelis can be rough and abrupt, when they ask these questions at the top of each conversation, they sincerely want to know how you are doing.

In the afternoon another electrician is at our house to work on some lighting problems. I pass Aaron's room in the basement when I see the lights flickering on and off. I yell up and ask him what he is doing and by accident we learn that the lights for the guest room are connected with Aaron's room two floors below. This discovery has put to sleep my fear that this castle was haunted and confirmed my belief that this place was simply incorrectly wired from the start.

* * *

The seawater is gray and the sky is gray—there is no line defining the horizon.

The cover of the newspaper shows a man holding a small boy killed by the bullets of a Fatah gunman who shot the backseat of a car suspected of transferring a Hamas militant. The lifeless boy looks angelic and peaceful as if he is simply asleep in his father's arms. Over the weekend in the town of Anata near East Jerusalem, a pretty young Palestinian girl with long black hair was killed during a fight between IDF Border Policemen and Palestinian stone throwing youth. She did not participate in the stone throwing and was simply in the wrong place at the wrong time. Slowly I stop to read the details of each and every occurrence because whether it is Jew against Muslim or Muslim against Muslim it is wicked violence controlled by men in hiding who direct aggression that kills innocent children really not much different from my Kobe or Eden.

I believe more strongly each day that we need women leaders in this world who have the empathy to heal and the wisdom to end the fighting that takes the lives of the innocent. In October of 2000 at the start of the Second Intifada, the UN Security Council Resolution 1325 on Women, Peace and Security was passed unanimously. It was the first resolution the Security Council passed that addressed the impact of war on women and stated that women needed to be a part of the resolution for a lasting peace. It has been over seven years since this resolution was passed, but never successfully implemented; the problems here in Israel painfully cry out for the active participation of empathetic Jewish, Muslim and Christian women.

* * *

All night long, a huge storm brewed outside causing the power to go on and off and the inactive house alarm to beep incessantly throughout the house. On top of this, Eden woke with a stomachache and in between the beeping, she complained and felt rotten.

I hide inside the creamy castle bundled in a warm sweatsuit under a thick blanket in the family room alone and reading, something I had planned to do, at which I have not succeeded. Just before I leave to pick up the children, a young man from the alarm company arrives to check the beeping problem. He kisses the mezuzah and with a blast of chilly air enters into my toasty domain. The repairman tells me his name is 'Areyeh' (lion), which is quite humorous because physically Areyeh is a tiny and very thin man. Areyeh lectures me for ten minutes on the alarm's features and value. "Are there a lot of break-ins these days?" I ask. "Lo," he says, but in the same breath he insists that I still need to use the alarm.

While I was in hiding, there was a pi-gua in the most southern tip of Israel at the Red Sea resort city of Eilat. A Palestinian suicide bomber left the Gaza Strip and walked through the Sinai Desert in Egypt crossing into Israel somewhere in the middle of the vast desert. An Israeli driving along the highway picked him up and once he dropped him off at Eilat, he called the police to report the odd man. Before the police could catch up with him, he entered a bakery and blew himself up killing three innocent Jewish workers and shattering nine months of no pi-gua. In Gaza, friends and family praised the suicide bomber for his martyrdom while militant groups announced that the bombing was aimed to stop the civil war between Fatah and Hamas and to unite all Palestinians against Israel and the Zionist occupation. This pi-gua was quite far away by Israeli geography at the most southern tip of the country and at the same time very close emotionally due to the nature of a country that feels many times like one large neighborhood where tragic events are personal and central.

* * *

Ferocious clouds fill the skies and the wind wildly sweeps the fallen leaves and branches across the small road in the kibbutz so strong, in fact, that I do not dare open my umbrella, as it will turn inside out. After I run with Kobe to the car pelted by large raindrops, we drive the back roads to watch the horses standing around bored on this stormy afternoon stuck in their covered corral. Kobe happily tells me a story about each horse, as they are all his personal friends.

The severe weather inspires me this afternoon to chop all the vegetables in my refrigerator and prepare a perfect winter minestrone soup to serve with the fresh whole wheat bread and mozzarella cheese I bought at Lechem Erez this morning. As I cut the vegetables with a Pokémon video playing in the background, I prepare for the different responses from each of my children; Noa will complain that there are potatoes in the soup; Eden will wish it were pureed; Aaron will think soup, bread and mozzarella cheese is an insufficient meal; and Kobe will remind me that he is allergic to vegetables. This is another reason I do not cook—four children and four critics.

Internally, my giborah struggles with her different offspring. President Katsav is required by the attorney general to move out of the Presidential

Residence during his forced leave of absence. Chaim Ramon, the former Justice Minister is found guilty of 'The Kiss'; the judges come down extra hard on the former minister who should have just said "sle-kha" (sorry) from the start and the case would not have spun out of control and taken up so much public time and money. After the judge's ruling, Ramon still does not apologize rather considers an appeal. Shimon Peres jockeys for the country's presidency, but he fears defeat once again, as he lost to Katsav six and a half years ago in a closed Knesset vote. While the job of president is mainly ceremonial, Israel could enjoy the mature Shimon's domestic nurturing and wisdom including his positive international public relations skills.

* * *

I have been going stir crazy for days in the castle watching the latest winter storm wage battle on Eretz Israel when all of a sudden, the sun manages to peak out through the clouds. In seconds, I throw on warm clothing and jump out of the house to take advantage of this precious opportunity. I desperately missed my khaver, my therapy and much needed exercise. I need very little to be happy, but this freedom is essential to my survival.

One thing that continues to make my Kobe joyful is Kinder Chocolate Eggs—the exciting combination of chocolate and a surprise toy is always appealing. Today is no different as I watch Kobe and his friend Ayehli sit at the table and happily remove the tin foil cover from each of their wrapped eggs. They devour the two halves of the chocolate egg and then excitedly open the plastic egg to see their surprise. As I prepare the children's dinner, I reflect on the simple happiness that Kinder Chocolate Eggs bring to children and imagine me and Kobe bringing truck loads of this magic to the Palestinian children of the West Bank and Gaza to take pleasure in; children sharing these little jewels could be a small part of the larger shalom that needs to permeate to the young.

* * *

My khaver is a big mess; the wind blows wildly and powerful waves rush toward the shore in many layers at great speeds. The wet uneven sand is blanketed with trash that the rough sea spit out earlier when the tides were higher. I see how Israelis leave their scattered trash all over the sand on a summer day and I assume they also dump in the sea while they sail along the Mediterranean and the storm aids the refuse's journey back to shore. At Daboosh Beach dozens of large arch shaped kites in bright colors fill the clear turquoise sky harnessed by ropes to the strong bodies of surfers gliding in between and over the barrage of enormous waves. While the kites dance like crazy in the frantic and furious wind, the kite surfers speed back and forth, jumping over crashing waves. One orange and green kite dips toward the sand and passes next to me; its sheer force and size is awesome and powerful.

The kite surfers are inspirational. After watching them and perhaps with Tu B'shvat approaching, I am acutely aware that I need some change in my life. Tu B'shvat is the Jewish New Year for Trees, a holiday about renewal and revitalization. I visit Zion, the hairdresser and tell him that I need a big change—I sit unemotionally drinking a tea as Zion chops off my beautiful curly brown hair I have taken great pride in for years. I simply do not care anymore and welcome a new beginning.

* * *

The huge hangar is dark. Four musicians walk on the stage and begin to play vibrant and exciting music with their violins and cello as the lights slowly fade on. After a few minutes, Achinoam, Ayehli's mom from the gan, appears in black leather pants and a lace white blouse with her long curly black hair flowing down her back. She sings beautifully; crystal clear high notes she can hold and play with and warm and raspy low notes that are long and deep, she beats drums as she dances and moves all around the stage. In one song she taps her chest to the beat and sings 'a cappella' until the other musicians join her to finish the song. The Israeli audience is delighted and engaged whether she sings in Hebrew or a menagerie of other languages; she infuses them with love and empathy, which they absorb like sponges.

I fall asleep renewed by Achinoam's concert as music and lyrics play in my mind. Noa wakes me to tell me that her friend Ruth's ear is inflamed. Noa and Ruth went to the very trendy Shenkin Street in Tel Aviv to get piercings and now Ruth's earring has disappeared under the red swelling. Ice does not bring down the swelling so we drive to the emergency room at Icholov Hospital in central Tel Aviv.

In the emergency room, we are placed in a cordoned off section and a young nurse who ironically has many ear piercings and a nose piercing asks us why we are here. After she and an ER doctor see Ruth's ear, we are sent to the 8th floor to see the Ear, Nose and Throat doctor by way of a dark and smelly service corridor that Noa refers to as 'a waiting hall for dead bodies'. On the 8th floor we meet a doctor dressed in his green scrubs with gray hair and bright red-rimmed glasses and without a word, he waves us to follow him. He points Ruth to the table to lie down. I ask him his name while he looks at her ear and he mumbles something like "Aryererf" with a Russian accent. He puts on sterile white gloves and opens the back post of the earring and extracts the tiny gold earring with fine tweezers. Now Dr. Aryererf warms up as we are no longer strangers and he speaks kindly revealing his excellent English.

We drive home in silence, exhausted from the late night emergency room. I think about Noa and Ruth's teen adventure on Shenkin Street where they each had piercings done. Noa had a piercing done in the upper part of her ear that she had wanted for a long time and is a popular trend in Israel. Tattoos are also popular and quite common for the young Israelis, but my daughter knows that permanent tattoos are prohibited in my home. Noa frequently enjoys reminding me that the youth here are free to go out all night, and are also free to get tattoos, but I hold to my values even when they do not mesh with the Israeli societal ones. The minute I enter the creamy white castle I cannot sleep. I lie on the couch in the family room and read. I doze on and off for a couple of hours before Kobe and Bob Sfog on the television wake me to start another day.

* * *

Another storm brews; cold and wicked winds stir the rough sea, but no rain parts from the angry clouds hovering low along the beach. Two black scruffy dogs, one small and one large, briskly walk on the sand. After about fifteen minutes this canine couple veers away from the water off toward the cliffs and the smaller black dog starts to mount the larger female, but the size difference proves a real challenge for him to perform his male duty and the female dog is not too excited by any of this activity. He unsuccessfully persists until they reach the most northern part of the beach and disappear. This little black dog's poorly received sexual advances are strangely symbolic and parallel to the news of sexual misconduct in the country although even with these headlines, Israel is amazingly strong and vibrant.

Tu Bish-vat, the Jewish New Year for Trees arrives; we celebrate and eat dried and fresh fruits, wheat and barley products, seeds and nuts and bread full of whole grains. At the kibbutz, Kobe and his friends plant trees; in the north of the country, trees are planted to fill forests that were burned by missiles during the Second Lebanon War last summer; near Nablus close to the Palestinian village of Salem, Israelis and Palestinian farmers join together as a message of solidarity to plant hundreds of olive trees to replace those they say settlers cut down. How I wish that Israelis and Palestinians on the Green Line could plant trees to mark borders replacing the cement walls that are currently needed for protection.

* * *

Ben, the mouse has returned for a visit to my kitchen leaving his mark on a nibbled apple in the fruit bowl. Back in November during a storm, Ben also visited, ate some fruit and moved on. I assumed we were just a stop on his travels and he preferred the kitchens of good Israeli households where food is traditionally left on the kitchen counters, easily accessible to nosh on at all times. The last time he was here, Kobe was so excited that he told everyone he had a new pet, but this time I refrain from sharing the news that his friend with beady eyes, whiskers and a tiny pounding heart has returned.

I take Kobe to gan early this morning. The sweet smell of pancakes meets us when we enter the magical second hand play world and Kobe runs off to join his friends who build a fortress out of wooden blocks. "Boker tov" (Good morning), I say to Alona as I admire her fragrant pancakes. She offers me one and I partake. I do not generally eat pancakes, but this one is delicious, prompting me to remember the pancakes my father would make for me on very rare occasions when I was a little girl. My father was a workaholic and did not spend much time cooking, so these pancakes were a special treat. Until this morning, I had not recalled this memory of my father for many years.

Eden and I attend Aaron's basketball game against a team of Arab kids from Jerusalem. The Jerusalem coach yells direction at his players in English with a heavy Southern drawl as though he coaches a team from Texas. The boys listen in English but speak Arabic amongst themselves. Their friends who have come from Jerusalem to cheer for them look like the teens from our school, who look like teens from America. The girls wear tight jeans and layered shirts and the boys wear baggie jeans and sweats very low with their boxers displayed on their rear, not a very attractive fashion on boys anywhere in the world. I am cognizant that through the Internet, the world for teens has become very small unifying their wardrobe and I hope their thoughts. Today they all scream loudly and excited by the game and each other. Eden who is trying to understand their conversations asks me if they speak a very fast form of Hebrew. On the court, the players battle, obvious fouls are all part of the game with coaches and referees keeping the young men in order. While the competition is fierce, there is no violence rather symbiosis. Aaron is one of the smaller players and the youngest, but he is quick and sets up plays with smart assists. I leave the game with two holy requests; please G-d let us find a way for the Israeli and Palestinian youth to lay down their Uzis and their rocks, and play competitive sports instead of participating in violence and please G-d let my thirteen-year old son succeed and feel confident off the court as well.

* * *

The pathway to the gan is full of dense fallen leaves and shadows from mature trees; it feels like a page out of the children's book, 'Where the Wild Things Are'. When I arrive to the gan, Kobe runs over to me eating a fresh pita and cottage cheese sandwich waving in front of my eyes a color photo of a baboon couple at the Haifa Zoo cuddling with their new baby, part of this weeks celebration in the gan and the country of She-vu-a Mish-pa-ha (Family Week). By the door lies a tray with more tasty sandwiches; Eden helps herself to an omelet sandwich and I grab a mashed avocado and cucumber stuffed pita—a perfect afternoon snack to celebrate She-vua Mish-pa-ha.

As I drive home, I receive a call from the junior high school secretary that Aaron's principal and counselor would like to meet with me to talk about Aaron. A few days earlier, I received a call from the science teacher who informed me that my son was missing assignments and in general was turning work in late. I spoke with Aaron who at the time promised to be on schedule with his work. I desperately wanted to believe him, but I am a fryer. I have no down-time to lament my failings as my afternoon continues with my most vital maternal job, driving. This part of life in Israel mirrors L.A. because no matter where in the world I am, I spend most of my afternoons driving my children. While the drives here are shorter, the traffic is rougher and I drive on narrow car filled streets and battle crazy drivers. In addition to the role of driver I also serve as an ATM, which means that I receive visits from teenagers when they need money, which is another job that has no borders.

* * *

Raindrops battered the windows all night long serenading my relentless insomnia. By morning, the sun shines brightly through scattered clouds with just enough of a break to steal a quick beach walk. The surfers have not wasted any time and have taken advantage of the large and powerful waves pounding the coast. I admire their energy and passion and while I used to be like these adventurers, now the thought of wearing a tight wet suit with my hands, feet and head exposed to the brisk water is distant. Many shiny phantom jellyfish have washed up on to the sand and lie stranded. I know that something is wrong, as I feel more like the jellyfish than the surfers.

I continue to make every attempt for a real social life with real people; I find I have friends to eat lunch with and enjoy their company as Eden does at school. I also watch with pride as my five-year old Kobe carefully legislates the swapping of small plastic Pokémon figures with his friends. I cannot resist observing the ironic parallel between Kobe and his young friends and PM Olmert and his political buddies who spend their days engaged in a game of ministerial swapping. Olmert also reminds me of my fourteen-year old son as he ignites fires to deter the country from pinning him down and holding him responsible for his actions. Aaron moves angrily from one activity to the next and blames everyone else—mostly his mother—when things go wrong, he takes no personal responsibility for his laziness and his faults. He currently has an injured elbow and I pay the price for it as he sits on the sidelines.

* * *

Eden is excited that her tiny feet have finally outgrown her old shoes and we drive to the Nike Store in the Herzelia Industrial Zone to celebrate. As I drive off the highway and turn onto the street where the Nike Store is located, a man in a blue Audi honks at me so I automatically assume I did something wrong. I slow down behind a pile up of cars and he pulls up next to me and honks again. He signals me to roll down my window and I do. "Ma ata ro-tzay?" (What do you want), I snap at him. He switches to English, "I wanted to say that you are very pretty." I am blown away and feel my face turn beet red. He smiles. I smile and stupidly say, "Sorry and thank you" and wave my right hand like a pathetic Ms. America. Eden laughs at me from the back seat. The pile of cars part like the Red Sea and I drive forward slightly embarrassed but secretly happy as this is the first person to pay me a compliment in seven months in Israel and I realize my ego needs it.

* * *

Aaron sits in the kitchen and eats cereal at 5:40am. He has practice in half an hour. All year I have struggled to wake him at 7:15am for school, but for basketball practice at this god-awful hour, he wakes, dresses and eats all on his own and in good spirits. The streets are dark and empty except for the Ethiopian street cleaners collecting their equipment to commence their day. The usually busy Rabin Intersection over the highway to Haifa is desolate. The road in Kfar Shmaryahu is empty until we arrive at the school and see a guard standing motionless outside the kiosk. Aaron silently gets out of the car. It is too early for either one of us to say much.

A few short hours later, I sit with the principal and the middle school counselor who tells me that Aaron is not doing his work. In a few weeks, the basketball team will travel to The Hague for a tournament and Aaron may not be eligible to join the group. They also inform me that Aaron does not seem happy. I mentally hit myself for allowing him to attend an all night Super Bowl party and a Maccabi Tel Aviv basketball game earlier in the week when he claimed that he had fulfilled his school commitments; come to think of it, he appeared quite happy to participate in these social sporting events. Now I know I am a real fryer. We invite Aaron into the meeting. He hears from all three of us that we are coordinated for his benefit so he cannot slip through more cracks. I leave the meeting numb from his teenage deception and disgusted that I took him away to Israel. It is hard enough to be a teenager, but I had to change his school and his friends for a year, changes which he apparently cannot handle.

Later, I return home to find Noa sitting outside with friends and the nargila we bought in the Old City that has lain dormant until now. Amir, 'nargila boy' has come over to initiate its use. Until now, I could not imagine my day getting any worse and now my almost sixteen-year old daughter who does well academically 'hangs out' in my backyard and smokes from a nargila. I am responsible for all of this. I have let the guilt of our move compromise my parenting and I have two entitled teenagers who have little self control and even less respect for me.

* * *

The recent rains fill the low-lying fields outside the entrance to the kibbutz creating a shallow lake. A large group of black egrets with long thin legs bathes in the lake amongst the thin tall reeds. On the bordering dry land, a group of white egrets appear to wait their turn to enter the water. Perhaps segregated by color like Jews and Palestinians, they do not share space?

I visit with my Blackberry today. I turn it on and within seconds, the gonging and vibrating symphony sends me into an excited frenzy. I immediately regret my decision to reconnect and for over five minutes as hundreds of messages appear on the small screen; I am appalled by my technological weakness. I sift through these messages saving important notes and immediately deleting endless junk mail that I have not missed.

The Saudi King Abdullah brings Palestinian President Abbas (Fatah Party) and Palestinian Prime Minister Haniyeh (Hamas party) to Mecca in hopes of motivating the Palestinians to lay down their weapons, stop battling one another and form a unity government for both Gaza and the West Bank. I do find it curious that the international press that scrutinizes every move the Israelis make when they battle Palestinians has taken a vacation from their meticulous efforts as the Palestinians needlessly and viciously kill their own people in a civil war on their streets each day. As I watch this royal attempt to bring calm, I know that the coalition is doomed as all the leadership consists of men with large egos whose concern appears to be the retention of power which would be seriously jeopardized by real concessions and by selling an optimal plan to the desperate people. Both groups also feel very different about Israel; Fatah is willing to negotiate for a two state solution but Hamas will not stop their terror until all the Jews are thrown into the sea. I want to offer King Abdullah my youngest son Kobe to help in the negotiations; he at five-years old is already a skilled negotiator. He thoughtfully negotiates with me to go and buy him Pokémon eggs at the mall each day and he can comfortably walk into a room full of familiar adults as well as strangers with a warm smile and receive respect and admiration. I have also witnessed and admired my modern day Biblical Joseph's cleverness and congeniality as he leads the swapping of prized figurines amongst his peers while forming his desired collection. Thousands of years of turmoil in the Holy Land and almost sixty years of battles between the Israelis and the Palestinians and still lasting coexistence eludes us. Perhaps my Kobe along side Israeli and Palestinian children will end this cruel story?

* * *

There is a terrible pounding outside. I jump out of bed and open the shutters to see a deluge of hail the size of ping-pong balls attacking my home; within seconds everything is a blanket of winter white. I slip on my Ugg boots and venture to the street and it is all white, but within fifteen minutes only random patches of white still appear. We drive to school and the hailstorm starts again as white frozen balls viciously attack my car making a terrible racket. I drive very slowly as I can hardly see the road and it is so noisy that I can barely hear Kobe's voice from the back seat. At Rabin Intersection, the sun shines through the clouds.

This evening we celebrate Valentine's Day with a dinner and some tokens of a-ha-va (love); Max Brenner chocolates and stuffed animals that I found at the mall marketed for this imported holiday honoring a-ha-va. Noa and Eden are in a competition to give me the nicest hand made cards with the sweetest messages—Noa even writes hers in Spanish. Kobe looks at me after dinner and says, "Mom, you know what the best Valentine present I got is?"

"No," I answer.

"You are the best Valentine present," and he hugs me tight. Aaron does nothing, which makes me think that one day Kobe will also do nothing, but in the meantime I hug my little son back perhaps a little too tightly and a little too long. The Israeli boy Noa likes does not show up to take her to a dinner because he has to work. She is crushed. I remind her that this is a foreign holiday and he is an Israeli. I hold my tongue and do not say that he is also a cute Israeli boy who happens to be a jerk, because this would not help anything.

* * *

The roads are empty this Shabbat morning as we drive to visit Saba and Safta at their kibbutz near the southern city of Ashdod. Once off the main highway, we drive along newly constructed country roads and pass clusters of new houses and neighborhoods settled in between vineyards and olive trees. None of these developments existed sixteen years ago when I first visited their kibbutz. We drive past the factory where the frozen pizza we eat comes from on the outskirts of Gan Yavne turning off on to a smaller paved road past a horse stable and a cemetery and we arrive at the entrance, where the guard station sits empty and the gate is left open. This kibbutz is where Yehuda grew up after making Aliyah from Iraq. As a child, he lived in special quarters with kids his own age and went to school; he worked the land, washed dishes and spent many years as a shepherd. Yehuda loved growing up on this kibbutz; he frequently describes the freedom he had as a child—he never felt restricted by the rigid structure or regiment of early kibbutz life that actually contributed greatly to the security of his youth. Yehuda and I often argue about the rules and boundaries that I try to set for our children as we do not have the natural kibbutz framework or support system; Yehuda looks at this structure like a form of child abuse and I as a way to cover my children with a safety net as they develop. While we do not agree and at times tempers flare, I appreciate the healthy value of discord between us knowing that we are working for the common goal of our children's development.

At Safta and Saba's small house, Eden and her Aussie friend Katie barely say "shalom" and are off and running. The kibbutz is one place where two young girls can explore alone and I do not worry. When I was their age, I was free to wander around my neighborhood, but I cannot offer this to my children in this day and age in L.A. Eden wants to show Katie the animals in the petting farm and the dining room. Kobe sits proudly in the basket at the rear of the Saba's electric cart as they drive around the kibbutz on their own adventure. Safta and I sit in her small and comfortable living room on the two well-padded easy chairs and she tells me stories—she talks and I listen which is a successful ingredient in our good relationship. As she speaks, my eyes travel over the magnificent photos of six generations of family adorning the walls of the room when suddenly the roaring sounds of fighter jets conquer the air as they take off from the military base just next to the kibbutz. She is accustomed to the intense booming sound and simply stops in mid-sentence and resumes after the jet has trailed off. I assume they are on military exercises and there is no need to be fearful, but their booming roar penetrates the body and soul while their pace is hurried and frequent.

The kids return from their adventures to a large pot of Safta's rice, which they happily eat before we head back home. Safta prepares a bag full of food for Aaron and Noa who she is sure will be hungry when they awake in the afternoon. Saba, at eighty nine-years old, amazes me as he takes all three kids for a final ride on his electric cart; Eden and Katie sit on his lap and Kobe takes the basket. The children's smiles reveal how happy they are on their final ride of the day through Saba and Safta's kibbutz.

* * *

At the gan, Nili has already started her morning meetings in the back room. I enjoy watching my small son run and take his place at his seat marked with his name in Hebrew on a small cut out seahorse. As I leave, I admire the dining tables full of fresh salads and enjoy the scent of the wonderfully fragrant pancakes; I smile knowing my young son is in a perfect place.

At the Rabin Intersection on my way home, a white and blue police car with a flashing light is parked at an angle, blocking one of the two exit lanes. One policeman stands with his arms crossed observing cars as they slowly drive by and the other policeman is speaking to a driver that he already pulled over. I assume they are searching for dangerous people or cars that carry suicide bombers and for this reason I patiently wait to pass assuming this delay is for my security.

Late in the afternoon, Noa and I go to Tel Aviv to meet with the Mayor to try to enlist his support for the charity event we are planning for the children of Jaffa. Noa is sick as a dog but committed to attend, she knows it was not easy to get a time on the mayor's busy schedule. Before we enter the City Hall, we pass the black stone Rabin Memorial marking the exact

130

spot where Prime Minister Rabin was assassinated. As I walk by, I recall the summer years back when we visited Israeli and on the weekends, I played tennis on the court next to Rabin and his wife. He was very congenial until he started to play and once in the game he was quite competitive and would roar loudly when he missed the ball and even louder when he hit a winner.

We enter the building through a metal detector and other than this, there is no security. It is quite empty at this hour—everyone has gone home. We take an old elevator to the 12th floor and a guard sends us down the hall to the mayor's office where the secretary has us wait. Ten minutes later, the mayor arrives with a half finished Sudoku game in his hands. He stops and greets us and then he disappears into his office. Finally, we are called in. The mayor warns us that there is a smell of a dead rat in the room and as he speaks the strong dead rodent scent becomes more pungent. Tomorrow they will find the culprit and remove him. The mayor sits behind a huge desk looking serious yet kind and with his large buggy green eyes asks, "Lama a-ten po?" (Why are you here) Noa thoughtfully shares some of her experiences about the children, the programs, the message of shalom and tolerance and why this program is important. The mayor listen as his assistant takes notes and then he lectures us on the many great causes his own Tel Aviv Foundation serves for urban renewal and children's services. I can tell we are being blown off by the mayor and even with the putrid smell of the dead rat; we do not budge until we have made our point loud and clear.

* * *

Half way up the beach, there is a dead sea turtle washed up on shore lying upside down on its shell. The large body of the turtle is still in perfect condition and I can see the beautiful anatomy of his underbody; his four strong flipper like legs and the greenish brown shell that envelops the back of his body. Last week a large baby whale washed up on the shores off of Haifa and was brought to a burial site for animals in the Holy Land.

I love my ge-bor-ah, but I cannot escape the bad news and scandals she is plagued with daily. The Israeli Police Inspector General (police chief for the whole country) Moshe Karadi resigns after the Zeiler committee cites him for bad conduct; taking bribes from Israeli underworld figures, mafia infiltration in the police department and cover ups and pay offs. In 1998, Mr. Kardi was involved in "Battery Affair" where the police negotiated and brokered payment to underworld figures for the return of gas mask batteries that they had stolen from IDF warehouses. The former Judge Zeiler, who heads up the Committee, announces that Israel is like Sicily because the police force works with organized crime. Even with all this news, I still feel much safer walking the streets in Israel than in L.A.

$$* * *$$

Yehuda and I walk and discuss the latest attempt to buy an apartment in Israel. We made an offer and the seller, a Jew from New York accepted it and then turned around two days later and increased the asking price by 15% after receiving a call from a secret real estate agent who told him he had a client for a higher price. We know that there are very few apartments to be found along the sea in Herzelia and debate our prospects. Yehuda grew up on a kibbutz and all the years he lived and visited Israel, he never owned a domestic property. We have discussed this prospect for years and it is now so close—pushing us to proceed even if the apartment is over priced.

Everyone in my family gets sick; Noa has strep throat and Dr. Shub of South Africa makes me look at her white puss-caked tonsils; Aaron woke in the night with red welts all over his body and uncontrollable itching; Kobe has a terrible cold and cough; and Eden has sympathy stomach pains. Even as I take care of the infirm, I wish I could join U.S. Secretary of State Condoleezza Rice as she meets with Palestinian President Abbas and Israeli PM Olmert. I simply want to know what they are really discussing. I am convinced that their agenda does not include the voices and the participation of women and those people on the streets who lose so much each day; without their participation I am convinced there can be no real progress.

* * *

A human bird with large green and orange wings glides through the sky, catching the wind by the cliffs above the seashore and enjoying the wonderful view of the sea. He has no engine; he is both in good control and at the mercy of the winds—a fine line between a wonderful journey of complete freedom and lunacy. I think my friends back home look at me and think I am living a wonderful journey but am a complete lunatic to reside in Israel where from CNN it looks like I live in a war zone.

The local news is full of stories about a Russian Israeli billionaire named Arcadi Gaydamak who has been helping the residents of cities and towns afflicted by war in the North and the South of Israel. Last summer during the Second Lebanon War, this live Tinkerbell, evacuated many residents of Qiryat Shmona from the barrage of Hezbollah Katusha Missiles being sent to their city from Lebanon and arranged for them to stay in hotels in the southern part of the country. Currently, he is evacuating hundreds of Sderot resident to Eilat to get a break from the Qassam Rockets being sent over from Gaza. There are many other stories of caring citizens who perform good deeds but they are hidden by the plentitude of bad news.

* * *

An army transport helicopter flies up the coast and about half an hour later two more army helicopters fly down the coast cruising comfortably, not at the frantic pace with the rapid, heavy rotors sound when rushing to or from any fighting. I imagine the soldiers inside, taking pleasure in the beautiful panorama on a day where their travels are not pregnant with anxiety.

This calm scene along the seaside is shattered in the middle of the day when Shin Bet, the internal security (like the FBI) receives information that a suicide bomber arrived in Tel Aviv from over the Green Line near the city of Jenin with a bomb in his bag. Upon hearing the warning of a potential pe-goo-ah, authorities close off the South Tel Aviv/Jaffa area. They find the suspect in an apartment housing Palestinian workers who live in Israel legally. The suspected suicide bomber tells the police that he panicked and left the bomb near the city of Rishon Letzion in a trashcan. The bomb is located and detonated, the frightened suicide bomber is arrested and life goes on.

* * *

Bountiful white birds glide across the water in a perfect line formation hovering close to the sparkling water. People sit at the beach cafés, small children run and play, couples walk arm in arm along the sand and a flock of black birds busily eats from a pile of trash left on the sand. Everyone relishes the beauty of this day as the winter hibernation comes to an end.

Kobe is invited to the fifth birthday of his friend who lives in Harsuf, a secluded neighborhood next to the kibbutz full of large beautiful villas set behind a guard gate on the cliffs of the Mediterranean Sea. An obnoxious clown performs in Hebrew to the delight of the children and many of the parents. Eden and I slip out leaving Kobe with his buddies and walk to visit our friends Killy and Gary who live down the road in a large old house with stunning sea views. Killy is the artist whose exhibit we visited a few weeks ago and her husband Gary develops computerized airport security systems. Killy and Gary are happy to see us, uninvited and unexpected guests. I love that in Israel, you do not need a formal invitation to stop in and visit friends on Shabbat. Within minutes, we are offered drinks and snacks; Eden plays with their dogs; and their two beautiful teenage daughters, Roni and Katya come in to say "Shalom". We passionately debate the current state of politics with candor and humor. While we spend Shabbat in this Jewish oasis over looking the sparkling blue Mediterranean, Qassam Rockets rain down on the city of Sderot and sirens warn small children, teens, mothers, fathers and the elderly to get off the streets, run for cover and find refuge in bomb shelters; indeed it is hard to personally relate to these people's suffering.

* * *

A large green tractor driven by a Thai worker moves over the vast green fields of the kibbutz shooting off water and fertilizer. A few weeks back, these fields were brown dirt, another sign that time is swiftly moving forward. Today for the first time, the black and white egrets share the natural rain-filled grassy swamp by the kibbutz entrance. I am thrilled that they do indeed co-exist.

The smell of baking bread with olive oil and zatar welcomes us as we enter the gan's yard. Kobe runs inside and proudly displays Torchik, his small bright orange Pokémon stuffed toy. Gordon in his rich Australian accent says, "Boker tov Kobe" as he sits by the front door and cuts out paper figures for an art project. Nili also calls out, "Boker tov Kobe" while she plays the memory game with some children at a table. Kobe disappears with Eli and I yell "Bye" as I help myself to a piece of toast with olive oil and zatar. Before I walk out, Kobe runs back and says as he hugs me, "You can't leave without a hug."

A few hours later I am back at Ichilov Hospital visiting my friend Joanna who had her baby in the middle of the night. This morning the bright hospital lobby is full of people and upstairs the maternity ward looks like a coffee shop full of newborn babies lying in plastic mini cribs with their mothers and families sitting around the tables. I expect to find a calm and nurturing maternity ward, instead it is loud and chaotic. We sit in the hallway where Johanna nurses her baby; the woman she shares her room with is religious and her whole family visits preventing Johanna from exposing her breast and nursing in her own room.

After the visit, Eden and I drive to South Tel Aviv to meet Yehuda at the attorney's office to sign documents for the purchase of our new overpriced apartment. While we wait, I stare out the window and notice an old and dilapidated building across the street that I am sure will soon obtain a facelift, as the trend these days is to buy, remodel and lease old buildings in Tel Aviv for exorbitant prices. While politics are a mess and corruption is rampant, the Israeli economy is strong and real estate prices are high which is proof that this country is driven by something unconventional and much more powerful.

"Mazel tov, mazel tov," we share hugs and kisses with each other and the attorney. This moment is remarkable as it marks the first time that

Yehuda owns a residence in the country where he grew up, fought in wars for independence and built shopping centers. We are no longer a Bedouin family who move from place to place; we are settled inhabitants of Israel where borders are scary and according to many the future is unstable. On this day as we establish our own personal roots, our family makes the proud statement; "Ha Ar-etz will never be taken away from us."

The day continues on a high as Aaron plays the basketball game of his life. He goes up against a boy six foot three inches and prevents him from making slam dunks, he drives the ball down the floor, sets up the plays, he even takes a few clean shots. After the game, he hurries home and runs to a new friend's Bar Mitzvah celebration at a nearby club. The words of the school counselor that "Aaron does not seem happy," still ring in my ears; quite incongruent with the active and social Aaron I am now observing outside of school.

* * *

It is dark outside when Eden and I leave with Doron at 5:30am for a day of skiing on Mt. Hermon in the Golan Heights. Eden knows we have a long drive this morning and has brought along the DVD from the TV show Friends. We drive north on Highway 6 next to the Green Line between Israel and the Palestinian Territories as the cast of Friends prepares for Rachel Green's move to Paris and buckets of water flood down on the car as though we drive through the rinse zone of a car wash.

Densely populated Arab towns fill the rolling countryside. The houses are white and large, usually three to five floors high each topped with a black water heater on the rooftop. Arab families traditionally build a new floor on their houses for each of their son's families to occupy hence the multiple storeys. Scattered through the Arab villages are mosques with their domes and tall minaret towers rounded at the top. Palm trees stand out as the primary and only substantial form of vegetation. Large fields filled with bright green crops separate the Israeli Arab towns from the Israeli Jewish cities while cement walls segregate the West Bank Palestinian towns. Driving north, the sprawling green farms turn into row after row of endless large white-tented greenhouses full of secret agricultural products. We wind through the mountains where Arab towns populate both sides of the narrow highway. A road sign directs traffic west to the Israeli port city of Haifa and east to Jenin, a hot bed of terrorist activity in West Bank Palestinian territory—an erroneous turn and one could definitely find oneself in the wrong neighborhood, yet another clear reminder that we are all so close in this region. A few days ago, Israeli soldiers stormed into the West Bank town of Nablus near Jenin searching for terrorists and explosive laboratories. Nablus and Jenin are two cities known for militant activity and stockpiles of weapons and bombs—many of the belts worn by suicide bombers are manufactured in Nablus.

Dark and ominous clouds fill the sky and touch the horizon but the rain stops falling. A slice of sun darts through happily landing on the rolling hills creating a lovely pastoral scene as we drive towards Nazareth. We crawl for a stretch stuck behind a tractor on the narrow highway where Arab vendors line up in small kiosks with green plastic roofs selling fruit and bread—all the signs are in Arabic and Hebrew. Skinny cows graze along the roadside and the sun continues to make great efforts to break through the thick gray clouds. The scenery becomes more idyllic with the biblical green rolling hills dense with rocks and boulders. At one intersection we pass, two more cows and three soldiers in khakis with their Uzis are waiting for a ride. We pass Kiryat Shmona, the city deluged by Hezbollah missiles last summer where the residents were forced to stay in bomb shelters. We watch Friends on the video monitor; the character Rachel says goodbye to all of her friends, which sparks tears to fill my eyes realizing how much I miss my friends in L.A.

At Mt. Hermon, we drive through two checkpoints with armed guards before we enter the ski mountain's parking lot. The first encounter at the base of the mountain is quite a surrealistic scene; an army commander barks orders at a group of twenty-five young soldiers in uniform covered with thin white plastic jump suits carrying both skis and Uzis. I have brought my daughter to ski on Mt. Hermon guarded by Uzi-carrying soldiers. Inside we rent boots and skis from Aymen, a young Druze worker who is curious about where we come from and why we ski in Israel. In a few short minutes, he shares his dream to come to America and work at a ski resort.

The lifts are old and slow two person chairs. After Eden and I ski a few simple runs with sticky white snow, Doron joins us with his snowboard. It is not a large resort, but what it lacks in size it makes up in the unique experience of skiing in the Holy Land. Eden takes a hamburger break with Doron and I head up to the harder Zion run on the side of the mountain, Mt. Hermon's longest run. I ski around a narrow cat track and stop to enjoy the incredibly beautiful white panorama when a young army officer, one I had seen earlier taking orders from his commander, stops next to me. I ask him if this is Zion. "Ken" (Yes) he answers pointing with his pole to the steep mountain in front of me and telling me that this is the Syrian border. It is a rugged snow-covered mountain and somewhere in the midst is the border between these two brooding nations. As I look at the beautiful terrain of Syria, it is hard to believe that on this same land Iran funds the development of 'surface to surface missiles' intended to destroy Israel. Also not far away in Damascus, Syria, Khaled Mashal, the number one man in Hamas leadership directs Prime Minister Haniyeh and Hamas in their war against Israel. At the bottom of the Zion run, two lift operators play cards inside the small hut and just below the lift an army jeep is parked on the narrow road and three soldiers dressed in green khakis with Uzis over their shoulders stand around in the cool air chatting.

After a few more runs on the mountain full of skiers with slushy snow, we call it a day. I say goodbye to Aymen and wish him mazal (luck). Before we leave the mountain though, we have to try Coaster bob. Eden and I sit on a plastic red sled, my arms wrapped around her little body as the conveyor belt pulls the sled up to the top of the hill and then we are released and careen down the winding track fast around the corners with fresh wind in our face back to the bottom. We do it again and let the Coaster bob run much faster and I hold on to Eden much tighter this time.

We drive down the mountain in Doron's cozy taxi and pass many kiosks lining the road where Druze women prepare and serve flat bread that they cook over a rounded hot table and fill with olive oil, lebane and zatar like what the Arab ladies in the malls of Herzelia sell during the holidays. We drive through Majdal Shams (the Tower of the Sun), the largest and central Druze city in the Golan Heights. Like other Druze villages in the Golan, their main business is agriculture; apples and cherries. Before the 6-Day War in 1967, the Golan Druze population resided in Syria and many still have family on the Syrian side of the border. There is a mountaintop nearby called the 'Shouting Hill' where families from both countries go to shout messages to each other from either side of the border. The Druze living in the Galilee are Israeli citizens, but the Druze of Majdal Shams declined Israeli citizenship convinced that one day that they will return to live under Syrian leadership where Israeli citizenship would be a disadvantage. Many talk in public about their Syrian loyalty and their desire to return to Syrian rule while they confess in private to the fact that they enjoy living free in democratic Israel. They recognize the qualities and opportunities that their lives have while their brethren in Syria do not. Their crops currently produce two tons of apples, and with help and financial support from Israel's Agricultural Ministry this fruit is exported to Syria and other Arab nations via the Quneitra Border Station.

Eden and I share a day together without her siblings, which for the kid in the middle is special and hard to come by. She is in heaven as she has her mom all to herself and I love the opportunity to spend the day with my eight-year old daughter skiing and careening around the Coaster bob tracks with my arms tightly wrapped around her small warm body. We talk and enjoy each other's company for three hours in each direction and the long ride does not bother either of us because we are together.

While Eden and I were blissfully gliding down the mountain, my gibor-ah was hit with more political tremors. The new Chief of Staff, Gabi Ashkenazi and Israeli Defense Minister Peretz were photographed reviewing troops on a visit to the Golan Heights, but there was one hiccup, Peretz's binoculars lenses were covered and made viewing impossible yet he acted as though he actual saw the military activity in the distance. How fitting for Israel's Defense Minister, who eight months after the failed Second Lebanon War, is still blind to his lack of leadership.

* * *

I sit in the kitchen reading the newspaper with a bowl of fresh juicy pomela wedges peeled by Safta, my houseguest for the week. I have learned that my mother-in-law is not happy unless she is taking care of others, cooking for her grandchildren, buying Kobe chocolate eggs, slipping extra cash to Noa and Aaron and advising me on what I am doing wrong in between indulging me with family stories and gossip. This morning before a day of cooking, Marcelle joins me with her cup of tea and enthusiastically shares all the details of her grandson Ilad's wedding, an elaborate one thousand-guest celebration my sister-in law Ora is planning for July. The number of invited guests does not shock me, because weddings in Israel are usually sizeable celebrations. Marcelle is having a dress made for the occasion which is perfect, as she is not only too large for a store bought dress, but she can chose her own fabric and dictate to the dressmaker her design preferences. The wedding Ora is planning also rejoices the conclusion of ten years of being the mother of three soldiers as her youngest son is about to end his mandatory army term this spring.

Once Marcelle finishes her tea, she returns to her position in the kitchen to start cutting and cooking for the feast she will serve this evening. I go back to reading the newspaper. The news today describes a large fairy tale wedding that took place in Jerusalem with ten thousand attendees. A nineteen-year old boy, the grandson of an ultra orthodox Gerrer Hasidim Rabbi, the largest Hasidic dynasty in the land marries a young nineteen-years old girl practically my daughter's age on a closed off street in Jerusalem high atop a building so that the masses gathered below can view the ceremony. All the men wear black suits and black hats and the women—well there are no photos of them in the designated women's section. We are not even treated to a photo of the beautiful young bride. The Ger sect has also imposed a new rule limiting weddings to four hundred guests to cut costs, but an exception is made for the rabbi's grandson with 10,000 invited to witness the ceremony, but only four hundred are invited to eat a real meal; the other nine thousand six hundred are served light refreshments.

* * *

Large waves, remnants of yesterday's storm, crash this morning under pale blue skies and the cool air blows on my face to wake me up as I amble down the beach. A group of kayak surfers paddle their special kayaks furiously; I admire these crazy people strapped into small colorful plastic vessels being hit by the spraying water and exerting great physical energy against the force of the water all for the brief moment when they ride the perfect wave into the shore.

After a meeting in Tel Aviv for the charity event Noa and I are planning for Friendship's Way, Doron drives me further south by the huge Dizengoff Mall surrounded by street vendors, pedestrians and street performers. We pass the trendy American Apparel store and on the other side of the street, a knife store advertising butcher knives for kosher slaughtering, knives for performing circumcisions, knives for hunting, knives for restaurants and knives for private use. The juxtaposition of these two vendors on the busy city street is the perfect analogy for existence here as modern and ancient and superficial and practical coexist in the frenetic pace of Israeli city life.

We drive a short distance to the Shook Ha Caramel (The Caramel Outdoor Market) and I jump out of the cab. In front there is a table surrounded by bars displaying black batman t-shirts, batman capes and batman eye masks. A few days ago, Noa sent me an SMS describing the batman costume she wanted to wear for Purim. Comfortably I can buy her the costume without having to enter the shook itself. As tantalizing as the shook is, I am ridiculously anxious about potential suicide bombers who lurk in these popular outdoor shopping zones and wait to blow themselves up in large crowds to kill and destroy with the promise of martyrdom. I purchase the shirt and batman eye cover, but the vendor does not have capes and refuses to sell me the one from his display. "Ta-voy ma-har," (Come tomorrow) he tells me. I take a deep breath and enter the shook to look for the cape while convincing myself that it is early and still quite empty—definitely not a good time for a pi-gu-a. Quickly the fear subsides and the excitement and pleasure win out. The shook is a feast of shopping pleasures; I quickly recall how I love the shook's narrow passageways with booths on either side filled to the brim with delectable items. I purchase a bunch of bananas and some cookies to hold me over until lunch. I buy Eden a bright yellow and blue clown costume and rainbow wig for the Purim Carnival at school, but I do not find a black cape. I walk along Nahalat Benyamin, a pedestrian street next to the shook where the many fabric stores are full of adult costume shoppers. I stop in one store and in a basket piled with fabric I find a black cape for thirty shekels—I am victorious.

* * *

Bright magenta wild flowers grow along the side of the road around the entrance to the kibbutz and inside on the large green lawn, I am surprised to encounter the black and white egrets once again separated by color as they engage in their culinary dance. I have a day full of teacher's meetings at AIS, but first Yehuda and I attend Kobe's Purim show.

Kobe's Israeli theatrical career continues as he portrays a court messenger in a gold and black costume with a thin black mustache and a thick black beard drawn on to his face. He sits on a small chair in the circle with the other actors until it is his turn to sing and dance and perform the messenger's duties in the Purim story of Queen Esther, Wise Mordechai and the evil Haman, who wants to exterminate all the Jews. The theme of this story dating back to the period between the destruction of the First Temple and the construction of the Second Temple is eerie in its resemblance to the current political theme of hate for the Jews. I know it is pushing it but even the names Haman and Hamas sound similar. After Kobe's performance, we eat a small sugar feast of candies and oz-ney o-man (triangle dough filled with either poppy seeds, fruit or chocolate), the traditional Purim treat found all over Israel. The gan has prepared mi-shlo-akh ma-note (wrapped gifts) with oz-ney o-man and other holiday sweets for each child to take home, as it is customary to give mi-shlo-akh ma-note to friends and family for Purim. Kobe proudly takes home his rash rash (noise-maker), a small plastic container he painted, decorated and filled with beans to make noise when shaken, especially when the name Haman is uttered.

After Kobe's show, Yehuda and I stand in lines in the American School gym, waiting our turn for meetings with each of the kids' teachers. I am happy that Yehuda is with me this time to hear directly from the teachers about our very diverse children. Most of the scripts are still the same; Eden and Noa are thriving and Aaron is not participating or doing his work, yet he shows up at school each day and attends classes. We break at one point for homemade soup and cooked salmon from the school's kiosk where Allen, the South African purveyor, serves us as if we dine at a fine restaurant and not at his simple food kiosk. We sit at a picnic table in the cool outdoors under the warm sun and eat alone like we were on a date in the schoolyard.

We have Friday night family dinner at Yakimono Restaurant on Rothschild, a beautiful old street in Tel Aviv lined with restaurants; down the middle of the road there is a charming passage landscaped with large old trees, park benches and kiosks selling fruit, coffee and falafels. We eat plates of raw fish and all agree that the food is delicious. This is good as I am finding it harder and also more important to discover things we all agree on. Kobe exhausted from his earlier performance, falls asleep. Noa and Aaron divulge their plans to visit Amir, 'nargila boy', who was injured at the last basketball game and is now in a full leg cast. Then they will go and 'hang out' at kikar Sharon with their friends. I hope that Aaron's decision to start a social life albeit this late in the school year will continue to make him happier.

All of these celebrations for my family are overshadowed by the awareness that an hour away in southern Israel, mothers and families in Sderot and surrounding kibbutz-eem and mo-sha-veem spend a good deal of time running to shelters with each warning that the Islamic Jihad or Hamas militia has sent more rockets from Gaza. It is a game of roulette; the terrorists do not have control of the rockets' destination, their simple goal is to send as many rockets as possible, hoping that some will kill and cause great damage and that all will wreak havoc on the psyche of the masses. While the Israelis have little success detouring these efforts, the world turns a blind eye to this aggression that results in whole flocks of Israeli children who are being raised frightened and hardened with hate and distrust as their homes are constantly under siege. Unfortunately, the simple rash rash is not sufficient to shake when Hamas carries out these bombings.

* * *

My khaver has many visitors on this festive Purim weekend. Yehuda and I walk south toward the Marina and look up at our new apartment in the Oceanus building to see the green windows and their design—some are flat and others concave. We study the building's layout to discover the possibilities of changing our windows from concave to flat. I am still amazed that in this crazy climate, we bought a domicile as if it were a safe country and secure investment. Holiday apartments in this area are hard to come by—a testament to the fact that Jews from all over the world believe in this country. We have some control over the windows and very little control over the animosity and physical advances of groups and governments that surround our nation and call for our destruction.

Back at the creamy white castle, Eden sits on the kitchen counter with her finger in the fish bowl. When I ask her what she is doing, she tells me that she is playing with her fish Mimi. I refrain from explaining that goldfish are not meant for physical play. Instead I prepare myself a cappuccino. A few minutes later, I look at the fish bowl above the sink and see Mimi floating on her side at the bowl's edge. There is still some movement in her tiny fish body but I know her minutes are limited. I am concerned how Eden will take the news. Perhaps I will flush little Mimi to goldfish heaven and maybe Eden will not notice? But Eden walks into the kitchen and sees Mimi on her side. She screams, "Not another dead one!" I cannot tell her at this time that her physical play with Mimi may have brought about her timely death, but instead suggest that Mimi had a good long goldfish life. Eden quickly asks, "Can we get a dog when we move back to L.A?" The kid has wonderful technique for an eight-year old.

At Kobe's kibbutz Purim party the first thing I notice is that the egrets' lawn has been taken over by enormous air filled sliding and climbing rides, a raging bull ride, a train and hundreds of happy people. The passion in which Israelis celebrate a holiday is inspirational and a main ingredient that fuels their existence. Kobe dressed as the Pokémon Treeko runs free with all the other kids. At one point I lose my five-year old Treeko, but I do not panic, as it is the kibbutz. He returns a short while later from a train ride with his buddy Eli who is dressed as Pikachu, another Pokémon character. I sit on the lawn with other parents and watch the array of rejoicing children in costumes and bright colored Crocs running around free, a picture I sketch in my mind and wish to hold onto tightly.

* * *

The drive to school each morning has become repetitious; Noa is angry that we wait for Aaron who arrives late to the car, still half asleep and Eden and Kobe are congenial and talkative. I try to focus on the little ones' happy energy and do not get too distracted by the teenagers' negativity. At school, Aaron gets out of the car without a word, Noa says "goodbye" and Eden tells me she loves me. Then Kobe and I drive merrily along the road through the mo-shav under the freeway and to the kibbutz. This morning, plentiful yellow and purple wild flowers line the road. The posters of a black hat rabbi with a thick gray beard who stares at me and informs me in Hebrew that the "Messiah is coming" have returned. Kobe sits in the back seat of the car eating string cheese, a new product in Israel as we listen to his favorite band, the Beatles and we sing 'Let it Be'.

Yehuda and I drive to meet Alex, the designer for our apartment at his studio in the old Florentine District in South Tel Aviv. We walk through the parking lot to the rear of the building to a metal freight elevator with heavy steel doors. Inside the dark and crude steel box we move slowly to the top floor and arrive with a good shake as it levels off. We push the heavy metal doors open and arrive on a bright landing where Alex greets us in jeans and an Abercrombie t-shirt. His studio is a white paradise with the only accents of color coming from his collection of small golden Buddha figurines, large dramatic canvasses, and a beautiful collection of old blue and white Turkish ceramic dishes. We review the designs for the apartment room by room confirming measurements. Yehuda makes changes and I mostly agree while I stare out of the tremendous floor-to-ceiling window at the vast Tel Aviv skyline against the light blue sky scattered with cotton clouds. I think physically building a home for my family is so much easier than all the non-tangible parts of this year's move like the challenges to my children's well being and trying to make the right decisions for them. Decisions I cannot pay someone to make for me. The words to the song 'Let it Be' run through my head and at the same time I realize that I also need to 'Let It Be' and things will work themselves out.

* * *

The white moon still gallant after a long night's watch hovers close to the horizon gently kissing the steel gray water. At the southern end of the beach, the sun's rays arrive from the east brightly reflecting on the green glass windows and balconies of the tall apartment buildings over the Arena Mall, but the rest of the sky and the water are not sun-filled yet. As I return along the beach, sunlight appears over the cliffs and highlights the long lines of foam the waves create along the shore. Even with the arrival of the sun, the moon remains perched in the sky, sharing the glorious morning.

All of my children assert their individual personalities in their choices of costumes for this Purim holiday. Eden refuses to wear the clown costume or the wig I bought her for the school's Purim party; she dresses more subtly, as a circus acrobat in hopes that the nine-year old boys in her class will not tease her. Noa on the other hand, is happy with male attention and wears the black Batman shirt, cape and mask. Aaron does not take any interest in this holiday and goes to school as a grumpy teenager with his customary pants hanging very low in the rear and exposing his boxer shorts. And with Kobe I definitely get my money's worth; he wears his Pokémon Treeko costume for the fifth day in a row.

I enter the Orange cellular phone store at the Cinema City Mall the minute it opens as my life support system is in serious jeopardy. My cell phone is broken and I am feeling deep pangs of anxiety. I am not proud of my behavior, but I have been in Israel long enough to know that I need oxygen to breath and a working cell phone for a life pulse. All the employees are in Purim costumes and the young cowgirl decked out with a hat and holster listens as I explain the problem in English. Before she can service the phone, she connects it to a machine that produces a short list of my saved phone numbers and once again I panic discovering that the extensive list of telephone numbers I have collected over eight months to all my Israel contacts disappears in an instant. The cowgirl explains very matter of fact, well she actually lecturers me that I did not save the numbers properly on the SIM card. I am both a victim of the rapidly advancing cell phone world and an addict who cannot live without her connectivity, which basically is a sign that I have become a good Israeli. Israel is a nation where small children have cell phones; teens text more than they speak to one another face to face; businessmen walk around with two and three holsters filled with different cell phones; and groups sit together at a restaurant speaking on their cell phones instead of to each other—there are more cell phones in Israel than there are Israelis.

* * *

The search is on for an Israeli national bird and the bul-bul (a songbird) with a radiant yellow tail, a white breast and black head and wings is in the lead. Ironically, a bul-bul is also the slang word little boys use for a penis in this country.

Aaron leaves to the basketball tournament at The Hague from the kikar very early in the morning at the exact same spot where I dropped Noa off half a year earlier for her trip to Poland. In the dark, next to the other players, Aaron seemed so small and young. He dreamed of joining the traveling team for the tournament and after injury and great discourse he accomplished this goal. Now I only hope he will have fun. I lay in bed a few hours later assuming his flight has taken off. I close my eyes and I swear I hear the pleasant rustling sound of Aaron's diapers when he was two-years old as he ran down the hallway in the middle of the night after a bad dream to climb in bed with me for comfort—the sound is so familiar and I am peaceful. While he is away, I call Aaron on his cell phone to check in, but he does not answer and he does not call us either. I send him text messages that also go unanswered. Finally, I give up trying and remind myself that I must exercise patience and understanding, but even in this enlightened stage it feels bad.

* * *

I run to the quaint flower shop I pass each morning in Moshav Rishpon to buy flowers for Noa's sweet sixteen luncheon. The air-conditioned glass house smells heavenly, full of beautiful cut flowers neatly filling large plastic buckets. I am tempted to buy many enticing flowers, but keep reminding myself that I am here for pink roses, my eldest daughter's favorite flowers.

I return home to find Noa on what is supposed to be the happiest day of her year, her sixteenth birthday throwing up. Her bathroom is a war zone, which I proceed to clean up. She is determined to be at her birthday party and goes upstairs to shower in my bathroom before fifteen girls arrive in pretty dresses and high-heeled shoes for lunch. Noa miraculously puts herself together and looks beautiful for the festivities wearing a new dress bought at the mall last week for this special occasion. I look closely at my beautiful sixteen-year old daughter and am a bit freaked as two images keep clashing in my mind; I remember being 'sweet 16', and while it does not seem like so long ago I am keenly aware that it was much more than a lifetime ago and I also clearly recall the moment in the delivery room when I first held my newborn daughter and kissed her soft forehead. It is hard to believe that time has passed so quickly. The girls sit at the large wood tables in our fancy dining room gossiping, giggling and enjoying their salads and lasagna. Dessert is served in large glass goblets—one filled with layers of chocolate mousses and brownies and the other with layers of cream and fresh berries—all displayed brilliantly through the glass cylinders. After lunch, the girls sit out on the Astroturf and enjoy the warm sunny day.

All weekend Noa celebrated her sixteen years; Friday a party at a club until three in the morning, Shabbat at the beach and a birthday dinner cooked by Safta followed by 'hanging out' at the kikar to celebrate the actual midnight hour of turning a new age. Finally at one in the morning, I got mad at her for staying out so late two nights in a row. "It's my birthday!" Noa answered as if turning sixteen was automatic adulthood. My response to my silly little girl was, "I know, but you are going to get sick and I am not going to be very nice about it."

"Mommmm."

I replay this conversation in my head as Noa sleeps on the couch in the bomb shelter a few hours after the luncheon and I clean her latest round of throw up featuring her lunch all over the bathroom. Israel for teenagers is truly Candy Land where there are no controls, no boundaries and plenty of unearned freedom. Slowly I have slipped into allowing this to be the norm for my children, I regret it and am desperately trying to regain some control and order.

The Israelis await the findings of The Winograd Report to get a handle on all that went wrong during The Second Lebanon War; this report will discuss Israel's pullout from Lebanon in 2000 up to the first five days of the Second Lebanon War in July 2006 when the Israeli leadership decided to initiate a large-scale invasion. Even without the report in hand, every journalist and every Israeli seems to have an opinion on the subject. Many say this will be the end of PM Ehud Olmert, whose poll ratings are abysmal. In his presumed absence, there is great debate as the whether Foreign Minister Tzipi Livni or Vice Premier Shimon Peres can hold their Kadima Party together or if Former PM Bibi Netanyahu, who leads the Likud Party, will make a grab for power. Even under this scrutiny, PM Olmert meets with PA Chairman Abbas and American officials to discuss the Saudi King's Initiative devised a few years back to establish a Palestinian state with East Jerusalem as its capital and the return of Palestinian refugees in exchange for full normalization between Israel and Arab states. The big problem and great obstacle to this Saudi Initiative is the inclusion of the UN General Assembly Resolution 194 that calls for the resettlement of the Palestinian refugees and their descendents in Israeli territory, which would be the beginning of the end of the Jewish majority in the Jewish state. At this point the Saudis and other moderate Arab nations are desperate to disable Iranian Shiite fanatics from exerting more power in the region and the Saudi Initiative is a tremendous unifying force.

* * *

Powerful wind and heavy rains prevent me visiting my khaver this morning. The front gate is broken again. The screen panel that controls all the lights in the master bedroom are broken and the shutters behind the bed are immobile. The chilly air reminds me that Eden's heating unit was never fixed. I take problems more in stride these days, they do not scream out to me from the top of my To Do List as they once did. I secretly have adopted the phrases, "Al-ti-da-gee" and "Ha kol yi-he-yay be-seder" that somehow ease the burden of what I have little control over. I appreciate the peacefulness in the castle; there is no construction noise from next door this morning.

We have begun demolition on our apartment and I visit daily to see the progress. Today from our fifteenth floor balcony, Eden and I look down and see a group of wind surfers enjoying the fantastic gusts of wind not bothered by the scattered raindrops that continue to fall late in the afternoon. One wind surfer and his arched sail sweep along the wild water rapidly and then he takes off from a giant wave and flies through the air for what seems like a whole minute. Eden is thrilled by the show. I am literally blown away by the natural passion and energy of the sea and the surfers.

Aaron returns from The Hague, but tells us very little about the tournament, the sites or any activities he participated in, but he easily complains that he did not get a good house to stay in. Aaron's terrible mood is matched by a photo in the newspaper of the dejected Prime Minister sitting in the middle of a group of fresh and happy young officers who fought in The Second Lebanon War—he looks almost as if he were photo shopped in to the pleasant picture. I actually think sometimes Aaron's negative persona is photo shopped into our family—it is an unnatural picture for so many reasons.

While my son and the Prime Minister may be at a low place, very exciting news fills the airwaves, the papers and the streets. Movie star Leonardo Di Caprio and his Israeli supermodel girlfriend Bar Rafaeli arrive in Israel for a visit. Surrounded by bodyguards, these two gorgeous celebrities tour the Western Wall Tunnels and other historic spots with the constant companionship of the Israeli paparazzi. The Israeli news lays siege on the Rafaeli home in Hod Hasharon, not far from where we live and the people on the streets enjoy living through this glamorous couple, a welcome rest from serious news.

* * *

Thick gray clouds haunt the shoreline preparing for a downpour. A large white fish has washed ashore, his bones poking out through his skin after being tumbled and thrown around by the rough waves. Two young men with large backpacks walk along the sand in Teva sandals, shorts and long sleeve t-shirts in training for their tea-yool (trip abroad). It is quite common after the mandatory army service and before commencing university studies that many young Israelis visit far off places like India, Asia and South America, where they can simply get away from Israel and its constant pressures to travel inexpensively for a good part of a year with little rhyme or reason.

This morning the gan smells wonderful; cheese rolls bake in the oven and eggs cook on the skillet. "Boker tov" Alona says congenially with a smile as she looks up from cooking. Gordon like a giant teddy bear sits at a small table cutting out paper figures for an art project; he has a gentle smile, a balding head, one earring and a quick tangy sense of humor. He arrived at the kibbutz many years earlier from Melbourne and has firmly kept his own customs living on the kibbutz with his Israeli wife and two young daughters; he speaks Hebrew with a thick Aussie accent, he is not Jewish and celebrates Christmas with a decorated tree in his house. A few weeks back, Kobe and I went to visit the bunny coop Gordon built for his daughter to house an abundance of white and black bunnies. Over the year, Kobe and Gordon have developed a very special relationship; Kobe delights in this rapport and I relish the fact that my young son has a wonderful role model in a fine male teacher.

* * *

The rain showers return so I spend the day inside eating a loaf of tasty khallah and answering e-mails. At one point I open an e-mail invitation from a friend in L.A. and instantly realize that it is a virus that within seconds spreads to all of the addresses on my computer. I have not been invited to many parties this year and the one invite I do receive is a virus—part of the irony of life in the Holy Land.

"Can we go to Egypt for Pesach?" Kobe asks me while I prepare dinner. In gan he learns the stories of the Jews in Egypt, this seems like a smart place to celebrate the Passover Holiday. He knows that Pharoah is dead, but he would like to see where he ruled the people and enslaved the Jews. It is a typical afternoon in our house; Eden is in the family room choreographing a dance; Aaron is hidden in the Trump quarters playing on line poker; and Noa sits with her friends in the bomb shelter and smokes from the nargila, which is very Israeli, but not what I want for my child. I give myself a private pep talk—'These teens are here in my house and not somewhere getting into trouble.' Their screams and laughter drift to the kitchen while outside it is pouring rain and freezing—I have grown tired of the abysmal weather and the teenagers who are running my life.

Ben and Dan, two old buddies of Yehuda's are over for dinner. Ben and Yehuda grew up on the kibbutz and then met Dan while they all fought together in the 6-Day War. Dan is a beekeeper in Israel, Ben has a television equipment business in L.A. and Yehuda builds shopping centers. Three very different men all strongly connected by their intense history together. After dinner I slip away leaving them together to share and remember.

In bed I read about a beautiful bride in a white wedding dress who passes through the Quneitra Crossing at the border with Syria near where Eden and I recently skied. This young woman is a Druze bride on her way to marry her Druze husband who lives in a village on the Syrian side of the Golan Heights. This border opens once a year, families are re-united and brides cross over to marry their grooms.

Israel continues to be attacked by missiles from Gaza.

* * *

Two young religious men wearing white prayer shawls with large dirty white knit yarmulkes on top of their heads and long pay-es on either side of their face solicit the passengers in waiting cars at the long Rabin Intersection traffic signal. They propagate 'their form of Judaism' selling religious books and giving away musical cds, bookmarks and bumper stickers all with a religious message. Once they hand the item to the customer, they quickly ask for some financial stipend to support 'their form of Judaism'. Today the short redhead tries to push a religious story cd to me through the closed window. I am bored and the traffic light is unhurried. I welcome the entertainment and open the window halfway allowing him to start his sales pitch. The light changes to green. He quickly asks for a donation and I pass him back his cd and say, "Lo, Todah" (no thank you) and carry on my way.

Kobe comes home with lice and instantly I start to incessantly itch my own clean hair. I panic at the thought of lice spreading though my house. I run to Oren at the pharmacy and buy the most recommended hair treatment program he sells and the finest comb he has in stock. Oren advises me on how to apply the shampoo and comb through his hair, pointing out that the quickest way to get rid of the lice is to shave his head. After an extensive shampooing and de-licing ceremony, I strip all the sheets to wash, place his stuffed animals in plastic bags for a two week quarantine and pray that he will be an isolated case within the creamy white castle.

* * *

After a meeting in South Tel Aviv, Doron invites me to join him for lunch at Ali Carivan Abu Hasan; a very simple restaurant he claims serves the best humus in Israel. The restaurant run for many years by an Arab family is in a poor residential area of Jaffa where laundry hangs along the building facades. It is quite cold and crisp outside, but warm and toasty inside the restaurant and in typical Israeli style very loud and energetic. The food choices are simple. They only serve thick and tasty humus with olive oil and te-hina, masa-ba-kha (spicy and chunky humus) and fool (a special bean dish). I order the humus and Doron the masa-ba-kha each doused in olive oil and served with quartered fresh onions and soft and doughy pita. We join two strangers at a small table, as there are no private tables and no empty seats, and mostly talk about our children's youthful escapades. Today the patrons at this Israeli Palestinian eating establishment are young Jewish businessmen, high-tech yuppies and a large colorful group of hippy kids with dreadlocks and many body piercings wrapped in alpaca blankets and shawls. I take humus, masa-ba-cha and fresh pita home to share this experience with my children replacing the typical store bought humus we enjoy at the house daily.

Aaron is invited by two classmates to a party at a nightclub in Herzelia that begins at 11pm and ends at 3am. I am happy that he is developing a social life, but I am not thrilled with the prospect of my fourteen-year old running around at these hours even if they are normal for kids by local standards. It is a recipe for trouble as I subscribe to the notion that nothing good happens to teens after midnight. I try to establish some ground rules before he goes out. I have to be precise as most of what I say these days is conveniently misinterpreted and I am generally told 'You never told me.' Instead of sharing his plans, he storms off mad. At midnight he is not home. I briefly attack myself for not locking him in and standing guard at his door even though I know this is unrealistic. I call him and as usual he does not answer the cell phone. I text him and fifteen minutes later he texts me back that 'He thought he had told me'. This is his teenage communication pattern, which I no longer fall for as I pay meticulous attention to my words. Either way, I fail terribly and fall asleep unsettled by this divisive behavior gnawing away at me.

The Palestinians have momentarily created a false relationship as Fatah and Hamas take a break in the fighting in Gaza and form a unity government. Nevertheless, Prime Minister Haniyeh and the Hamas Party still do not recognize Israel or support any of the demands that have been made on the Palestinians in order to drop the international boycott against the Palestinian people. Palestinian lawmakers who are not in Israeli jails (46 Hamas lawmakers are currently in Israeli jails) vote overwhelming for the new government.

Qassams Rockets continue to rain down on Sderot, authorized by Hamas leadership in Gaza.

Aviv (Spring)

Thick white beach sand covers the entire theater stage and under dimmed lighting, men and women in colored bodysuits dance on the stage like fluid rolling over, under and through one another as figurines in a glass shaker where the sand swirls around the water. I watch from the audience in awe of their talent and the beauty of their bodies and their movement. The performance is fantastical and takes me away from the continued frustration I experience with my teenage children's freedom. I am trying to choreograph my own family but I am definitely not graceful. I want us to dance with ease and beauty, flowing like the dancers on the stage, but instead I question if I am steering our family ship well through the rocky passages. There is friction; Noa announces to me that she would like to stay in Israel for the next school year; Aaron avoids me so that we cannot discuss his late night out; Eden reminds me daily that she misses her friends and her school in L.A.; and Kobe loves both homes and still unconditionally loves and respects me. Kobe is proof that I am not the lunatic many thought me to be for having a forth child.

* * *

I stop in at Sabor coffee shop to warm up after my chilly sea walk. I admire the friendly blond owner as she prepares my cappuccino and places a tiny sugar cookie on top of the cover. Even after the endless cappuccinos she makes, she prepares this one with great care and no matter how many I make at home, hers always taste better.

A notice arrives from the school that the Bahai community celebrates Naw-ruz festival, the Bahai New Year and a very holy day that symbolizes the spiritual renewal brought by the teaching of the founder of the Bahai Faith. Noa's friend who is a member of the Bahai community is fasting for nineteen days from sunrise to sundown to celebrate this holiday. Naw Ruz also coincides with the first day of a-viv.

* * *

I go back in time a couple hundred years as we drive through the streets of the Mea Sharim neighborhood in Jerusalem. I feel as if I have landed smack in the middle of the movie Yentle where men and little boys in black suits with black hats and pe-yas fill the narrow old stone streets. They walk very fast with great purpose and many talk on cellular telephones—proof that they know we live in the 21st Century, and the modern world is ticking away outside their shtettle. Groups of little girls with long skirts and braided hair walk along the narrow sidewalks pushing children in strollers. Small stores that look more like caves with dull storefronts line the sidewalk; upstairs the balconies along the dark building façades are packed with hanging laundry. I am bothered that I do not see any women on the streets. I am sure behind the walls I will find women scrubbing, cooking and taking care of the kids. Mea Sharim has the feeling of a ghetto, which is another name for this neighborhood.

At the grand old King David Hotel in Jerusalem, I find myself again in a completely different world from a different era. I feel the immense and intense history of this hotel as I walk through the lobby and read the floor tiles with the names of world leaders, peacemakers, celebrities and deposed leaders who have worked and stayed here over the last eighty years. During the British Mandate one wing of the King David Hotel became the military headquarters of the British; in 1946 the Irgun, an underground resistance group led by Menachem Begin, later the Prime Minster of Israel, bombed the hotel. Tonight, in the spring of 2007, I escape from the creamy white castle and the teenage subjects who live there and find refuge in this enchanting hotel.

Early the next morning, I look out the window and see the beautifully manicured hotel gardens and the wall of the Old City shining in the sun, a live picture of a vibrant historical city full of texture, rhythm and beautiful sounds. The fresh Jerusalem air carries the chime from the bells of the church; the chant of the Jews who pray; and the voice of the muezzin from the mosque as he calls worshippers to prayer. I happily listen as these lovely sounds arrive within a short period of time at the small window in my room. After experiencing the Old City many times over the years, I am still mesmerized by the view and so happy for each brief and energizing experience. We spend the morning with Jewish leaders from the United States and Israel in meetings discussing how Reform Judaism can flourish in Israel alongside the Orthodoxy offering all Jews the freedom to worship, as they believe in the Holy Land.

* * *

I am invited to Aaron's family class at school to participate in a course on communication between teens and parents. Just as the class commences, the warning sirens for bombs blare through the school and through the entire country—an exercise for a nation that is painfully aware that it is not a useless drill but could satisfy great need in the near future. Hundreds of students and adults move through the campus. I follow Aaron's class to the designated bomb shelter that daily serves as the music room for the high school students. Somewhere in the crowds of students are Eden and Noa. All three of my children are in one location where if a bomb were to arrive, I would be powerless, as would the security guards at the front gate. Growing up we in California, we had earthquake drills and upon hearing alarms, we would get under our small wood desks; I am sure my mother felt helpless against the ills of Mother Nature. Once all the 8th grade students are accounted for, we are allowed to return to class with our teens to work on our communication issues— a truly explosive topic.

Aaron sits down next to me nervous and awkward which is a common theme of his teen years. I look around the room at other anxious parents eager for some panacea and realize I am in a gathering of my peers. Aaron and his classmates take turns making a presentation and then we sit face to face and with model situations written on a piece of paper; we talk with the focus to use the "I" statements and not to use the accusatory "you" statements or to attack the other person. Aaron begins by choosing situations that have no familiarity to our lives and I suggest we try one that is more pertinent to us. Slowly we start to listen and talk to each other, my son speaks to me and looks me in the eye and a rush of achievement comes over both of us—I want this class to never end.

This victorious sense of accomplishment is blemished when I return home and discover that my front yard is flooded. The Astroturf is saturated and water runs on to the street, looking as though I am draining my pool. The flood causes the outside lights to short out, which triggers the entire electric breaker to shut off when I turn the lights on in the house. I call Zohar who comes over, shuts off the water and looks for the cause of this flood. A couple of hours later, as I prepare to boil pasta and steam broccoli, I cannot get the stove to light up. Instead, I order an Italian dinner from Joya, which without a doubt is much tastier than the dinner I attempted to make on my own. Amidst the flood, Kobe has his first sleep over in Israel with Ayehli. Even our great flood will not stop two young Pokémon warriors from this great coming of age ceremony.

After I put the kids to bed, I sit on the phone and wait for the Bezek (the Israeli phone company) Internet technician to help me get the Internet working. I speak to three very nice technicians, but they cannot help me as our computers are Macs and not PCs. Bezek appears to be the Mea Sharim of Internet service not dealing with the modern computers just the old ones.

* * *

A lone soldier in khakis with an Uzi on his chest stands looking out to the gray sea in the tan early light. I am not sure if he protects or dreams. After I walk past him, a group of soldiers calls down from the cliffs above where the Sidni Ali Mosque stands. He looks up to them briefly and then his thoughts and his glance return to the sea. When I return down the beach, this group of soldiers stands at the edge of the cliffs talking to an

Arab with a white keffiyeh wrapped over his head and a matching white robe. On the beach a second soldier with a shaven head stands by his comrade clutching the Uzi on his chest. These soldiers look exhausted standing side-by-side peering out to sea. They remind me of the stories that Yehuda has told me many times over the years about exercises he performed as a soldier walking through the desert all night long carrying a heavy backpack with little water and few breaks, the importance of comfortable socks and boots, and the sheer exhaustion of not sleeping for twenty four hours or longer. I cannot relate to any of this.

Rich and robust Pesach gift baskets start to appear in all the markets, shops and coffee houses full of tasty holiday goodies; plain, and chocolate covered matza, Golan Winery Wines, grape juice, chocolates, coconut candies, fresh fruit, dried fruit, honey and nuts. Shortly, all markets will clean the kha-metz (breads, grains and leavened products) off their shelves and many religious Jews will also remove kha-metz from every nook and cranny of their houses.

At eighty-four years, my mother-in-law like a spring chicken starts to plan a family Seder at our creamy white castle, her second home. Marcelle will do most of the cooking and give the rest of us jobs to bring this Seder to fruition. We are faithful followers under her strict and loving stewardship and I am happy to host the dinner as long as my role does not require me to actually cook. Yesterday disgruntled workers throughout the country went on strike for ten hours protesting salaries and conditions; once again this shut down the airport, the trains, the trash collection, the schools, and other public services. University students are still on strike, bringing higher education to a stand still all across Israel. My sisters-in-law and I are all happy (unpaid) workers who fear and respect Marcelle with no chance of going on strike ourselves.

Even the excitement and spirit of the holiday cannot temper political corruption. This week Finance Minister Avraham Hirschson, a good friend and close political ally of PM Ehud Olmert is accused of embezzling tens of thousands of dollars a few years back when he was politically active in the Likud party. He is currently in the Kadima Party and is questioned by the police and as customary, the press intensely dissects the story for the nation to follow.

* * *

Eden, Kobe and I walk unhurriedly along the beach soaking in the cool spring day. After all these months, I am still stunned by the splendor of the bright blue skies and the energy and varying texture of the waves, which today are large and wild. The children are excited to see a young man sail leisurely along the wet sand on a homemade wooden board with a sail atop four large rubber wheels that he maneuvers to catch the wind. As we pass Taboon Restaurant alive with customers, the children convince me to buy them their Shabbat ice cream. Inside Taboon, we open the fully stocked self-serve ice cream freezer, a vital component of any eating establishment along the beach, and after a few minutes of serious deliberation each of the children chooses an ice cream. Before we return to the creamy white castle, we visit the new apartment building; all of the walls are gone and almost the entire floor has been removed—we now own an overpriced large cement box with a lovely view of the sea.

By late afternoon, Yehuda has still not returned from a lunch meeting with business associates from Spain; Noa and Aaron are 'hanging out' with friends; and the little ones and I watch television, cuddling on the couch in the family room. I am reminded how much I love Shabbat as it is a perfect day in the modern crazy world to recover from the old week while recharging for the new week. I enjoy the warmth of my children's bodies so close, but am not focused on the their program; rather it triggers me to think about a new television program that is popular with Palestinian children called Pioneers of Tomorrow featuring a charismatic Muslim Mickey Mouse character named Farfour. The show takes place in a child-friendly pastel romper room where Farfour, the black and white mouse and a pretty little girl dressed in pink with a pink head cover discuss the Israeli occupation of Palestine and encourage the Palestinian children to rise up against the Jews in the name of Allah, to shoot and annihilate the Jews and to conquer Al Aksa and Israel. Palestinian children, the age of Kobe and Eden, call into the show and sing songs about liberating Jerusalem and all of former Palestine with AK47's at the will of Allah. In a congenial manner, Farfour and the little girl impart to the children that throughout history people have lived happily and successfully under Muslim rule and that Muslims are good people. I am incensed that they are using my beloved Mickey Mouse to manipulate young minds and saddened to think about the high degree of hate that these people are teaching little children; it is as natural as the air they breath and imprinted deep in their genes.

* * *

Hardly any other soul is at the beach at 5:30am except for a group of young men in black carrying large white surfboards. The sky is full of clouds with a denim blue background. I pass a large bag of soaking wet white onions that lie unopened appearing to have arrived from the sea earlier with the strong and deep waves. I do not get too close to it—as I am overly sensitive to abandoned items and bombing strategies from the enemy. Fresh in my mind is one morning on the beach when I watched the bomb squad detonate an unidentified bag believed to contain a bomb. Even years later, I simple cannot stop my mind from taking these crazy journeys. Half a mile up the beach I pass another large bag of soaked white onions convinced it is nothing more than wet onions and still hesitant to approach it. I see Popeye running this cool morning in tight black training shorts and a thin white t-shirt; he is built like the cartoon character with round and muscular bowl shaped legs and muscular arms that bulge from his body. Popeye smiles each morning as he passes me on his beach run—all he is missing is the pipe hanging from his grin.

In the afternoon, I proudly pull into my reserved red and white parking spot on the sidewalk in front of the school. In front of me, a petite Asian woman in a powder blue suit busily scrubs dirt from her blue Audi A4 with the white diplomat license plates. She holds her light blue handbag over her left elbow and with a dry tissue in her right hand wipes the rear of her car in perfect round motions. We all suffer from very dirty cars as ham-seen (dry desert winds) have arrived, blowing dirt and sand and this combined with the frequent rain pretty much glues sand and dirt to our vehicles covering them with an orange tint. I watch this woman's dedication knowing it is a pointless effort to clean cars during periods of ham-seen and rain. I resist the temptation to tell this woman that her efforts are futile because I see that she really believes her labor will make a difference even if just briefly and she looks quite content.

We all arrive to this community from such different places; I enjoy the American School as a population rich in cultural and religious diversity. It is the beginning of spring and my children are exposed to the celebrations of Easter, Naw-Ruz Festival (Bahai New Year's Day), Ram Navami (Hindu Festival—the birthday of Lord Rama) and Pesach (Passover) learning about their schoolmates' customs and religions not from textbooks, but from shared life experiences. Even though the issues are more complicated, I wish this theme could permeate the Jews and the Muslims aiding understanding and perhaps even tolerance. I watch the children pour out of the campus and also wonder how we can apply the lessons I enjoyed in Aaron's class about speaking with confrontational teenagers; I would propose a dialogue where Jews and Muslims, men and women, leaders and people on the streets would use the "I" statement and not the accusatory "you" in their negotiations.

* * *

Throughout Herzelia and the country, blue and white flags hang from the light poles along city streets, storefronts, office buildings, apartments and private homes. Cars, trucks and buses drive with small Israeli flags attached to their windows all in celebration of Yom Hatz-ma-oot (Israel's independence), a true confluence of blue and white although the holiday is still a month away. I feel the contagious pride and excitement that shortly we will celebrate Israel's birthday on her soil knowing the dedication, the hard work, the loss of lives and the fight so many have made for her survival, which is still delicate; all of this is blended with the rewards of creating and building a beautiful and thriving nation from the desert sands in such a short period of time.

The independence that my two teens enjoy here is truly hard for me to accept. They have little homework and lots of free time. Aaron has abandoned basketball and 'hangs out' with kids from school. While I am relieved that he has friends and leaves the Trump Office, he continues to live in a secret teen world where he intentionally pushes me away and I carefully watch from just beyond his self-imposed barriers. Noa's social life leaves little time for her family, but she is pleasant during the limited amount of hours she spends with us. Her very generous free time is mostly dedicated to 'hanging out' at restaurants, clubs and parties where she joins her friends in drink and smoke and returns home showered in these scents. If I ask for help with the dishes or taking the trash out, I am met with incredulous looks and degrading comments. Teenage independence in our home is a hoax. It is all about being free to party with very little hard work, dedication and creation, but a lot of talk and expectations about what comes with independence.

Israel's independence, like my children's, cannot be taken for granted. The Arab League Summit takes place in Riyadh, Saudi Arabia. Palestinian President Abu Mazen joins the majority of Arab leaders by voting for the Saudi Peace Initiative that calls for recognition of Israel's right to exist, a permanent peace as Israel withdraws from land captured in 1967 in the 6-Day War, a Palestinian State with East Jerusalem as its capital, and a just solution to the issue of Palestinian refugees. Hamas does not vote for the Saudi Peace Initiative, which does not bode well for the Palestinian unity government or peace in the Middle East.

Qassams land daily in Sderot.

* * *

A large abandoned me-do-rah (bonfire) is still ablaze early this cool morning as the many walkers pass by and inhale the smoke blowing in the direction of the seawater. It is the beginning of the Pesach Holiday and many young people journey to the beach and 'hang out' all night long around the me-do-rah sleeping in silver tents that populate the sand.

Kobe now collects and trades Yugioh cards. I have not learned what they really are, although he returns home excited each day with a new one, which I know means Gordon succeeded in getting him to try some new type of food. Kobe, like Israel, is a confluence of modern and ancient stories and while Yugioh cards entrance him so do the stories from the Bible that he recites for me about the Jews escape from Egyptian slavery.

Last night he woke at 4am and climbed into bed telling me that he was having a bad dream about Pharaoh. His little body snuggled next to me; I could feel fear in his tiny tight body until he slowly he relaxed and fell into deep slumber.

* * *

On my early walk a group of soldiers perform exercises with a few ferocious German Shepherd dogs. When I approach, one soldier prevents me from passing as I watch another soldier bundled in a thick jumpsuit walking through the seawater while being attacked by a dog on a long leash held by one of the soldiers on the sand. After the ferocious dog is pulled back and calmed down, I continue my walk. I am not sure if this exercise should appease my fears or actually increase them.

Corruption in the Israeli government seems to be more at the forefront than terrorist attacks these days. In addition to Finance Minister Hirschson's embezzlement troubles, former Justice Minister Chaim Ramon, is found guilty of 'The Kiss', fined 15,000 NIS ($4000) as compensation to the victim and sentenced to one hundred and twenty hours of community service working at a horse ranch with mentally challenged adults and children, which once he finishes will allow him to return to politics.

We attend an evening hosted by the bank at the Tel Aviv Art Museum to celebrate a new exhibit by the Latvian born Jewish American painter Mark Rothko. Although he never visited the country, his son Christopher speaks about his father's love for Israel. Excited energy buzzes through the hall; Israelis truly appreciate when fine art arrives in their small nation especially when a fellow Jew produces it. The museum tonight is a 'who's who' of Israeli culture. I have no idea who many of the players are, any more than the characters on Kobe's Yugioh cards, but Yehuda knows them and works the museum. I return gracefully to the role of 'trophy wife' for a couple of hours. After viewing the exhibit, I sample some scrumptious chocolates as compensation for my award-wining performance this evening.

Pesach (Passover)

Two long, thin rowboats glide along the calm sea this morning in rhythm one after the other. Their bodies are camouflaged so that the oars appear to move by themselves while the boats slither through the lively seawater at a much faster pace than I can walk on the sand.

Today Kobe celebrates the Pesach Seder at gan with Saba and Safta. Alona has been cooking for a few days preparing the Seder feast for the children and their grandparents, and the small low tables are garnished with matza, grape juice and Seder platters. Kobe dresses in nice pants and a button down long sleeve shirt and proudly announces, "I like to dress fancy". He is fascinated by the stories of Moses, Joseph and his brothers, Jewish slavery and the Jews walking through the desert on their way to Israel, which leads him to ask many questions. Kobe like most children loves stories and characters, he believes in them and understands their plight even after thousands of years. I keep thinking about the message of Farfour, the Palestinian Mickey Mouse and the beautiful little girl who together spread hateful stories about the Israelis to the Palestinian children. I realize that our circumstances are different, but I cannot imagine teaching Kobe or his young friends about hate, let alone encouraging them to partake in the destruction of a country and its people, but I am cognizant that young minds are ripe to learn. Hamas is as well.

Stores throughout the Holy Land fill with matza. I buy whole-wheat matza, thin matza and a holy box of large matza that is completely inedible. Jews all over the country buy matza and it is reported that Arabs also love matza and can't keep enough stocked on the shelves of their neighborhood markets. Arab markets continue selling bread during the entire eight-day holiday providing many secular Jews with a place to buy bread during Pesach. I love to see the culinary interdependence between Jews and Palestinians.

* * *

Fluorescent green seaweed washes up along the shore covering large sections of the soft beige sand. In the north, a yellow tractor works to clear this seaweed and prepare the sand for the flocks of Israelis who will visit my khaver over the Pesach holiday. At the end of the walk, my shoes are stained by black and chunky tar that is also scattered all over the beach sand. Soon the metal bins with rotating rough brushes at the beach entrances will be full of acetone to remove the tar.

Kobe leaves for gan wearing Yehuda's white t-shirt that serves as a tunic on his tiny frame. Today he will reenact the Jewish peoples' exodus from Egypt with his gan tribe as they walk along nearby sand dunes. They will eat flat bread made on a taboon (outdoor oven) and feel the hot sand under their feet, as did our ancestors thousands of years ago. I hope this departure from Egypt will symbolically relieve Kobe of his fear of Pharaoh. I also learn that Pesach in Israel is an important gift-giving holiday as Safta prepares presents for all the kids and they happily await this pleasing tradition. Yehuda returns from the office with beautiful wine glasses and champagne flutes from the bank, bottles of wine from business associates, a beautiful hand crafted Haggadah in English and Hebrew and a vase with an unusual rock decoration inside.

I arrive at the kikar equipped with a long shopping list for our Pesach Seder; we are now hosting thirty-two family members. It appears as though the majority of shoppers in the kikar are European tourists in Israel for the holiday. I am amused that as I listen and look at all these foreign visitors, I do not see myself as one of them, rather I am the real Israeli and they are visiting my home.

* * *

Pesach arrives. The sun shines bright in our backyard filling the large dining room with an abundance of natural light. Yehuda, Shabtai and I place cushions on each seat and add the seating cards that Eden has written in Hebrew and English. I adorn the table with white candles in clear glass holders between the purple and white flowers that I have arranged in twelve small glass vases to symbolically represent the twelve tribes of the Jewish people. I place kosher wines from the Golan Wineries, bottles of grape juice and an assortment of matza. I chop up apples adding wine and cinnamon for my Ashkenazi khoroset that I have loved to eat with matza and horseradish since I was a little girl. Marcelle also prepares an Iraqi version of khoroset; thick with honey and chopped walnuts sprinkled on top. We boil three-dozen eggs. We clean parsley. We chop a large salad with cucumbers and tomatoes. Marcelle has prepared fresh chicken broth and small hard matza balls reminding me of the small hard matza balls that my grandma made forty years earlier for Pesach— a fundamental Jewish grandmother treat whether from Baghdad, Iraq or Omsk, Russia. Marcelle prepares enough food for an army. We celebrate a Pesach embracing both Ashkenazi and Sephardic Jews, which allows different food to be served—Sephardic Jews eat rice on this holiday and Aunt Shula will bring a large caldron of Ti-beat, her flavorful rice with the sweet crunchy bottom layer.

My sister-in-law, Shlomit and her husband Eitan arrive half an hour early with children, grandchildren and lots of strawberries from their home on the kibbutz bordering Gaza. Yehuda's brother Roni and his wife Ora arrive with gefilte fish, an assortment of Ha-ga-dote (Pesach prayer books) accompanied by their fifteen-year old daughter Michal and their son Tom, who just served four years in the army and is off to South America. Another son, cousin Dan arrives a few minutes later to the delight of Kobe and Eden, while their oldest son, who will be married this summer, currently lives abroad in London. Yehuda's cousin Iris arrives with her husband, Israel and their three children. Yehuda's brother Giora and his wife, Nira come in with roast beef, horseradish, cakes and chocolates. Yacov and Shula enter with their Ti-beat. The castle is alive this holiday with excitement and energy from the large and lively Iraqi tribe.

I welcome four generations of our family and thank them for filling our home with love and warmth as we celebrate this holiday together. I could not have imagined nine months ago our creamy white castle would feel like home and tonight it does. I look around the large dining room, my eyes as a camera lens carefully filming this special night carefully documenting everyone and everything. Celebrating Pesach in L.A. each year we say, "Next year in Jerusalem" and here we are in the Holy Land. Yacov, our family patriarch tries to lead the prayers and follow the Ha-ga-ddah but it is his wife, Shula who keeps us going. We tell the story of the Israelites leaving Egypt, we pray, we laugh, we eat abundant and delicious food and most important we are together celebrating with our family—in my opinion, the true value and meaning of a Jewish holiday. In the spirit of the evening, Kobe brings a baby doll in a basket to the table and announces that he has brought Moses to dinner. We are all stuffed, yet we continue to eat dessert; platters of fruit, kharoset balls covered with white chocolate, moist and tender coconut cake and an assortment of flourless cookies. Presents are given. Eden finds the hidden afikomen (hidden piece of matza) and Kobe cries.

We spend a magical evening with the family celebrating Jewish freedom in the Holy Land. Even in our happiness, I cannot help but think of Gilad Shalit who spends his Pesach in Gaza as a prisoner. There has been talk of trading him for thousands of Palestinian prisoners, but there is no successful outcome and he is not home tonight reclining and enjoying his holiday meal with his loved ones.

* * *

"In Israel, in order to be a realist you must believe in miracles." David Ben Gurion

My khaver is a live Monet masterpiece; millions of dashes of paint dancing through vibrant shades of blue as a tinge of sun highlights the water's shimmering texture. A soft hum from the calm seawater whispers softly to me, and my thoughts are free to roam wherever they wish. On the Northern Beach, large flat boulders usually hidden under the seawater are fully exposed and covered by green slimy algae. At Shablul Restaurant, music blares from speakers at this early hour. A group of gray haired beach elders in bathing suits sit on the restaurant's yellow plastic chairs drinking coffee, engaged in a lively group conversation.

Today we take a break from the constant running that has overtaken our lives even here in the Holy Land and eat Shabbat lunch together as a family. It is apparent that with the welcome comfort we experience, we have all reverted to this chaotic behavior making the simple ease of organizing family dinners or eating Shabbat afternoon lunches together complicated and all the more appreciated. Simply sitting together in the dining room around the table eating, talking and laughing with my family for more than ten minutes is blissful. Today I share preparations in the kitchen with my mother-in-law and two daughters; Kobe and Saba are busy building a Lego spaceship in the other room; and Yehuda is studying his Orange Business Newspaper. Aaron currently avoids me with even greater effort as he conceals his third quarter report card. Noa has her grades—does he really think I do not know he has his? All quarter, he told me he did his work, but I know that he has academically checked out of school—an executive decision Trump Jr. made all on his own. When I go to his room, I find him listening to his music and working on his computer, which means he is playing on line poker or researching NBA (basketball) statistics and scores. He does come out of his room to eat and in between his constant complaints that there is nothing good to eat, Aaron consumes great quantities of food. For months now, I have made excuses for his 'cranky teenage behavior' and the lack of schoolwork, because of the guilt I felt taking him away from his comfortable and familiar life in L.A. If I had a backbone and were not such a freyer, I would come down hard on him or at least take away his computer.

Today is no different. Lunch is served and Aaron arrives in a timely manner, piles food on his plate and focuses on his feeding exercise with a couple of grunts and sly-sarcastic comments. He may not be engaged with us, but I know he is listening. Noa happily talks about her friends, her busy social life and school. After ten minutes, Eden cannot sit still at the table; she needs to dance and to move. Kobe takes five bites of schnitzel and asks me when he can have dessert; he still resists any green colored food and considers ketchup to be the only edible vegetable. He won't touch fresh fruit, but loves meetz petal (raspberry juice), a standard kid's drink in Israel. Today the highlight of the meal is a heated and intense verbal battle between my husband and his mother. We all watch and listen knowing it will pass over once all the hot air is let out on both sides. On a larger scale, we watch as the Israeli and Syrian leaders make heated statements and accusations against each other in the news threatening to start a war this summer. We all watch and hope it will pass over as well.

Israel is the land of miracles. There are endless scandals, great public discontent with the government and public frustration with the country's leadership, but the Tel Aviv Stock Exchange, whose director is a woman, and the value of the shekel both hit new highs.

Yom-eem Me-yo-he-deem (Special Days)

Ha Aretz is alive with an abundance of colorful spring flowers; empty fields along the roads are packed with millions of dainty yellow flowers and tall wild purple flowers; city landscapes are carefully manicured with green topiaries and white, pink and red flowers; and all around the kibbutz old and gigantic hibiscus plants are dense with bright flowing flowers creating a gorgeous and vibrant wall of color. On the surface, the country feels fresh and alive with spring regardless of tough political times domestically and internationally.

This morning Kobe and I stop for a moment to watch a yellow tractor pass back and forth in the fields of the kibbutz. Inside the kibbutz, parents riding bicycles, bring their children to gan on handlebar seats and rear baskets and others push their babies in metal playpens set on four wheels along narrow trails making it necessary to drive very slowly. As I walk with Kobe hand in hand, the natural scent from the re-fet (cow farm) arrives with the breeze. It is actually a putrid smell but feels fresh and stirs me today.

In the afternoon, two Israeli teens in jeans and t-shirts—a skinny blond girl and a tall dark haired boy stand on the divider of the Rabin Intersection selling blue and white Israeli flags for Independence Day. As I wait at the intersection, I buy an Israeli flag magnet to adorn my car door and two Israeli flags with plastic holders to attach to my windows. These kids have encroached on the territory of the young religious men in tfillin and skullcap who daily greet drivers and promote their religious items. I am thrilled to see representatives of state and religion respectfully working side by side in their perspective jobs at the intersection named after the great leader, Yitzhak Rabin who dedicated his elder years to shalom and tolerance. The light turns green and I drive off to the American School with a large blue and white magnet on my door, and two Israeli flags blowing in the wind as I hum Ha Tikva. Many of the cars I pass are also adorned with the magnets and flags. We are all in the spirit of celebrating this young nations birthday. My children of course get in the car and tease me about how Israeli I have become.

* * *

A chorus of happily singing birds outside makes it difficult to focus on the words in my newspaper. My eyes travel around the castle's beautiful backyard and focus on an orange cat that visits us frequently and sits on the blue and white lounge chair cleaning himself. This cat reminds me of one of my first visits to Israel with Yehuda when Noa was a baby and I walked into a store and asked for a box of diapers, which in Hebrew are hcc-too-lccm, but instcad I askcd for a box of ha-too-lccm (cats).

Aaron's new friends are mystery children who frequently appear, but are never introduced. I am sure that they have been given names by their parents so today when an apparition of the loving son I used to have appears in Aaron's jeans and white t-shirt, I suggest that if his new friends walk in the house right in front of me that it would be nice if he introduced them to me. He agrees in concept to this old-fashioned notion.

* * *

High tides envelop the beach and saturate deep beds of rocks and shells making it a challenge to walk today and each footstep produces a crunchy sound. The Arab man I have seen many times in a long white dress and head cover stands proudly on the cliff by the old stone Sidni Ali Mosque holding a walking stick in his right hand staring out at the impressive sea as rays from the setting sun on the horizon spray orange light on him.

Aaron finally hands me his grade report after I enter his 'dungeon' and make it obvious that I will not leave without it. He received a 'D' in family life, the same class I joined to learn how to communicate better with my son—the irony here literally smacks me. Across the board he does not work. I calmly ask him "Why?" and Aaron responds that there is no point as these are 'things' he does not need in life. I naively talk to him once again about why school and his studies have value in his life. He agrees, but I know he is intent on getting me out of his room more than he is about an earnest commitment to actually doing some work.

At 8pm a loud siren blares in our neighborhood and all through Israel everyone stands silent for two minutes in honor of Yom Ha-Sho-ah (Holocaust Memorial Day). Yehuda, Eden and I rise from our seats at the dinner table without a word and stand silently with our heads bowed down. Yom Ha-Sho-ah actually began at sunset throughout the country when all the restaurants, markets and entertainment venues closed for the evening to honor the lives of the six million Jews murdered during the Sho-ah. For twenty-four hours radio stations' airwaves are empty and television screens are blank to remember, to contemplate and to say to ourselves, our nation and the world, "Never Again". Eden innocently asks if we had any relatives who died in the Sho-ah. While we did not, I explain that all the Jewish people are a family and when Jews are attacked or killed for being Jewish anytime, anywhere in the world, it is personal and feels like a close relative. The 8pm siren leaves me somber. As I crawl into bed tonight, I am frustrated by how the crazy people of the world, like President Ahmadinejad of Iran, can deny or even question that the Sho-ah happened. In the near future, there will be no survivors to personally recount these details. The documentaries—life accounts from survivors and film footage will have to be the testimony that these atrocities took place.

* * *

At 10am on Yom Ha-Sho-ah, I stand in my dark closet and the loud siren blares all through the country once again to memorialize and pay respect to the six million Jews murdered by the Nazis. For a second time in this twenty four hour commemorative period, we stop whatever we are doing and stand with our chins to our chests and our arms flanked by our sides motionless; cars stop in mid drive, school children stand silent, construction workers stop pounding and people in mid-sentence stop speaking. I stand at attention alone in my closet and tears well up in my eyes for all my murdered and abused extended Jewish family.

All throughout the country on Yom Ha Sho-ah children perform in memorials; survivors and leaders light candles; stories are read out loud as are the names of victims at the Knesset, cemeteries, local community centers and Yad Vashem; Vice Premier Shimon Peres speaks of parting from his grandfather, a rabbi at the railway station in Poland; older men and women vividly speak about the moment they were separated from their parents as small children; other speak of the hunger and the cold still fresh in their being; and most remember the distinct faces and the voices of Nazi hate. These survivors represent the children and young people who survived the concentration camps. Six million Jews are remembered as all of our family members who perished.

* * *

Loose papers and food wrappers fly through the air while monstrous waves pound the shore this dark gray morning. Out in the sea, a flock of white birds congregates on a large patch of the rough water next to a school of small sailboats. A large coast guard ship with a gray-green metal exterior blends with the water's color as it passes like a giant sea creature on its way to the Herzelia Marina.

Aaron continues to attend school, but does no work. I run into his humanity teacher who tells me amongst other things that Aaron has the demeanor of a Detroit used car salesman. Recently Aaron approached him with a smile and asked earnestly why he did not make honor roll for 3rd quarter. Six months ago, he made honor roll, but did not like the kids and now he does no work and wants to be part of the social scene. I feel like one of those birds on the rough seawater; I must be gme-sha (flexible) as the water currents go up and down convinced that my kid's adolescence will not drown me. I am careful not to rush time and am much more patient than when I arrived here in August, but I fervently await the finish of Aaron's academic year.

* * *

Strong gusty winds sweep the light grains of sand into smooth land waves; I struggle as though I carry a heavy load behind me while each footprint is quickly covered with fresh sand that flies in to replace the mark leaving no indication that I walk today.

After dinner, Yehuda and I are sitting at the kitchen table when Noa runs by and yells that she is off to meet friends on the street for the siren to mark the beginning of Yom Ha Zi-ca-rone (the National Memorial Day). Within seconds the 8pm siren blares through the country; we get up from the table and stand in silence with our heads tilted downward and pay tribute to all of the people who lost their lives fighting for Israel's freedom and survival in the many battles and wars since the inception of the state. Since achieving statehood, 22,305 Israelis have been killed in battle and just in the last sixty hours of the Second Lebanon War, 33 soldiers were killed including one female soldier. I am pleased that a nation of 6 million diverse Jews, struggling to be harmonious, succeeds on these occasions to be cohesive even if it is for only two minutes.

Kobe's gan visits the kibbutz cemetery to honor those members who died serving their country. As an American, I feel a bit 'creeped out' that my son visits a cemetery, but for Israeli children it is part of their normal educational experience. Kobe returns home to tell me quite naturally, as though he is sharing a story he learned from the Bible, about all the people who died and which of his friends they were related to. Children sing and perform in Yom Ha Zi-ca-rone ceremonies in schools and community centers throughout Israel. A large memorial ceremony takes place at the Western Wall lead by acting Israeli President Dalia Itzik. 600,000 flowers are donated for memorial services throughout the nation honoring those who have given their lives for Israel's existence in a Muslim controlled

175

region where it is clear they are not wanted. Yom Ha Zi-ca-rone is one of the days when I feel the intense power of being Israeli. Israelis love their country with great passion and pride and while they disagree on many things, today they are united for this small land that has been the home of the Jewish people for a few thousand years.

* * *

At 11am the next morning, the long eerie siren blares again and I stop in my tracks as I walk on the street by Yehuda's office. I see no faces. A light breeze blows. The siren finally dies down and I move again.

At sunset, we move from Yom Ha Zi-ca-rone to Yom Atz-ma-oot (Independence Day). The Jewish people have inhabited these lands for 4000 years but the country; home to 7.15 million residents (80% of them are Jews) is a very young 59 years old. In 1948 when statehood was declared, 806,000 residents resided here and as we celebrate Israeli's 59th birthday one third of the original residents are still alive. All night long throughout the country, Israelis partake in parties and fireworks celebrating this difficult-to-come-by-independence. The feeling is dafka (despite) existing in a part of the world where neighboring nations and religious fanatics threaten our existence and daily put our security in peril, Israel survives and thrives—even tonight, security throughout the nation is increased in anticipation of terrorist attacks.

Noa and Aaron continue thoroughly to enjoy their independence. On Yom Atz-ma-oot, like many weekends, they are out with their friends all night long. I try to accept this practice on the surface, but truthfully I lie in bed not sleeping well and worrying until I hear the door open and know that they are home safe. On Yom Atz-ma-oot, I am up early with Kobe and Eden and my teens who arrived just before the sun are now fast asleep and will be for most of the day. Yehuda and I walk with the little ones to visit my khaver joining many other walkers where bonfires flicker in the cool air and small silver tents full of young Israelis are scattered on the sand. Israelis picnic all over the Holy Land from the coastal beaches to the Golan Heights, the shores of the Sea of Galilee to the forests around Jerusalem, the vast Negev Desert to the Red Sea, in backyards and city parks. While Israelis struggle with the 'hard to come by independence', I struggle with my children's 'too easy to come by independence' that living in this country offers young people—it is a constant battle for all of us.

* * *

Summer encroaches with muggy warm weather and my khaver once again fills with the young; surfers now liberated from their winter wet suits congregate out in the water; bald seventeen year olds run along the sand in preparation for the army; and others sit on blankets with friends drinking and smoking from a nargila. Each group surrounds a boy with long black curly hair who strums his guitar serenading the group's conversation. I walk by the Gaudi house below the cliffs as the creator returns from a sea swim, dripping wet and disappears through the metal gate into his compound. At the end of the stonewall, a group of young Ethiopians sit at a long table and celebrate Friday afternoon eating and laughing as the sun sets.

The concept of a calm life that I naively imagined for this year is long gone. The pace of activity with four children and an energetic husband keeps me well occupied. I have become acutely aware that it is not the setting, but rather the characters that create the drama. I still take pleasure in not being a slave to the gentle Blackberry 'gong'. I also do not miss the bundles of mail or the endless catalogues arriving at my house beckoning me to buy items that I do not need.

The charity event that Noa and I are organizing for the Jewish and Arab children of Jaffa is a week away. Achinoam has volunteered to perform ensuring a warm and delightful evening yet I start to feel great anxiety and question what I got myself into. This was the year I was going to be selfish, take care of myself and not volunteer for anything. As I watch the movie of my life, I realize that my character is well defined and helping others is a vital part of me. There is also a part of me that desires in a small way to help promote the message of tolerance and coexistence between the Jews and the Arabs. I am also proud of Noa, who embraces this message and works hard to help create this event.

* * *

As we drive down streets, Kobe plays a game where he points to teenage soldiers in military uniform with Uzis slung over their shoulders and excitedly calls out "army girl" or "army boy". He is still very American and unaccustomed to the sight of teenagers just a little older than his big sister who take an active role in ensuring their nations survival, which is not a game at all. In America we keep guns out of the hands of our youth and off the streets and in Israel it is a serious responsibility given to these young soldiers and the mass circulation of firearms does not result in civilian casualties.

Kobe also plays with Pokémon figures like crazy. Many afternoons we stop at the Gilgi Toy Store in the kikar and Kobe buys a clear plastic egg with a tiny Pokémon figure from a small machine. He works with great fervor to assemble the entire collection while trading duplicates with his buddies. I happily work as his accomplice remembering when I was little and after school each afternoon my mother would drive us to the local convenience store to buy Wacky Pack trading cards with a slice of sugary gum in hopes of assembling the entire collection. I continue to dream that I buy thousands of Kinder Chocolate Eggs, filled with tiny toys to distribute to the young children of Gaza as well as arrange for teenagers to receive computers to empower themselves with knowledge instead of weapons.

* * *

The pull of the gentle tides encourages my listless body as I make my way along the sand. At the Sharon Beach, a new fence surrounds the lifeguard station, the Hasakays and oars are neatly propped up on wood stands and the permanently tan lifeguards convene on the decks waiting for the mass of summer swimmers to arrive. Today children from a nearby nursery school play ball with their teachers on the beach; a young man practices Tae Kwan Do kicking and spinning around all alone; and an old man with a cigarette pursed between his lips fishes by himself as a red balloon drifts and dances in the slight sea breeze over the sandy beach. I continue to relish in the fact that everyone belongs here and enjoys my khaver.

Late in the morning, the repairman returns to fix the front gate lock again. He tries to convince me that someone is coming and kicking the huge iron-gate, which in turn breaks the lock. I am perplexed by this thought, yet with regards to this domicile, I have resigned myself to accept the absurd and ridiculous, and chose not to argue too much. A few hours later after meeting with the contractor at the new apartment, I return to my creamy white castle to find the whole top part of the front door's wooden frame, a thick piece of wood weighing about seventy pounds, lying on the floor leaving a large gaping hole. The American in me whips out the camera to photograph the scene for my Israeli attorney as proof of the incident; I know full well that this is a futile exercise and we are very lucky that this piece of wood did not land on someone's head.

I continue to be mystified by my surroundings—all of a sudden, my teenage son is charming and sweet. After weeks, actually months of miserable and crappy behavior, I am completely suspicious. I wait for him to attack or to make a verbal assault, and for a shouting match to ensue. At dinner, Aaron tells me he is getting A's now. I look at him incredulously, but not a single word escapes from my fallen mouth. The punchline he continues is that he has straight A's so far this week, but it is only Tuesday. I am not sure about the marking of a 'used car salesman', but I am becoming more and more convinced that my older son's constitution may suit him well to become an Israeli politician. Just this week, the Winograd Committee reported to PM Olmert that he has failed in his job and his popularity is at an all time low yet he acts like a success, insisting that he will not resign.

Noa is thrilled with her prom dress and shoes, but she has no date. She is convinced she needs Prince Charming. I am convinced that she has seen too many Hollywood movies. I mention to her that a nice date or a friend is the best option to have a good time with at the prom—someone who is dependable and may arrive not dressed in torn jeans and tennis shoes. I realize I sound like my mother when these words leave my mouth—further proof that I have become antiquated in my daughter's eyes.

* * *

Tan dry earth is all that remains of the kibbutz's thick green fields, which turned out to be potatoes. A tractor with large black wheels rotates the earth for the next crop. Yehuda, who was also a farmer growing up on his kibbutz when the members actually did the work, has informed me that potatoes are a healthy crop that fertilize soil for future crops. Kobe wears his yellow Bob Sfog pajamas to gan today. I say nothing as I have been to meetings at the gan where kibbutz fathers arrive barefoot and mothers wear housedresses and slippers.

On my drive home, I am stuck in traffic caused by a police-security checkpoint. I spend this time watching the charades of the village crazy man, a small balding red faced gentleman whose daily uniform in rain or shine is Bermuda shorts and a t-shirt as he walks the streets of Herzelia attempting to achieve his simple goal—to get a ride in someone's car. This morning he is fully engaged in his routine of soliciting rides from the cars slowly passing the police. One time he approached my car and when I refused him a ride, his face became beet red, his eyes bulged and he started yelling at me, but I knew he was harmless, as I had been observing him for some time.

In the afternoon when I turn the corner by Yehuda's office, a policeman calls me over for talking on the cell phone while holding it in my hand, which is against the law. The policeman speaks Hebrew but at this moment, I only speak English. He then conveniently switches to English and asks for my driver's license. I show him my California driver's license. He then asks for my passport, which I do not carry with me. He then lectures me for five minutes in a serious tone that I must drive with my passport. During this whole drama, I sit patiently. I know he cannot give me a ticket because I am a tourist (fines for Israelis are $250), but he can lecture me none-the-less in his heavily accented English and my punishment is to listen.

We sit down to dinner and Aaron has not returned. When he left, we confirmed he had to be home at 7:00pm for dinner and now it is 7:15pm and we eat without him. At 8:00pm, it is pitch black outside and I start to panic and call him non-stop on his cell phone. Then I proceed to call the two houses of friends whose names I have learned, but I still do not know the parents. I think about all the police I met today and consider a call to the local police station to report a missing fourteen year old. I get in my car and drive to the two kikar-eem, but do not see him. No one has seen him. I slip into mother 'hell mode' imagining he has been hit and is lying on the side of the road injured with no helmet on. After half an hour driving around, Yehuda calls to tell me that Aaron is home. He does not reveal where he went; he will barely speak to me and is very angry, but he is home and safe. The charming Aaron period is short lived.

* * *

Sha-rav (hot desert wind) brings cruel and punishing heat—it is already 30' Celsius (85F') at 8 in the morning. The air is heavy and full of sand and the sky is filled with thick dark gray clouds. Yehuda and I walk to escape the high temperatures, but find no sanctuary and instead the sand starts to swirl and lift and there is no way to turn around without sand attacking our faces and our bodies. The small drops of rain become large raindrops and assault us. We climb up a crevice just beyond the Gaudi stone house to avoid the flying sand and pass Apollonia Park's ancient stone ruins soaking from head to toe. The rain slows as we walk along Wingate Street where a golden retriever adopts us and accompanies us back home. My new furry friend walks next to me until I arrive to our gate, but he does not make any efforts to come in. Perhaps he is like the crazy man who hitches rides around town daily and in between walks the streets alone.

Noa texts me on the cell phone all day long panicked about the rain, as our charity event is this evening and the reception is outside in a sculpture garden. Each time there is a downpour I tell myself unconvincingly, the sky in clearing up and soon it will be cooler and less humid. Achinoam sends me a text message that she has a herniated disc.

She is in terrible pain, but will perform. I spend the day feeling sorry for her, worrying about the rain and encouraging myself to believe that the event will be a success for the children of Jaffa.

Noa and I drive along Hanassee Street to Zion's Hair Salon to get a fan for this evening. We pass a group of Ethiopian street cleaners walking slowly with their loaded carts after spending the workday outside in the rain. In the middle of the migrating group, I spot my favorite gentleman, an older man who always wears a purple knit cap. On many occasions, I have passed him admiring his magnificent smile as he cleans and carries on with his associates. Today is no different, I catch his bright smile as he pulls his cart and chats with the others. I am not sure why, but his smile calms me and I resign myself to stop worrying about what I cannot control.

Achinoam arrives for a sound check stiff and in pain, but reassures me that she will give a wonderful concert. The sculpture garden shimmers with candles in the warm dark air, pizzas fill one table and humus salads fill a second table. Our friend Dana and her college friends, all young Israelis who have come here this evening as volunteers, work the large shiny white bar. The clouds are pregnant with moisture but produce no rain as the sculpture garden fills up with many people happy to be a part of this special evening.

The warmth and love carry into the auditorium. Noa speaks to the audience passionately about children who benefit from this program and the tolerance it encourages. We show a video of the Arab and Jewish children playing and learning side by side and we hear the words of a young Arab Israeli man who credits his happy youth and success to his experience in this program. Then we are delighted with a performance by Achinoam, who once she takes the stage does not reveal to the audience that she is in pain. She literally entrances us with her voice. She performs for our small charity as though she is performing for the Pope or world leaders, which she does in between her extensive European tours. She sings with the accompaniment of Gil Dor, her partner and guitarist and Zoar Fresco, her percussionist. Their music is a feast for the ears and for the soul. They all donate their performance to the children of Friendship's Way.

I am very proud of my daughter. She worked hard to make this evening a success and stood up to seventeen-year old boys at school who expressed their dislike for Arabs and made her feel bad that she wanted to help them. Noa learned that she must do what she feels strongly about and not be affected by what others may say or do. She has been motivated to make a clear difference by her actions embracing tza-da-kah.

On the balcony in the cool late night air, I sit outside alone replaying the events of the evening in my head while a cheesy Israeli singer belts out American classics and Israeli standards from our neighbor's bar mitzvah party, a great contrast to the enchanting music of Achinoam. The sky is now liberated from the large gray clouds that I feared all day long. I also reflect on my growing premise that women need to be more involved to attain real and lasting peace and it needs to include everyday women from the local communities, as well. Arab women came this evening to support a program that helps their children and their community. Not a single father attended the event.

* * *

I cannot sleep—I am up at 4:00am and at my khaver just before 5:00am. On the northern beach, a large yellow tractor is stopped in the distance by the water's edge. A jogger runs toward me waving his hands over his head and at first I think this is part of his physical exercise. I am slow to realize that he is signaling to a police truck driving along the beach from behind me. As I approach, I see a large man with a round belly lying on a ha-sa-key surrounded by a small group of people while one officer performs mouth-to-mouth resuscitation. I walk by leaving the greatest distance I can, as I know I cannot help. On my trip back, I realize the man is dead; the paramedics cover him with a black blanket.

At noon three Arab Israeli couples arrive at our creamy white castle for lunch bearing a plenitude of gifts; fresh olive oil in Sprite bottles, two jars of green olives marinating in seasoned olive oil and a beautiful blown glass and bronze sculpture of flying birds. These families are our partners in the newest BIG Shopping Center being built in Nazareth, Jesus' childhood village. Aunt Shula and Uncle Yacov also join us for the lunch. I appreciate that in my living room sits a diverse group—Jewish Israelis originally from Iraq, a Muslim Israeli Arab couple and Christian Israeli Arab couples all from Nazareth and perhaps I add the greatest diversity being the Jewish American in the group. Distant cousins sit and eat, discuss business, share stories about children and families and what is very apparent is that no matter whether Christian, Muslim or Jewish we can all relate to each other. Shula speaks with these women in Hebrew, but it could just a well be in Arabic. Our guests appear to have more in common with us Jews than they do with their Palestinian brethren in Gaza who call for our demise. The Arab population of Israel is 1,140,000, Arab Israelis make up 10% of the Israeli Knesset and Nazareth is the largest Arab city. Today, we only skim the surface, but I yearn to hear their thoughts on what they believe needs to happen to achieve peace and if they even believe it to be feasible. Our lunch is yet another reminder for me that we are all similar and need to find common dialogue for coexistence.

* * *

Large wooden frames of a bonfires stand in the middle of the empty field in preparation for Lag Bomer. On the walk to the gan, Kobe searches on the ground for tree branches to make a bow and arrow, part of the tradition in celebrating Lag Bomer. Kobe learns the story and the songs of Lag Bomer and the children make small fires and roast marshmallows as they practice for the real celebration when under the moonlight and around the blazing flames of the bonfire, Israelis sing, eat pita and humus, meat and potatoes, and most important, they roast marshmallows.

It is dark at our friend's Killy and Gary's neighborhood, Arsuf where we are celebrating Lag Bomer. On a vacant lot stands an impressive fifteen-foot tall bonfire that looks like the shell of an Indian teepee, filled with wood scraps and papers. The bonfire is lit and within seconds the whole structure is enveloped in bright orange flames that dance in the sky shooting off orange sparks in the direction of the wind. Kobe and other small children run excitedly to this area and we evacuate them. Potatoes wrapped in tin foil are placed at the base of the fire; kids stand with long sticks and roast marshmallows on a smaller more gentle fire where Gary prepares different meats. The strong smell of smoke fills the cool air. Arsuf is an enclave of wealthy and successful Israelis many of whom grace the covers of the country's business and gossip news daily, but tonight they are practically faceless Israelis enjoying a holiday, eating pita and humus and drinking wine while the orange flames provide the only light on this dark night. Noa and Aaron leave early to meet school friends gathering on the beach back near our house—even the international children partake in this Israeli holiday. The religious also celebrate Lag Bomer; three hundred thousand ultra orthodox male revelers attend a traditional feast in Meron, a religious mo-shav in the Upper Galilee where their revered Rabbi Simeon Bar Yochai is buried. They build and dance around a bonfire and the rabbi's grave while being guarded by thousands of policemen. No women partake in this celebration. Also on this holiday, the religious celebrate with wine and candy as they ceremoniously cut the hair of three-year old boys for the first time. Throughout the night, the dark country is ablaze and the scent of smoke permeates every inch of the Holy Land and into our skin and clothing too.

* * *

A dense fog sits along the calm waters of the coast. On the beach, large piles of trash and the charcoal remains of bonfires mark the many spots where celebrants spent the evening. In one of the many shiny silver tents scattered along the sand, two feet stick out the draped enclosure. Nearby, a group of five boys all with long curly hair sit on plastic chairs in a semi circle surrounded by bags, trash, four nargilas, and bottles of vodka. Other young people in a haze slowly begin to leave the beach wrapped in blankets.

The morning after Lag Bomer is a vacation for Israeli schools, but not for my children who wake up cranky and slow and tell me it is 'not fair' that they have to go to school. I have truly come to hate when my children tell me what 'is fair' and what 'is not fair' but I refrain from too much comment as I battle with myself not to engage with my teens in contentious conversations. Marsha is outside the school this morning with her congenial smile waving as though she is the beauty queen on a parade float. After many months, I am still happy and at ease that she welcomes my kids each morning, alongside the force of good-looking security guards.

I return from morning drop off and before I enter the creamy white castle, I watch as a young man and woman walk down the middle of our street pushing an elderly woman in a wheelchair whose wispy red hair blows in the wind. The young man, who I guess is her grandson, sings out loud "Shalom Aleynu, Avinu Shalom Aleynu" and the old woman reveals a content expression on her otherwise vacant face. I watch them and instantly think of my grandmother, who sang Russian lullabies to me when I was a little girl. Years later when her health and body failed, she could barely hold baby Eden, but she still sang Russian lullabies which pleased her greatly and enchanted me.

While bonfires burn through the whole country, the political environment is also ablaze; former Prime Minister Ehud Barak, who was considered politically dead after the failed Middle East Peace Summit at Camp David in 2000, is back running for the leadership of Labor and denounces the Olmert government. Barak left politics with his head hanging low, spent time in the private sector and even visited an Ashram in India. Foreign Minister Tzipi Livni and PM Olmert both leaders from Kadima Party have been battling each other recently in the media. She has even called publically for his resignation as leader of Kadima. At the same time, 100,000 Israelis hold a peaceful rally against PM Olmert calling for his resignation. University students throughout Israel continue their vocal and angry strike against planned increase in tuition. An Arab Knesset member is accused of sharing secrets with Hezbollah intelligence during the Second Lebanon War by identifying where the Israelis were aiming their rockets and revealing that the Israelis wanted to murder Hezbollah leader Nasrallah, which I am not convinced is such a big secret. Meanwhile from Lebanon, Nasrallah who is alive and well praises the Winograd Report for Israel's acceptance of failure in the war and says, "When the enemy acts honestly and sincerely, you cannot but respect it."

* * *

At sunset, orange and purple rays fly through the light blue sky above the tanzanite seawater speckled with sea scouts paddling around on tiny kayaks and sailing on mini sailboats while Kobe, Ayehli, Eden and Shiraz build a primitive sand villages on the beach in front of the sea scouts headquarters. At the small snack stand where I bought the kids ice cream, the young tan and shirtless worker stacks lounge chairs and tables. A lone windsurfer glides up and down the coast as the orange sun ball meets the horizon.

I retired my Blackberry earlier this year and since have become advanced at sending text messages from my cell phone, a powerful and timely form of communication that I once thought was just for teens. I may not be as fast as Noa or Aaron, but I am closing in on this trend. I debate if this actually qualifies for my list of accomplishments this year in Israel. One thing I am very clear about is that life moves very fast in this country and Israelis are in a hurry to get things done. My family has also fallen into this pattern especially as the school year winds down and we begin to plan our departure. The warm weather returns and I start to visit my khaver many afternoons with the kids. At the sea, time is slow and easy; I feel as though we value the moments. If not, I worry we will become part of the whirlwind, and time will fly by with little opportunity to stop and appreciate this country and these times.

While the nation is very young, I continue to be amazed at how ancient the stories, the sites, the people and the traditions are. After thirty years of looking in the wrong places, archeologists announce that they found the real tomb of Herod the Great, the King of the Jews who expanded the Second Temple, built Caesarea, Masada and many other monument beauties. Herod, one of the first real estate developers in the Middle East, died over two thousand years ago (he lived from 74 B.C.E. to 4 B.C.E), but he still remains a huge player in the Holy Land.

Olmert secretly speaks with Palestinian President Abbas, while the IDF attacks the active rocket launching sites of the Hamas terrorists in Gaza. I worry that the Palestinian militants will conveniently place women and children as human shields at these launching sites while waiting for reprisal attacks by the IDF, a despicable feast for journalists, who fear being kidnapped in Gaza but thrive on reporting these happenings. I do find it curious that international news agencies like CNN do not care to cover the local violence, poverty and abuses by the Hamas leadership in Gaza; they prefer to promote news directly related to demonizing the Israelis. The press also skips over any positive humanitarian news to the credit of the Israelis who sent two floating pumps to Gaza to lower levels of sewage that flooded residential areas near the village of Umm Naser and that Jewish Israeli doctors treated over one hundred needy Palestinian children from the territories over the last year through a program called Save A Child's Heart. I note as well that Farfour, the mouse also does not share this message with the Palestinian youth.

* * *

Five young men in jeans and t-shirts with the word 'security' written on their chests in bold letters sit with their Uzis in front of the school waiting to escort my son and his classmates on a journey to the Negev Desert. Aaron has forgotten the water bottles that he is required to bring, but he does remember a hat—one out of two is not bad. I bid him farewell as he unenthusiastically takes his bag and slowly meanders over to the group of waiting students. I drive away from the school feeling a tremendous freedom. I surprise myself—I do not feel a bit guilty that I am actually thrilled to have a break from my fourteen-year old son who I have to believe is in the good hands of these former IDF soldiers.

As I begin to bask in my freedom, my cell phone dies on me. I know that I cannot make it through the day without my warm, live electronic friend and the connectivity it offers me. At the Orange store at Cinema City I am reunited with the cowgirl I met during Purim. We greet each other like long lost friends. Now that we are friends, I have pro-tec-zia (protection), which is one of the most valued commodities in Israel. She will look out for me and make sure my problem is solved. Once I reconnect to the world, I feel much better and go to meet my friend Tzipi at Running Sushi where plates of sushi go round and round on a conveyor belt. I am not a big fan of pre-prepared sushi, but it is wonderful to speak to another mother, an adult, and someone who needs nothing from me nor I from her.

* * *

Menacing dark gray clouds produce a warm and humid tropical storm with bulky, round raindrops. My dark blue car is caked with a thick layer of brown mud as the dirt and water fly through the air leaving their mark everywhere. I think of the Asian diplomats' wife and hope her car is safe in a garage somewhere. By midday, the rain dissipates and the scorching heat returns. Hundreds of birds fill the trees around our back yard singing to each other a happy tune from a Disney movie.

The serenity of the afternoon is broken with the arrival of a text message from Noa—"I need to see a therapist." I am not sure what to make of this electronic notification from my dramatic daughter. I resist the urge to panic, and I have to assume the crisis will terminate prior to her return home in the afternoon. I have learned that my children recover from their stressful activities much quicker than I do. In the afternoon, I join Eden and Kobe in the swimming pool to resuscitate myself. As I float in the water, my mind races to my daughter who needs a therapist and then to my ti-pesh-es-ray (slang for stupid teen) who left for a trip to the Negev Desert with no water. I listen to the joy of Eden and Kobe throwing a ball in the pool water and my thoughts skip to Farfour, the Mickey Mouse 'wanna be' who continues to poison Palestinian children with a message of hate for the Jews. In the latest episode, Farfour is caught cheating in a classroom. When the male teacher asks Farfour why he cheated, he blames the Jews, who destroyed his house, which caused him to lose his notebook—a Hamas version of 'the dog ate my homework'.

In the evening at the Greek Ambassador's estate, I attend a fundraiser for Neve Shalom (Oasis of Peace), a unique village where an equal amount of Arab and Jewish families live in coexistence. David Broza, a well-known Israeli performer strums his guitar and sings with great passion under the stars in this sprawling backyard for an audience of distinguished diplomats and foreigners. As I sit and listen, I truly believe that music and the other arts where people can communicate in a common language and embrace their differences will make great strides in the quest for shalom. I have lost faith in these foreign diplomats whom I earlier believed could be the key to shalom, but now appear simply to sit and watch from the audience.

I still hold out hope for one Israeli leader, Shimon Peres, to bring shalom. During the Oslo Accord in 1993, Peres partnered with Itzhak Rabin to negotiate a peace treaty with Yasser Arafat and the Palestinians; they all won Nobel Peace Prizes, but Rabin was murdered, Arafat died and shalom was not realized. Currently Vice-Premier Peres wants to be the president of Israel, but is unsure that the Knesset Members who hold a secret ballot will give him enough votes to win. PM Olmert is not about to let Peres lose the presidential race and goes to meet with Rabbi Ovadia, the spiritual leader of the Shahs Party to request that his party's twelve Knesset members vote for Peres in his bid to be president.

Shavuot

This morning Kobe tells me he needs to drink a lot of milk in preparation for Shavuot, the holiday that celebrates the wheat harvest and when G-d gave the Torah to Moses for the Jewish people on Mt Sinai, which is exactly seven weeks after Pesach. Kobe hears that he needs to drink milk and eat cheese, bread, fruit and vegetables, but the only part of this scenario that Kobe likes is the milk and therefore he promotes this as the 'milk holiday'. After I drop Kobe off, I run to the kikar for Shabbat shopping and order breads at Lechem Erez for Shavuot. I find myself walking across the congested parking lot like a bag lady laden down with a heavy load. It is Friday morning and the coffee houses are packed with happy and energetic patrons flowing out to the tables that line the sidewalk. I admire these people who purely take the morning off to sit in the kikar, drink coffee, eat breakfast, smoke and appear to have nothing more pressing to do than catch up with friends at the end of a work week. It is clear to me that my role as mother, wife, worker and general caretaker in a hybrid of lands has forced me into living on a roller coaster that does not begin nor finish. I need to get off, but the ride moves very fast and simply keeps going.

Friday night we eat a quick family dinner at the Italian restaurant Joya. I am happy that we are all together, although I am aware that the big kids only sit with us now as a duty—they act like they are Shabbat hostages. Noa counts the minutes until she is free to have a second dinner with friends at the sushi restaurant and Aaron is simply pleased to have a good professionally cooked meal. I have to keep asking them to not send text messages and not to answer the cell phone for the brief time that we sit together. I quickly recall my idea to spend this year abroad, together as a family, but due to hormones and Israeli teen freedom, this plan has been derailed and these days their goal is to spend as little time with us as possible. After dinner, Aaron has a bunch of kids show up and they submerge into his dungeon space. When they all leave an hour later, I ask Aaron where they are going and he mumbles, "I dunno." Noa leaves dressed in a mini skirt and ridiculously high pumps she can barely walk in. She is mad at the onset, as I will not let her go to a party in Tel Aviv, but she curbs her comments, as she needs to ask for money before she leaves. A few days ago, Noa sent me the SMS that she needed to see a psychiatrist, but this does not seem to slow down or hinder her active social life. She has moved on and I am reminded that I must as well.

While I joke about my children being Friday night dinner hostages, the news of 'real hostages' is not a humorous part of our lives; Alan Johnson, the kidnapped BBC journalist, is detained somewhere in Gaza and has not been heard from for eight weeks; Gilad Shalit, the young kidnapped soldier is still being held in Gaza; and the two soldiers who were kidnapped by the Lebanon border remain unheard from, their whereabouts uncertain. At the same time, the Palestinians continue to build tunnels from Gaza into Egypt to smuggle weapons while Hezbollah in Lebanon rearms for the next battle against my giborah.

* * *

My khaver is full of walkers who like a parade of ants, walk up and down the sand in long steady lines engrossed with partners in lively conversations accompanied by grand hand gestures. The sea is full of surfers, sailors and fishermen. The restaurants are packed. My khaver is back in full business this beautiful spring morning.

Eden and I experiment with whole-wheat flour in our chocolate chip cookies that we prepare for our Shabbat lunch guests. I love Shabbat more and more as this year moves on. It is the one day each week where time almost stands still and we invite different friends and family to enjoy the time together.

While we take pleasure in our friends, great food and beautiful weather, not many miles away from here in Gaza, Hamas and Fatah battle each other making the streets unsafe for civilians. The Israelis are not responsible for this civil war, but I have a feeling they will be blamed at some point along the way. Even as Palestinian factions battle for control, Hamas militants launch Qassam Rockets into the city of Sderot sending the residents running to their bomb shelters each time the siren sounds. The militant branch of Hamas publicly and proudly takes credit for the attacks. In September 2005, Israelis evacuated Gaza, leaving behind all of the military posts and over twenty settlements where Israeli citizens had lived. Prime Minister Ariel Sharon, now in a coma for almost a year and a half, believed back then that the Israeli departure would halt the fighting. Even at this juncture it is very clear that the Hamas leadership wants more from the Israelis than just Gaza back and their efforts are supported and funded by the Iranians, whose leader has been completely clear about his goal to wipe Israel off the map.

* * *

Pink and white azaleas and bougainvilleas blissfully envelop the border of the kibbutz like bright wrapping paper accented with a fresh green bow of leaves. As Kobe walks along the familiar path at home on the kibbutz he has adopted this year, he greets all the dogs by their first names.

I visit Yigal in the kikar to buy schnitzel. We talk tennis, because in a few minutes the Israeli female champion, Shahar Peer will play at the French Open in Roland Garros. It is a small country and everyone knows Shahar Peer like the girl next door. I see my friend Caty with her wild blond hair and array of gold bangles and diamonds sparkling in the sun as she hurries home to watch Shahar. At the pharmacy, Oren boasts about Shahar Peer like his sister and asks me if I am playing any tennis—"Lo," I answer, although I wish I were and that life had not become so busy.

* * *

Large green metal cages full of plastic bottles wait by the roadside to be recycled and next to them are green trash bins stuffed with used newspapers. These metal monsters are not aesthetically pleasing, but they represent an opportunity for people who are concerned about the environment to recycle. They are always full—a huge contrast to the trash left on the seashore. As so much, it goes both ways in Israel.

The news is also this way—daily there are reports of Qassam Rockets landing in the city of Sderot; one hit the Sderot high school and the roof of a classroom completely collapsed, one killed a woman walking down the street, and another Qassam killed a young father as he drove down the street. The city's youth burn tires and thousands demonstrate against the mayor and the Prime Minister, while in separate incursions the IDF soldiers battle Hamas gunmen along the border and other soldiers bomb terrorist launching sites and the Hamas Headquarters in Gaza. Once I get past the cover articles each day, there are so many wonderful stories about Israelis who create and invent, volunteer to help others, and in small meaningful ways work towards shalom and co-existence, but the old news adage, 'If it bleeds, it leads' unfortunately is still true.

* * *

Wild waves crash exuberantly into shiny white foam spraying the scent of salt water into the fresh air. I selfishly and optimistically look for Aphrodite, the God of Love to appear in the white bubbly wash. Instead fresh purple graffiti welcomes me with the words 'Locals Only' written in bold letters with skulls and fancy borders on the cement walls down the beach path. Rarely do we see such artistic graffiti written in English here. As I walk, I ponder the meaning of the skulls and the written words 'Locals Only'.

Herzelia Pituah reminds me of small town America; everyone knows everyone on a first name basis, kids go to school with the same children practically from birth until they go into the army at eighteen-years old and most of the retail establishments have mom and pop proprietors. Even with many transient expatriates and embassy families, the neighborhood is cohesive and happy. I continue to take pleasure in the fact that my children walk safely down the streets to their friends' houses whether in broad daylight or late into the night and they are safe. And like any small town, rumors travel very fast, people know each other's business and cars stop in the middle of the street so friends can greet one another.

Not all neighborhoods in Israel are this harmonious—in the Halisa neighborhood of Haifa a feud brews between two known Bedouin crime families—a modern Middle Eastern story of the Hatfields and the McCoys. Last year two sons of one family were murdered and now they seek revenge exchanging gunfire and tossing grenades at each other. The police raid both homes, confiscate weapons and arrest eight family members. Ironically women from one family have married into the other family. It is said, "A Bedouin can wait a thousand years for revenge."

* * *

Jerusalem celebrates the 40th anniversary of reunification. Downpours and major floods in the city cancel many of the planned activities.

Four years ago, an injured female stork at the Bet She'an Zoo attracted the attention of a migrating male stork. All these years, the male stork has waited for his love in a nest he built nearby on an electric pole and has not participated in any of the bi-annual stork migrations from Europe to Africa. The female stork has never been able to leave the zoo to join him and now another female stork has moved into the nest and has her own babies that shortly she will teach to fly and they will migrate to Africa. Will the male stork migrate with them or stay by his old love who remains in her cage? Storks are one of a hundred species of birds that cross Israeli skies twice a year. Basra reed warblers traditionally migrate from Africa to Iraq, but due to the war in Iraq they started to arrive to the HULA valley region of Israel. Last year they were banded and now after a winter in East Africa, they return for a second year as they opt for the relative Israeli tranquility rather than the Iraqi chaos.

* * *

Hot summer weather has arrived even if the season does not actually commence for a few more weeks. Purple graffiti still boldly blemish the wall along the beach path and the shore is full of walkers. Just off the coast, a lone bright red fishing boat with two men aboard bobs up and down in the gentle moving sea. A large gathering of beach elders wade in the calm green tinted water wearing bright-colored swim caps, while another group sits on plastic chairs in front of Shablul's eating breakfast joined by two lifeguards for spirited conversation and their morning coffee.

I secretly envy them leisurely sharing the morning, eating and drinking with their feet in the sand and enjoying the fresh sea air. I on the other hand rush home to meet Zoar, the contractor to fix the refrigerator's handle that has broken off and now we have to bend down and pull the heavy door open from below with a strong yank. I have adopted the phrases, 'Al-ti-da-gee' and 'Ha kol yi-he-yay be-seder' in order to live in Israel and not go crazy when it comes to fixing things that I have little control over.

* * *

Weekend shoppers hover around the market's seafood counter waiting to buy fish for Shabbat meals. Like an artist, the fish man with his arsenal of knives and equipment prepares each fish with a ritual performance; he scrapes the fish's skin, slices it down the middle and gently plucks the large bones from the innards as a woman plucks eyebrow hairs one by one. He repeats this activity time after time honoring each fish like a treasured prize. Afterwards, he carefully wraps the fresh fish and proudly hands the package to the waiting customer. By the time it is my turn, I have waited over fifteen minutes but have enjoyed the live show, better than anything I have seen on the cooking channel in America. Finally I order my two branzino fish and enjoy the ceremony once again.

Israel is a place of wonderment and miracles. Even as Qassams land and the nation faces troubled political times; the Israel Stock Market remains strong; the quantity of North Americans who make Aliyah is higher than in recent years; apartment sales to foreigners are greater even with the looming threat of another war with Syria; and French Jews, who face tough times in their native country, buy second homes like crazy. There is no formula for how life works here, but many Jewish people definitely want to be a part of this Holy Land.

* * *

Two loud army green apache helicopters hover close overhead and muffle the shrieks of joyful children in the pool. Even from my backyard, the pounding sound of their rotors vibrates through my body causing me to feel uneasy; I think about the pilots and soldiers safety in the helicopter, whose ominous responsibility it is to protect my family, their families and our country.

School is in the final days. Noa and her classmates, like members of the United Nations representing countries from all over the world, sit around the wood tables in our dining room studying all weekend. My only jobs are to serve food and drink and keep Kobe and Eden away from them. Trump Jr. simply does not turn in work rather continues to beat to the tune of his own lost drum. In a moment of delirium, thinking in the final hour I can remedy the situation with Aaron, I pressure him to turn in the last bits of homework, but his computer crashes and he is left with a blank screen—a perfect ending to the abysmal second semester of his 8th grade year.

* * *

Driving down Keren Hayasod this afternoon, the tall shady trees are full of bright yellow and orange flowers and these same colorful fallen petals dye the otherwise dreary sidewalk and street below with some cheer. The village crazy man stands in front of the Tavola Restaurant seeking rides from cars backed up at the street kikar and the two religious men in white congenially solicit stalled cars at the Rabin Intersection. Everything feels in its place today.

In the evening we attend Aaron's junior high school graduation ceremony. I feel cheated, as Aaron has made very little effort. For lack of a better reason for his problems, the school has told me to have him tested for ADD or ADHD. When he made honor roll first semester, he did not have signs of these disorders—perhaps he has a 'latent' case. In the graduation program, he gets mention for 'Persistent in Ceramics' while all the other students receive titles highlighted with the words excellence, enthusiasm, or even 'most persistent'. Aaron is simply 'persistent' in 'ceramics', an art class he never mentioned, causing me to laugh and cry at the same time. In my Pollyanna attempt to look at the bright side, I play the 'glad game' in my head; Aaron did not get caught cheating like Hamas's Mouse Farfour and he does not blame an entire nation for his problems—just his mother and father. As I watch the ceremony, I am comforted to see that Aaron looks happy with his group of friends.

Israel continues to be a great dichotomy for me; the quality of life is rich and interesting and yet a tinge of fear always flickers. This week, the threats that Syria will start a war with Israel this summer moves through the news causing me to feel great alarm and fear, yet at the same time, PM Olmert says he is ready to speak directly with Syria.

* * *

No waves and no ripples appear on the enormous translucent green sea offering a perfect view of the sandy sea floor. Droves of young Israelis congregate on the sand enjoying each other's company. As the day heats up and little clothing is worn, many tattoos are revealed. Israeli youth are in love with the bright colorful and decorative markings all over their bodies. I cannot help but make the odd comparison that the elder segment of the population was forced by the Nazis to be tattooed while today's youth independently and brazenly chooses to brand their bodies for life.

My teenage son does not join in any of the activities at the sea because he sleeps all day and is awake all night. Zoar, the contractor tells me his fourteen-year old son like many teens in Israel also has a nocturnal life. I have great difficulty accepting this for my kid even though it certainly cuts down on skin damage from the sun and potential altercations between us as we briefly meet alternately at the end of the day and in the early morning hours. Unfortunately for the sleeping prince, the Russian Ambassador and his wife come to tour the creamy white castle today in hopes of moving their ambassador's residence to our home when we depart. I have warned Aaron that the Russian Ambassador will enter the Trump Office and to be respectful. When they leave, the sleeping prince makes a midday surprise appearance to express his dismay that the Russians entered his room a couple of times and I had only warned him of one disturbance. After registering his complaint, he of course, goes back to sleep.

A couple of days later, I drop by the school to pick up the children's year-end records, and see a table by the front office with student's ceramics work. I call and wake up Aaron to ask for a description of his final ceramic work. Naively and maybe in maternal desperation, I think I can at least savor his work in a class that he received 'persistent in ceramics'. From his description I bring home a picasso-esque 'S' nosed figure with a black square around the left eye and a hat in the shape of George Washington's wig all in a lovely orange ceramic background color. Proudly I carry this art from my car and place it on the bookshelf in my office. Aaron notices the ceramic piece a few hours later and is shocked and reacts quite dramatically that from his description I have brought home this artwork that is definitely not his. As a mother, I fail once again not even able to preserve his ceramic glory at the American School.

* * *

A fresh breeze from the sea passes through the kibbutz and gently pushes dense orange-petaled flowers to drift off the large tree in front of the gan. They land forming a brilliant orange blanket on the dull cement. Many small children are outside laughing and screaming while playing in their second hand magical yards, as parents arrive by foot, bike and with carts to drop off their little ones for the day.

Yehuda and I sit with Kobe's teacher Nili whose tiny frame bursts as she commences her 8th month of pregnancy with twins. She enthusiastically shares with us Kobe's development and progress this year. He arrived at five-years old speaking not a word of Hebrew, he could barely hold a pencil, he did not paint much and he knew not a soul. Nine months later he flourishes, speaks native Hebrew, writes Hebrew letters, paints five-year old masterpieces, and has made dear friends. Spending a school year in Israel makes it feasible to mark the time and changes for each of my children and Kobe's development in this period of time is remarkable; moving around the world has enriched my smallest child who on his level has soaked into his essence the language, the land and the people.

Farfour, the man-size Hamas mouse, becomes a martyr in the latest episode. His dying grandfather played by a young actor with a keffiyeh on his head sits with Farfour under a tree and gives the white mouse, his grandson, two very symbolic items; a large key to use when the Palestinians liberate all of Israel and a rolled up paper document that shows their land before the Jews took over Palestine, he tells him to safeguard these items until the day they return to their land. Then the pretty little girl in a soft and lovely tone shares with the viewer despicable words about the Jews. The camera returns to the interrogation of a fearful Farfour by an Israeli agent in dark sunglasses who angrily tries to make him reveal his secret document. The Israeli agent proceeds to beat up the scared Farfour and in the midst of this violence, the scene once again cuts to the sweet girl who kindly tells the young and impressionable viewers that Farfour is a martyr who died at the hands of the Israelis.

* * *

Beautifully formed waves crash evenly on the shore this morning as I walk south to Daboosh Beach. In one of the small bays created by the man-made rocky breakwater, a lifeguard stands on a ha-si-kay paddling over and through the waves while a little girl sits cross-legged in front of him on the bow with a pastel colored life preserver around her waist. Nearby, an older woman lying over the front of a red sea kayak holding on for dear life is being safely returned to the shore by a kayaker wearing a blue helmet who swims in the water guiding her back to land. Spectators line up on the shore and watch the rescue mission of the safta and granddaughter who apparently drifted too far out to sea.

We sit outside with all the other parents and grandparents under a large tree for Kobe's graduation ceremony from the gan. All the children dress as different animals and Kobe is a proud pig. While pigs are not kosher, Kobe's version is delicious—besides strict dietary laws are not observed on this kibbutz. Kobe fidgets with his pig nose while he sings and dances with his friends in other animal costumes. Nili, who today looks like she swallowed a whole watermelon sits and narrates the show. Achinoam sings for us. Little children in the audience move around freely and we all enjoy our graduates and the warm air. Personally I am overwhelmed by the richness of experience this year has afforded my son and what a pleasure it has been for me as well. I have tried to hold on to time and experience, but markedly I realize they are fleeting and I must relish the moments like this one with my beautiful little pig before they pass.

Ar-ba-yeem Yo-meem (Forty Days)

In forty days, Noah built an ark and loaded it with two of each animal species. I now have just forty days until the finish of our year in Israel. The year has passed with great speed and at this point, it appears I will blink and my time will draw to a close. I have long given up on the naïve concept that this year would be a vacation. It is evident that life with four children and a busy husband does not allow for a great deal of down time regardless of what land I live in. The energy and the pace of the year have been exhilarating and there are still many things I want to do before I leave. Noah must have worked steadily and fast to finish his project and I now will make every effort to finish in my last forty days what I set out to accomplish at the beginning of the year.

* * *

Hundreds of young families bathe in the seawater, which appears to be an enormous clear bath this morning. Kobe, Eden and I join the festivities, floating effortlessly very far out to sea on our pink and blue water noodles with a pure and rare pleasure in the motionless water. We drift so far out that the people on the beach start to look like little ants and yet we still see the sandy sea floor just beneath us. The three of us enjoy our lazy sea journey together under the watchful embrace of my khaver— we laugh, we talk and we dream. We are free.

A few hours later as I watch the kids and their friends swimming in the pool, I read about continued fighting between Fatah and Hamas in Gaza.

The Palestinians appear to be engaged in a civil war, but no one is ready to mark the fighting with this title. Gaza's beaches must resemble ours here in Herzelia; I wish that Palestinian parents and children could also enjoy the sand, the sun and the water and mothers could drift with their small children out into the sea and talk and dream as we did. Instead, I fear the young are locked inside watching the likes of Mouse Farfour spread messages of hate and violence directed at my children and me.

Late in the afternoon Noa and Aaron appear. I have enjoyed a full day of activities and they have yet to begin anything. Last night they were at the United States Ambassador's residence playing poker with friends from school. Noa left early, but Aaron ignored his curfew, did not call and won lots of money. Aaron is definitely not a kid with ADD, but rather a disease called 'Entitlement', his passionate online poker training and live success with kids a few years older is proof that he can focus and succeed at whatever interests him.

* * *

Eden and I walk on the beach. I try to get her to walk a little faster and she reminds me she does not like to sweat. We run into Eden's classmate Austin and his mother Mary and join them for a pancake breakfast at C Restaurant on the sand. Mary's husband is with the US Army and they have lived all over the world and are currently stationed in Israel. After a large pancake meal, Eden and Austin run down the beach to watch another friend from school who is at surf camp. I enjoy the remarkable nature of the moment; Eden at nine-years old is unsupervised away from me safely on the sand and I do not worry that someone will harm her as I would in L.A., or for that matter, in most locales I have visited around the world. Until they return, Mary and I sit and talk about the school year and share stories about our lives on foreign soil.

* * *

Two fishermen wade in the shallow water at the northern beach checking their nets for fish and tangles. There are no waves in this rocky area of coastline, but the water is rough and bouncing all over these men. On the shore, many of the concave seashells I have collected all year line the beach and I quickly gather as many as I can hold. As I walk back down the beach, I feel something slimy against my palm and discover a live creature in one of the shells that has been caught off guard and popped his head out to say "shalom."

Eden and I have a farewell lunch at Rocca with Shiraz and Johanna who are leaving for the summer in Switzerland. Eden and Shiraz have become inseparable this year playing, dancing and sleeping over at each other's houses every weekend. They have developed a lifelong friendship and Eden will miss Shiraz, but the Internet and travels will surely re-unite these two young women. Likewise, I shall miss Johanna and her friendship as well—she has been an important part of my journey this year.

After lunch, the children are swimming in the pool when a delegation of Chinese businessmen descends upon our creamy white castle. One of these gentlemen with a congenial smile says "Shalom," to Eden, as she is about to jump in the pool. The large contingency walks through the castle checking every nook and cranny with their American broker, a woman I recognize from my walks each morning. When the Chinese finish their domestic investigation, the broker returns to inform me that they love the castle and will be putting in an offer. I smile to think the Chinese are up against the Russians, who desperately want the castle and are waiting for approval from Moscow—the making of an international confrontation.

* * *

After a short drive form Herzelia, I find myself in another world called Bnei Barak, a predominantly Haredi city where Doron the taxi driver has brought me to find an authentic silver tza-da-kah (charity) box that I want to bring back to a friend in L.A. The large boulevards of Bnei Barak are lined with stores that sell kosher food, kosher clothing and a wide variety of religious items. Everything in this overpopulated and poor city is under rabbinical supervision and on Shabbat the stores are all closed and the residents walk to synagogue. There are no blue and white Israeli flags in sight. I find it fascinating to be in this ultra orthodox neighborhood where the men are dressed in black suits with black wide brim hats and the women are modestly dressed in long skirts, long sleeved tops and wigs, scarves and hats. The Hare-deem population believe themselves to be directly in line with the teachings of Moses and the giving of the Torah on Mount Sinai—the name 'Haredi' means 'one who trembles in awe of God'. I know these folks believe me to be far from an authentic Jew and honestly, I am not sure I have much respect for their lifestyles either, but I do prescribe for everyone being free to chose for themselves a level and form of religious observance. I also find it amazing how the religious control their followers' use of Internet, believing it poisons their minds. One group of religious Jews, the Gerrer Hassidim are trying to remove completely Internet access as computers bring 'spiritual danger' to their followers. I cannot imagine trying to remove Internet access from my children. Actually, I would fear for all of our 'spiritual well-being' if it were taken away from them.

Ky-tz (Summer)

The heat and humidity of ky-tz (summer) truly arrives. Up until now it has been hot, but suddenly the temperature is cranked up and the air fills with dense moisture. We have come full circle, as this is the weather that welcomed us when we arrived in Israel almost one year ago. The windows of the house in mid afternoon are layered with water as the hot moist air outside meets with the artificial cold air inside along the glass. A year ago we did not have working air-conditioning and now as we plan our departure the air-conditioning works brilliantly.

I also see changes in my nocturnal adolescent son. He appears to be happy even if he still cannot reveal this emotion to me. His group of friends now includes a beautiful redhead named Tamara who spends a great deal of time at our house. The tall beauty actually speaks to me and Aaron is much nicer when she is around, which is a definite bonus in the last 40 days; Tamara is another 'unspoken' reason why Aaron prefers to live in Israel and attend the American School next year—I am certain it is not the academics that captivate him.

Hamas militants have taken over Gaza and they patrol the streets killing the Fatah opposition. A group of masked men ransacks the office of President Abbas in Gaza City and proudly poses for photos victoriously standing on his desk. President Abbas who resides in Ramallah these days calls for a state of emergency and solidifies his hold in the West Bank. There are essentially two Palestinian governments on two different Palestinian territories with Israel wedged in the middle. Bombings take place at Palestinian refugee camps in Lebanon as leaders try to root out the Al Qaeda forces that have infiltrated and spread the beliefs of Osama Bin Laden among the locals. The term 'refugee camps' always strikes me, as these are in fact cities where people have worked and lived for many years, but the term is utilized to hold on to the fact that the original residents were displaced people by the creation of Israel. It would be the equivalent of making many cities in Israel 'refugee camps' for the displaced Jews of Poland, Germany and Russia after World War II or the displaced Jews from Muslim Arab nations like Egypt, Syria, Iraq and Yemen who left penniless over the last sixty years due to religious intolerance and persecution. The Palestinians have never been assimilated into the other Arab nations in order to keep the plight of the Palestinians alive and it is apparent that the neighboring Arab nations have not wanted to absorb them.

* * *

Thousands of jellyfish that look like little extra-terrestrial space ships have landed on the beach. Dangling tentacles surround their large round translucent bodies and smaller jellyfish have a streak of purple running through their bodies. They arrive at the warm sand riding in the waves at high tides where they are abandoned to slowly dissolve like the Wicked Witch of the West at the end of the Wizard of Oz. Others still alive fill the shallow water and move at the mercy of the current. Only a few very brave souls enter the dangerous water during the days of the jellyfish, as their sting is painful and scarring. Even in areas where there are no apparent sea phantoms, particles from their tentacles break off and easily sting the unsuspecting.

Yehuda is on a business trip to Italy and Spain. Kobe's best friend Eli comes over with his family to swim and I sit with his parents speaking in Hebrew about our children, their lives on the kibbutz and politics in Israel while the children's laughter and screams emanate from the pool. I no longer break my tongue to speak the language and feel the ease of stating my opinions in these foreign words. We eat cold watermelon, bamba, sunflower seeds and Yigal's schnitzel. It is Shabbat and this is all that is meant to happen on this pleasurably forced day off from running, working and shopping. I will miss this tradition when we move back to L.A.—I feel like a true Israeli today.

Eden prepares for her ballet and hip-hop recital dancing through meals, in the pool, in the mall and in her dreams. She is in constant motion and exudes pure pleasure in her movement. She plays with her friend Jade from ballet class whose family made Aliyah from England last summer. I look at Eden and it is hard to believe that she is the same little girl who started school almost a year earlier with no friends. Her experiences this year have made her fiercely independent—all that she was before but now acutely so.

Noa is in typical Israeli teen mode; she goes out all night and sleeps most of the day, waking to tan a few hours when her busy schedule allows. Even after this year in Israel, I am still fearful when she is out at a club or sits at a coffee house late at night, but ironically I feel she is safe walking with a girlfriend down the dark streets in the middle of the night. At sixteen, Noa is indifferent to any danger. She reminds me of the swimmers who continue to enter the water regardless of the hundreds of poisonous jellyfish. I know that young people in this world must be resilient and unafraid in order to stay happy and healthy, but secretly I would like to hold her close and tight. As I learn to accept that which I have no control over, I hear in my head the phrases 'Al-ti-da-gee' and 'Ha kol yi-he-yay be-seder'.

Hamas has gained control of Gaza and all foreigners have departed with the exception of Gilad Shalit, the kidnapped Israeli soldier and Allen Johnson, the kidnapped BBC reporter. From Damascus, Hamas leader (Khaled) Mashel declares that this period of anarchy is necessary to bring calm to the people and that Hamas intends to uphold the Unity Government once the violence is under control. Meanwhile on the ground, it looks like senseless killing of Palestinians by Palestinians. In Ramallah, President Abbas appoints Salam Fayad as Prime Minister to lead the new Fatah government in the West Bank creating two Palestinian Prime Ministers—one for Fatah and one for Hamas. The Israelis prepare to release $300 million dollars to President Abbas who desperately needs these funds to pay for government workers and breath some prosperity back into the West Bank; Abbas also promises that some of the money will be used to support the poor people of Gaza.

* * *

I join a group of Jewish leaders from L.A. who are on a mission to Israel; today they learn about PACT, Parents and Children Together, a program that is designed to support and help Ethiopian Jews integrate into the Israeli society. My friend Beryl is one of the group's leaders and I happily tag along to learn and to enjoy a friend. Many of these Ethiopian families immigrated to Israel in the last few years with no formal education; they arrived unfamiliar with modern appliances, but through PACT, the children and their parents receive extra training and support. We arrive to a gan in the city of Bet Shemesh (house of sun) where Ethiopian children learn amongst Sabra children. I meet Gideon, a native of L.A. who runs these assimilation programs with great passion and I hear heart-warming stories of local families who personally get involved to make the transition for these children and their families happier and more successful. Throughout the morning, Gideon guides us through the program as we watch five-year old children happily ensconced in Israeli life and language regardless of origin or skin color. We meet Stella, one of Bet Shemesh's deputy mayors and a Russian immigrant who is an enthusiastic advocate for this program. The image of Farfour remains with me even after his recent dramatic death as a Hamas martyr. I think about the time, the money and the dedication that programs like PACT require to work with children and make them productive and successful members of society, while Hamas finances the Al Aksa TV station which through programs like the Pioneers of Tomorrow instead of raising the people up, keeps the Palestinian children down, teaching them to hate the children of Israel.

In the evening Beryl and I eat dinner together on the terrace of Manta Ray, a fish restaurant on Tel Aviv's beach well known for its platters of delicious salads and mouth watering salty flat bread. I admire Beryl greatly; she is a widow with a flock of beautiful grandchildren, who dedicates her life to the Jewish people. As we discuss her work, I am more convinced that we need women like Beryl and Stella or community organizers like Gideon who work with children and their families in the field to cultivate shalom and coexistence through local programs. These individuals are desperately missing in peace efforts in the Middle East where the predominant focus is on men in suits negotiating and making agreements. I sit drinking my wine and breathing in the warm sea air; this day has served to energize the hope I have for shalom and tolerance in Israel and personally I enjoy the nourishment of an old friend sharing this evening with me.

I drive home late at night along the busy Tel Aviv boardwalk packed with people walking in the hot humid air, a great escape and no doubt a cooler destination than their naturally heated sticky apartments in the city. Crowds stroll along the brightly lit Mediterranean boardwalk; people eating ice cream, parents pushing babies in strollers, children chasing balloons, couples walking arm in arm and street vendors selling art and jewelry. A simple, easy happiness mixed with energy and passion emanates from the crowds on this warm evening as everyone appears to enjoy the night together—images I capture and will carry next to the inspirational ones I took earlier of the varied children joyfully learning side by side.

* * *

White puffy cotton clouds outlined by a streak of orange light fill the darkening gray sky at dusk along the horizon. Handicapped children in wheelchairs visit my khaver; some sitting in their wheelchairs while others sit and stand with help in the shallow wash of seawater. Further up the beach, families celebrate the end of the school year (public schools are just finishing) making fresh pita on two taboons set atop fires, as the kids run around on the sand and their parents recline on straw carpets. Nearby, two large Arab women wearing long black dresses lounge in the shallow water and gleefully converse while a few little boys in shorts and tank tops swim and splash around them.

Aaron and Noa's funds have dried up. They are united in their effort to argue with me and attempt to persuade me to sign on to their Israeli

Teenage Freedom Plan which entitles them to lots of freedom, no responsibility and great volatility, all of which I am to fund. I watch the Palestinians battle each other and the Israelis and it reminds me of my teenagers who fight me and each other with little principle and no real goals other than to stir things up and evoke frustration and anger. Once President Abbas of Fatah announces the new Palestinian government he has established from his Ramallah headquarters in the West Bank, President Haniyeh of Hamas in Gaza claims the new West Bank government is illegal. Before the Israelis could not make shalom with one Palestinian government and now we have two separate governments on two separate territories each with its own very different agendas.

I still yearn to meet with Israeli and Palestinian mothers who want shalom; we could share our frustrations while we work jointly to discover ways to guide and help our children, our men and our nations. Whether we lie in the shallow waters of the Mediterranean fully dressed or sit eating watermelon and cracking sunflower seeds, we need to unite. We must say "Lo" to destruction and hate. I remind myself that this is the land of miracles and while shalom seems unattainable, one can dream the impossible in these parts.

Katusha Rockets hit Northern Israel—the first since the end of the Second Lebanon War last summer.

* * *

Doron arrives at the creamy white castle early in the morning dressed in a bright orange t-shirt and even brighter orange Crocs to take us on a journey to the Yam Ha Me-lakh (Dead Sea). We drive for an hour south toward Kastina, the city where the accused rapist and ex-president Katzav lives and home to the newest BIG Shopping Center in its final days of construction. The sites are intriguing as we drive away from Kastina on a country highway; we pass a Bedouin shepherd tending to a huge flock of brown and white sheep grazing on cleared wheat crops; fields of yellow and brown sunflowers drying in the scorching sun; a group of soldiers with heavy backpacks engaging in training exercises on a hillside in the depressing desert heat; a sign directing us to Hebron in one direction and Gaza in the other; and a patch of my grandfather's pine tree forests on the gentle hillside. Just before the city of Dimona and in the middle of nowhere there is a yellow camel-crossing sign on the side of the road and a few kilometers later three camels sit out in front of a small Bedouin village with their heads propped up proudly. Doron tells us that the Bedouins are camel traders suiting their typically nomadic existence. Traditionally Bedouins travel from place to place but Israeli Bedouins have learned to build and settle in villages and cities and this land becomes theirs after many years of populating the area—squatter's rights.

Doron drives his white Mercedez cab along the winding and narrow roller coaster road framed by the dramatic brown and orange sand-swept rocks; we pass two burros tending to a herd of goats and on one curve alone there are four separate metal monuments honoring lives lost in automobile accidents. As we rapidly descend to the lowest point on the earth our ears fill with pressure and there are no more signs of life until the hazy Yam Ha Me-lakh comes into focus, which in itself is not really a sign of life. All of our phones start to beep; welcome notices from Jordan's Fastlink Cell Phone Company. The Jordanians appear very happy that we have arrived at 400 meters (1312 feet) below sea level, the lowest land point in the world shared by a Jewish and an Arab nation. Their cellular phone company obviously has no issues with borders. The Yam Ha Me-lakh is flat and murky and filled with vast and thick white salt deposits and its shores are lined with a row of shiny hotels offering wonderful spa packages. We continue further along the hazy sea and stop at a snack stand and souvenir store. Eden, alongside two German tourists, rummages through all the products along the shelves; Dead Sea Salts, mud skin treatment kits, beauty creams and wooden figurines in the shapes of Christian Crosses, Stars of David and camels. Three young Bedouin girls with their heads covered walk by at the same time as five Israeli soldiers in their khakis each carrying the three tools for survival in Israel: Uzis, bottles of Eden Water and cell phones.

We drive further along the receding tan shores until we arrive at Kibbutz Ein Gedi, a simple spa set in a large building with dressing rooms, a cafeteria and lounging area. The girls and I huddle off to the side of the large changing room. I watch Eden's curious eight-year old eyes studying the older rounder women as they change their clothing. I am quickly reminded of a trip I took to a spa, Murieta Hot Springs with my mother and grandmother when I was a little girl and my first shocking encounter with older naked women and their large and drooping breasts. I am amused to think I understand my child's surprise and at the same time when I look in the mirror I realize that each day I am closer to being one of those women.

Outside in the incredibly intense sun, we cake our bodies with dark brown gooey mud rich in sulfur and other natural minerals leaving only our eyes and lips exposed. We are surrounded by many other visitors chatting and waiting on plastic chairs in the shade of wooden gazebos also covered in mud. I move like a stiff robot as the mud aided by this brutal heat dries quickly and tightens on my skin. After, I stand under the pounding outdoor shower, which is a mixture of naturally warm water and nasty smelling sulfur, a similar scent to rotten eggs. I tolerate all of this as I've read that sulfur works to promote metabolism and communication between nerve cells and for thousands of years has aided skin ailments and chronic arthritis. At this point in my life—thankfully this treatment is only a preventative measure. The next shower is fresh warm water and finally I can comfortably re-open my eyes. The shore of the Yam Ha Melakh used to arrive at the edge of the Ein Gedi Spa, but due to evaporation and decreased rainfall, the waterfront is now about a kilometer from the Spa. Noa, Eden and Doron take a small shuttle bus, but I set off in my wet bathing suit walking through the desert on the parched road with a bottle of Eden Water. The dry air cooks my body; I feel very small and alone as I walk along this desert road, but the vast, beige scenery is tremendous. At the sea we float in the warm, dense salty water and no matter what position we find ourselves in, the thick saltwater forces us back to the surface. The salty water burns Eden and she runs out to hose herself with fresh water from the side of the lifeguard's station. We lounge in the water with a few Arab couples, a family of American tourists, a large group of Russians, and two girls floating and reading books. Noa and I dream that we float hand in hand all the way across the sea to Jordan where we meet and greet the Jordanians who had so warmly welcomed us earlier in the day.

We depart Ein Gedi and drive by the majestic ruins of Masada high up on the mountain, the world-renowned Ahava skin products factory and the Qumran Caves that remained sealed for almost 2000 years until a Bedouin shepherd discovered them sixty years ago. Forty years later, the Qumran Scrolls, the oldest manuscript of the Hebrew Bible were re-discovered and celebrated. The ride toward Jerusalem continues as we pass a group of proud camels loitering the side of the road, stores selling ceramic garden pottery, the Palestinian cities of Jericho and Ramallah in the distance, vacant police check points and Wadi Keli where monks live in isolation. We pass another military checkpoint staffed with young soldiers equipped with Uzis and arrive at the Palestinian neighborhoods of East Jerusalem where the landscape fills with dense apartment-packed neighborhoods set behind barbed wire fences bordering the road recalling to my memory the paintings on exhibit in Tel Aviv a few months back.

While East Jerusalem appears calm, Palestinians in Gaza gun down their brethren trying to escape into Israel at the Erez Checkpoint where looters already pillaged the checkpoint facilities; disparage across the border results in truckloads of bananas and plums not being delivered into Gaza. Trash piles high through the cities. Hamas killed and murdered to achieve this control and now blames all the problems on Fatah, Israel and the West. I have learned that this is the mode of the Islamic terrorists; they are never responsible for societal problems and they are not held to any standards of accountability by fellow Palestinians, Muslims, world leaders, the press or some free democratic nations throughout the world.

* * *

Rushing seawater meets me as I descend to visit with my khaver. I enjoy our solidarity and relish the cool morning air that I know is brief and worthy of appreciation. Thousands of rusty tan sea sponges formed like sticky wads of pasta and full of twists and caverns have washed up on shore adding beautiful texture to the shells and rocks on the wet sand. On the sea, a small white fishing boat sways with the motion of the water; its sole passenger sits on the stern of the boat peacefully fishing and waiting.

I return home as Aaron, who is officially nocturnal, begins his slumber. He and his friends find refuge in the Trump Office after they hang out in the kikar or at the beach late at night, but none of them appear to do anything productive or active during their summer. I note with some appreciation an impressive and carefully constructed sculpture featuring hundreds of Dr Pepper cans on his desk. Shortly I will send Aaron to camp in the USA where I hope he will become reacquainted with reality before school in America commences in September. Life for the rest of us is a composition of activities; Yehuda travels to Spain; Eden and Jade spend their afternoons choreographing dances; Kobe spends a great deal of time with his friends on the kibbutz; and Noa's friend Jessie arrives from L.A. on a mission to learn the behavior of Israeli teens before they leave for a program in Greece. I continue to juggle everyone and everything finding humor in my original premise that this year would be a break for me to unwind and regenerate myself. Late at night I get into bed glued to my mini-iPod catching up with The Daily Show and my friend John Stewart, who with humor, reminds me to poke fun at the intensity of my family's life as well as political life in Israel.

$$* * *$$

I wake at 4:00am to drive Noa and Jessie to the airport; they are leaving for a two-week program on the Greek Island of Lesbos. When we leave, Aaron and Noa hug and exchange secret best friend whispers. Their screams and battles make me nutty, but I appreciate this brief moment where they display true affection. I am comforted and reminded that underneath the veil of fighting, my children depend on each other intensely and appreciate each other. I drive along the dark highway drinking my coffee to wake up; the girls who have not slept all night are still fully awake and chat excitedly—they will sleep well on their flights to Lesbos.

The airport is a loud and bright Mecca of activity with crowds of pilgrims at this painfully early and dark hour. Noa is in a hurry to check in and say good-bye to her German Ecuadorian friend Eric who also travels this morning. This is the same Eric who I found lounging on Noa's bed when we first arrived this year and whom I feared might be lice infested. At the security zone, Noa says goodbye to me in a quick business like motion. I know I am up against Eric, who waits for her by the Arcaffe Kiosk inside the terminal to share a final teen moment. As I watch her walk through the glass doors I start to cry confused tears; I am happy for the break in teenage drama but sad to see my child leave.

I return home to walk along the dim shoreline joined by schools of phantom jellyfish abandoned over the night to melt into the warm sand. The only sign of active life is a large group of black birds feasting on left over trash. As I walk, I replay the Hallmark moment where Noa and Aaron embraced and said goodbye. They will be separated for two months. I remain melancholy throughout the day; struggling with the uncanny parallel I find between my battling and many times warring teens and the Palestinians and the Israelis who both under completely different circumstances, fight intensely and yet really do depend on each other. The embrace Noa and Aaron shared did not end the battle but cohesiveness and the need for survival were present. I know that the Israel— Palestinian conflict is utterly complicated and long-fueled and it is a bit ridiculous that I trivialize it and compare it to my offspring, but I watch the divergence intently and study those who strive for resolutions; there is great disconnect between the people who need shalom and the leaders who need to retain power and have their egos massaged. At the end of the day, the Jews and the Muslims are ancient cousins. We are all the children of Abraham and we need to embrace each other.

* * *

Thousands of petite yellow flowers creep along the rough limestone ridges of the beach cliffs. Within a few miles of rocky coastline are hotels, apartments, homes of poor beach dwellers, villas of wealthy Israelis, the American Ambassador's residence, ancient ruins, a mosque, a marina and a mall—all coming together and demonstrating a diverse coexistence in a small territory.

Marcelle and Shabtai stay with us even more frequently these days. Time is running out to properly feed and spoil their grandchildren before they depart; Safta is on standby to cook for Prince Aaron when he wakes and Saba is on standby at eighty-nine years old to run to the market for Safta and to buy Kinder Chocolate Eggs for Kobe.

We go to see the musical Mama Mia at the Nokia Theater, a converted basketball stadium owned by the phone company Nokia. Even after renovations, the theater acoustically still sounds like a stadium, but the beauty of the show is that five thousand Israelis as the background chorus sing each word of every song in English with a Hebrew accent in this energetic production imported from London.

I fall asleep reading an article about destitute Bedouins living in Egypt near the Rafah Crossing who dig tunnels to aid Palestinian weapon smugglers bringing goods from Egypt into Gaza. While the majority of Palestinians live in poverty and medical care is inadequate, Hamas leadership has funds available to dig tunnels and pay for weaponry to fight and bring destruction to Israel. One of the greatest ironies perpetuated by a conveniently blind world.

* * *

Large tarps that have covered the fields of the kibbutz for the last few weeks have been removed to expose the rough tilled soil. The old days where the members of a kibbutz worked the land with their bare hands are long gone and have been replaced by imported Thai workers dressed and draped in bright colored cloth from their heads to their toes like multi-colored fabric dolls. Rows of these faceless individuals bend down, inserting small plants in straight lines along the tilled dirt and while I have no idea what they are planting, I am intrigued and pull over to the side of the road to watch.

Late in the afternoon I meet Kobe for another year-end gan party. Kobe has a blast with his posse of friends jumping, climbing, and swinging on blow-ups filled with water. For a while, I sit alone under a broad tree enjoying the shade and the celebrating children. I am keenly aware of the amazing indulgences granted to the youth juxtaposed to the crazy and dangerous nature of life in Israel. Kobe and I roll out bread dough and hand it to a boy fourteen years old, my son Aaron's age, who then places it in the portable oven. After a few minutes, the free-formed bread comes out crisp on the outside and doughy fresh on the inside. Kobe proudly spreads Nutella all over the surface. I cannot help but stare in awe at this teenager who participates responsibly and happily with an activity on his kibbutz; Aaron and Noa cannot wash a dish in our house without rolling their eyes let alone helping their siblings on a project without voicing discontent. I blame myself for enabling this to occur. Before long, Kobe discovers Gordon dishing out ice cream and in his second hand, he takes a small cone as well. A fitting example of indulgence, my Kobe is in gastronomical heaven.

* * *

I stand with my husband and small children on the hot and windy beach holding many red and orange balloons with hand written messages on their surfaces to release in honor of my father's birthday—he passed away four years ago, but his memory is still very much alive in all of us. Even Kobe who was very little when he died reveres his grandfather. We stand in front of the Oceanus building just below our new apartment and the children release the bright balloons. Watching them fly, Kobe asks with concern, "What if they go to someone else and not to grandfather?" I assure him that he will get our messages and that he is smiling somewhere up in the sky enjoying his grandchildren's attention.

In the Western Galilee, thousands of people release white balloons with blue strings to show solidarity for the three soldiers who were kidnapped last year and to mark the one-year anniversary of the abduction of Gilad Shalit. Over the airways, we have just heard a brief message from Gilad telling his parents and his country that his health is failing him and he needs an extensive hospital stay—this young man is being held prisoner by Khattab Shaheed Iz Al-Din Al-Qassam, a military wing of Hamas in Gaza. Near Gilad in Gaza, Alan Johnson, a BBC reporter is being held in a neighborhood controlled by the Doghmush Clan members of The Army of Islam. He appears in another released video wearing an explosive belt telling Hamas not to invade the compound or the captors will kill him. While Hamas oversees Gaza and Fatah the West Bank, each party and territory consists of different splinter groups with their own agendas and strategies wedged into the social fabric. At the end of the day, I am confident that my deceased father will get the message that his grandchildren sent to him, but unconvinced that the live captors of these men will receive the message that these white balloons carry.

* * *

Lounging in the shallow water each morning, a large old lady wearing a bright pink bathing cap holds court with a few other older women all sporting different colored bathing caps; none of the head cover as bright as hers and none of the women as large or domineering as the lady in pink. I am not a jealous person but today as the pink cap woman lounges in the comfortable shallow water, chats with her girlfriends and enjoys her time, I silently envy her. In contrast to her ease and comfort, the sand where I walk is rich and difficult to pass through. With each step my shoes sink deep and quickly the sand particles fill in my socks and between my toes.

Before I take the stairs up to the street, I stop to remove the tar that has collected on the bottom of my shoes. In the summer months, tar is abundant along the sandy beaches and the metal bins with rough rotating brushes are filled with acetone to aid in this removal process. It would make sense based on the excessive tar on the beaches that Israel would have its share of oil reserves, but unlike her neighbors Eretz Israel is not rich in oil. As I clean the caked-on tar from my shoes, a tall older gentleman with white hair and a large Cheshire cat smile asks me in Hebrew why I am cleaning my shoes. In my defense, I lift my foot before I realize that he just wants to talk. He introduces himself, "Ani Victor" (I am Victor) and comes over to shake my hand while another older gentleman approaches and yells out to him in Hebrew, "I am going to tell your wife." We all smile. I have seen Victor and his friend walking for the last year and time has created familiarity, which changes everything in Israeli society.

* * *

At night while the intense sun rests and the temperature decreases, the humidity rises creating a powerful natural sauna. Storks in the Jordan Valley where it is 40 degrees Celsius (104 degrees Fahrenheit) work intensely to ensure that their newly hatched chicks remain cool; the male storks carry water in their beaks to spray the chicks in between shading them from the sun and placing small water soaked bales of hay by them to decrease the temperature of their immediate surrounding. Many people in mass flock to the malls escaping the oppressive natural conditions into the artificially cold shelter where they play, eat and enjoy their 'time', which is a precious commodity that cannot be wasted in an unpredictable Israeli world. The kids and I spend hours idly in the pool and by the warm sea eating watermelon and sucking on popsicles while feeling wet and dirty. Under normal circumstances I would complain, but here in Israel I actually enjoy and seize the time to be sweaty and shiny.

Over the last month, six hundred refugees from the Sudan, Eritrea, Ivory Coast and Ethiopia have entered Israel from Egypt walking through the brutal Sinai Desert to escape the poverty and killing that takes place in their homelands. While the IDF and government agencies publicly spar over who is responsible for the care of these refugees, most of the work falls on benevolent private individuals and organizations. I cannot help but find a grain of humor thinking that Jews in the Bible wandered the desert for forty years and these desperate souls arrive by foot to the Holy Land in just a couple of weeks.

* * *

We drive to the hotel Mizpe-Hayamim (literally 'view of the seas') in the North to join our family for a pre-nuptials celebration the week before my nephew's wedding. In less than two hours, we pass the large coastal city of Netanya, the fisheries near Hadera, the hills of Haifa, and up to Rosh Pina near the border of Lebanon and then make our way East. The summer landscape has turned from green to yellow and brown, as many fields lie fallow in the baking heat.

We stop at the BIG Shopping Center in Karmiel (literally the 'vineyard of G-d'), a Jewish Israeli city in the Galilee surrounded by many Israeli Arab cities and villages. The shoppers as well as the salespeople are a healthy mix of Jews and Arabs who live side-by-side appearing to get along and respect each other even if it is simply in the bubble of a shopping center. This energy reinforces my belief that Jews and Arabs can co-exist; the simplicity of walking through the stores and seeing people getting along elates me. In the parking lot, I admire three beautiful, young Arab women in long black dresses with white tight fitting head covers accompanied by two young men in black pants and long black coats with white caps (like ski caps) on their heads. It is over one hundred degrees and terribly humid; they look fresh carrying their bags while I, sweaty, dirty and in awe, admire them. My excitement is tempered, however, when I recall that last summer, Hezbollah sent hundreds of missiles from Southern Lebanon into this region with no regard to the fact that their Muslim brethren populate this area and these folks did not speak out against these attacks on them or their country.

Leaving the highway, we twist around the mountain roads arriving at the empty streets of the mystic and artistic city of Safed where in the late afternoon the locals have retired to their homes to prepare for Shabbat. The religious believe that the Messiah, when he arrives, will come to Jerusalem from the city of Safed, but for the time being many tourists visit Safed for the religious flavor, artist galleries and stunning views on their way to Jerusalem. On the other side of the city, we wind down the narrow road until we find the hotel's camouflage entrance along the barren hillside. Inside Mizpe-Hayamim is an oasis; lush plants and fruit trees, crops of fresh vegetables and small barns and enclosures full of farm animals that produce milk for fresh cheeses—all of the food here is homegrown and organic and the field to table time is limited to hours.

We sit with Safta and Saba in the lobby and enjoy cake and tea from the large bar featuring teas, herbs and spices with descriptions of the natural remedies they produce. We walk to our room through hallways full of mature trees and plants and I feel as though I am in a fragrant and fresh jungle. Our room is beautifully decorated with elegant, handcrafted furniture. Mizpe-Hayamim is one of two Relais & Chateau Hotels in Israel, and while it has all the finest details, it is very down to earth and symbolic of the Israeli experience of turning a Biblical desert into a green and livable country.

The views from our balcony are stunning; the city of Tiberias and the Sea of Galilee, where Jesus once walked on the water and now resort hotels line its shores; the Golan Heights where Yehuda and his division climbed during the 6-Day War to capture the land from the attacking Syrians; Mount Hermon where Eden and I skied a few months earlier; the Hula Valley, a wetland of flora and fauna where birds, migrating and local all thrive; and the city of Rosh Pina where vast yellow and green fields are filled with houses and villages. Early in the evening, the yellow full moon hovers low along the landscape and as it rises over the Sea of Galilee the round ball becomes lighter and brighter. I watch everything this weekend through the lenses of a movie camera viewing both families—the Iraqis from Ramat Hasharon and the Georgians from Ashdod—over one hundred people many meeting for the first time and now merging into one large family which is a distinct fabric of Israel. Through my camera's lense, I realize that I am getting older; the growing lines at the corner of my eyes should have been enough of a sign that I am farther removed from the younger generation getting married and having babies. The weekend is an enchanting and loving celebration—lots of meals, speeches, songs, ice cream and a serious ping-pong tournament, which in the final round is won by the Georgians.

* * *

We drive back through Nazareth, where Yehuda and his Arab partners are building a BIG Shopping Center in the same neighborhood where thousands of years ago, Jesus of Nazareth, the Jewish son of G-d ran around and played as a child. Nazareth is divided into Upper Nazareth, a city mostly populated by Jews and Lower Nazareth, an enormous sprawling Arab city with narrow streets crowded with old stone residences, mosques, churches and museums; men and women dress traditionally in burkas and abayas; and storefronts with all the signs in Arabic overflowing with merchandise. Driving through Nazareth is a journey to a foreign land—I recognize little of the Israel that I have lived in and traveled through this year. We arrive at the huge vacant lot of the next BIG Shopping Center to be shared by the Arab and Jewish citizens of both Nazareths. They have just finished very complicated and expensive leveling to prepare the ground for a large shopping center. I look at the enormous dirt field and imagine a beautiful mall and even more impressive, I see the potential that a Jew, a Muslim and a Christian have when they work together.

* * *

2500 years ago, Phoenicians first settled in the Apollonia ruins overlooking the Mediterranean Sea and over the years many different groups of people conquered and settled in this prime real estate constructing cities full of villas with a sophisticated water system and surrounded by a moat. I have admired Apollonia's fortress walls from the beach this year but today after a two-minute drive from our castle, Yehuda, Kobe, Eden and I actually climb amongst the partially excavated ruins exploring every nook and cranny. The remodeling of our apartment actually looks like the remains of Apollonia these days; walls are partially erected to frame the different rooms. And even in disrepair, the views of the Mediterranean are stunning.

Sof Sof (The End)

At the edge of a grassy bluff overlooking the Mediterranean a family of robins flies around the lunch table happily singing; they are not bothered by the incredible heat, but enjoy the fresh sea air and the gentle breeze. Today the sun-drenched panorama feels as though a painter has brushed the scenery with a broad stroke and accented every color— radiant green grass, a shimmering aqua sea and gorgeous bright blue skies. I dine with my new friend Joan at Rocca, the restaurant that has become like my second kitchen. We eat breakfast as our feathered friends steal bread and cheese straight from our plates. Not even a 'shoo' deters the robins from their mission; these birds like so many in the Holy Land are adamant about their right to stay and eat. Joan, the wife of the United States Ambassador and a weathered expert on living in foreign countries shares a similar story with so many Israelis; she too lost family during the Holocaust.

I return home from lunch to find the creamy white castle taken over by the Russian Ambassador's staff measuring rooms and investigating the property. The Chinese Ambassador also fell in love with the elegance and glamour of the creamy white castle, but in the final hour, the Chinese realized that they could not take the residence, because there was no gas to operate the woks required for their cooking. I know the Russians will appreciate the rich design and the complicated Bite Ha-ham technology as they have the staff ready to operate all the systems that I single handedly have failed to master.

Alan Johnston, the BBC reporter is free after being held as a prisoner in Gaza for 114 days. He is delivered at dawn to Prime Minister Haniyeh's house and photographed eating breakfast with prominent Hamas leaders before he leaves Gaza by car with British consular officials. Johnston was held by a man named Mumtaz Doghmush, the leader of the Army of Islam who controls a dangerous Gaza neighborhood closed off by burnt out cars, trash and barbed wire and patrolled by his armed followers. This group kidnaps foreign journalists to bargain for their concerns like the release of a Moslem cleric held by a foreign country. Johnston explains that Doghmush became very nervous after Hamas took Gaza over by force, as he could not operate without the cloak of chaos that had previously existed. Johnston was ultimately released after Hamas militia encircled the Doghmush compound and a religious figure issued a fat-wa (religious decree) demanding Doghmush free Johnston. Doghmush, a very religious man was greatly impressed by this fat-wa and was assured that if Johnston was unharmed his group could keep its weaponry. Many believe that the Doghmush clan was involved in Gilad Shalit's kidnapping, but he remains a prisoner.

In the evening, Yehuda and I meet PM Olmert at the United States Ambassador's 4th of July party. We arrive by foot and wait amongst hundreds of guests in long security lines on the closed off street to go through medal detectors—at least we all do not have to remove our shoes. Inside, the sprawling estate is decorated with red, white and blue balloons and American flags and the yard is packed with thousands of Israelis, foreign ambassadors and expatriates who mingle on the rolling grass lawns eating food from American vendors like McDonalds and Domino Pizza. Even with a cold beer in hand, Yehuda is miserable with the crowds of people and the quality of the food—he would be happy watching television at home eating a pita stuffed with humus. I on the other hand, feel like I have arrived in America and I love the pomp and circumstance of celebrating my country's independence. I still look around crowds full of foreign ambassadors and hold out hope that one of these foreign leaders will aid in the Middle East peace process. I equate it to the book—Where is Waldo?—where viewers search on pages full of detailed art work and after a long hard look find the small blended-in

Waldo character in a variety of scenes. From the stage, US Ambassador Jones, Acting Israeli President Dalia Itzik and PM Olmert all speak in English about the special relationship between our two countries. Both nations' national anthems are followed by a spectacular fire works show that lights the sky. As we walk home on the sidewalk above the Mediterranean Sea, I realize how much I loved visiting America for a few hours, but I am not yet quite ready to go back.

* * *

Ha-vat Ronit (Ronit's Farm) was once a working farm, but now is a popular party venue; many dunams of a lush and green oasis surround a large lake with floating lily pads creating the feeling of Monet's Giverny Garden in central Israel. Silver-serving dishes and flickering candles garnish the crisp white linen covered tables that accent the fresh green landscape of the wedding my sister-in-law Ora has been planning for the last year. Tonight, her oldest son Ilad is getting married, but Ora also celebrates that her youngest son has just finished his obligatory army service—she has been the mother of an Israeli soldier for over ten years straight—a feat I could not imagine. Eight hundred guests arrive for the celebration, a large number by many standards, but not unheard of for a Holy Land wedding. Avigail, the beautiful bride in her long and tight white gown and Ilad, the handsome groom are surrounded by their family and friends and are married by a black hat, religious rabbi who ensures that the wedding is traditional and their union will be legally recognized in the Holy Land. The heat this evening is as palpable as the love and happiness in the night air. After the ceremony, we sit at elegantly decorated tables eating designer food as though we dine at a royal ball. After dinner we make our way into the well air-conditioned indoor hall designed as a dark and smoky night club with a huge central bar full of large and colorful bottles of alcohol, clear drinking glasses, jars full of cigarettes; all around the room buffets serve desert, sushi and roast beef. Videos are shown, speeches are made and the dance floor is full. I am aware that while it is a celebration of Avigail's and Ilad's union and a celebration of freedom from the army—it is also a celebration for every person here tonight that we are ha-zak (strong) and we ki-yem (exist); two vital statements for all Israelis. The festive celebration continues all night long.

Shimon Peres is finally our president and I instantly feel happier. There is a huge sense of relief and proud recognition from the Israeli public that this octogenarian well deserves this honor; Peres is warmly embraced as the Saba of Israel, a leader whom younger generations can look up to and who can ceremonially lead this country to heal and soothe the wounded image and the political corruption that is rampant in the Knesset these days. Peres' character uniquely represents the value of shalom and coexistence with the underlying need for safety and security within the nation's borders.

* * *

On the Nof Yam beach, two fishermen in shorts and t-shirts work to untangle a large net they have laid along the sand full of shells, seaweed and fish that continue to flip flop as they live out the final moments of their existence. Once they clean the net, they return it to the shallow sea for another day and night of activity re-fastening it to the wood beams that jut out from the water.

Aaron wakes early this afternoon at 3pm. After he eats a bowl of cereal and life seeps back into his body, he and his friend Eitan prepare to go swimming. I ask the boys to wait for the pool cover to open all the way before they jump in, but when I look outside, they swim like dolphins under the cover and it freezes half way open. According to the boys, it is mysterious that the cover broke as neither one of them touched anything—another item I add to my end of the year To Do List.

Aaron leaves for camp tomorrow. Selfishly, I am happy that he will be in a safe place where he will have to follow someone else's rules. He will shed his nocturnal existence and actually re-learn what it means to engage in physical activity and fun. Aaron is sad to say goodbye to the incredible freedom that he leaves behind in Israel—I cannot blame him, it is ideal in his teen eyes and exactly what he wants, yet regretfully too much to handle and he does not thrive as a result of it. For Israeli parents, the army arrives at eighteen years of age and helps to guide young Israelis, among many things inherently teaching them about hard work, responsibility and commitment.

At two in the morning I awake from a deep sleep by the front door buzzer. From the intercom I learn that it is Pizza Domino with a delivery. Aaron manages to order pizza and open the side door by his Trump Office, but forgets to mention to the delivery person not to ring the buzzer and wake up the whole house. It is another all-nighter and this time, Aaron, Eitan and Idan play Who Wants to be a Millionaire, a Hebrew board game in the Trump Office eating pizza and drinking Dr Pepper. Aaron leaves for camp tomorrow, I remind myself as I drift back to sleep annoyed at the sleep interruption.

* * *

Wicked Sharav desert windstorms arrive and mix into the already intense summer heat driving up the thermometer. The great humidity holds the heat and dirt together in the air; everything everywhere changes to a sepia color and as I breathe, I taste the unmistakable flavor of soot in the air. There is no escaping this condition for a few days.

As the year winds down to a finish, Kobe's enthusiasm for Kinder Chocolate Eggs does not wane and each time he gets one in his little hands, his face still lights up and his blue eyes sparkle; the clever little guy also has a team of agents working to buy him these eggs; Saba and Safta top the list. Kobe's mini-plastic surprises that he has collected all year line the shelf in his bedroom. They simply have to be colorful and fit neatly in his little hands for control and he is thrilled. I often wish something as simple as a chocolate egg and toy could bring some happiness to my teenage son who once also relished in Kinder Chocolate Eggs.

Late in the night, I drive Aaron to the airport. As happy and relieved as I am that he is leaving to embark on a more productive life, watching my son walk through the final security where I cannot accompany him any further makes me melancholy. All around me are others saying good-bye to their loved ones and I feel very alone. I am frozen in place until well after he passes from my sight, then uncontrollably tears fill my eyes and run down my cheeks.

* * *

'As sands through the hourglass so are the days of our lives,' the opening voice over for the soap opera, Days of our Lives that I used to watch in college comes to my mind, as the top of my hourglass is almost empty. At this point, I cannot skip any visits with my khaver who has offered me freedom and unconditional acceptance all year long. Even after all of my time at the sea, I am in awe of the incredible beauty surrounding me and continue to feel like the most fortunate woman to enjoy such a unique alliance.

While Kobe runs his mini-plastic toy empire and Eden dances hip-hop, the Palestinian children continue to watch the Hamas show, Pioneers of Tomorrow. A new character, Nahoul the bee replaces the martyred mouse Farfour. Nahoul, the yellow and black bee is welcomed to the show by the pretty little girl and as he flies around the set, he clearly explains that his purpose is to continue Farfour's Jihad (Holy War) against the Israeli occupation and to take revenge on the enemies of Allah; the Jews, the Israelis and the Western World.

After my walk and with a clear head, I decide I am ready for my personal jihad—cleaning Aaron's room, which is a job too bloodcurdling to ask of someone else. A few hundred Dr Pepper cans are scattered all over the Donald Trump desk and the floor—needless to say the sculpture I once admired is long gone. I find a milk carton that is half full of black rancid and putrid smelling leftover milk that must have been up on the side shelf for couple of weeks. How did I let so much get out of hand? Truthfully I had smelled a scent over the last week when I poked my head into the room, but I assumed it was dirty socks and the stench of a dark and closed up teenage boy's room. I almost pass out as I remove the milk carton from the shelf and place it in a plastic trash bag. How Aaron could have lived with this stench is unbelievable. Is this simply because he is a teen? Green double mint gum wrappers lie all around the cabinet. An assortment of lighters and coins are left in the many drawers of the Trump desk highlighted by a pack of flavored tobacco for the nargila. Is all of this because we moved for one year to another country? Most of his school papers he ceremoniously burned in an empty lot when school finished, but the remaining ones are still scattered around the room. Am I simply ill equipped to be the mother of a teenage son? My personal jihad continues as I move to his bathroom where he has left piles of hair all over the sink after he shaved his hair short for camp. Around the laundry basket are four white shirts that Aaron upon his departure snapped at me that he could not find. As I clean up, it is more and more apparent that Aaron needs camp. He has not lifted a finger and now he will share a bunk with ten guys where he will not be able to leave a sprawling mess or ignore the counselors. Is this one of those experiences where one day in the future, I will look back and laugh?

Aaron is in a much more productive and stimulating place now. I wish that Palestinian and Israeli teens could join Aaron at camp in California for a few weeks of sports, good times and camaraderie far away from war, mistrust and hateful rhetoric. The majority of youth in this region would benefit and develop with powerful messages of shalom and tolerance in a safe and controlled environment.

* * *

The kibbutz air feels a bit cooler along the tree-lined pathways under the generous branches of old oaks and pines. Cherry Blossom trees full of pink flowers are shadowed with pink patches from the fallen petals. School children on summer vacation ride skateboards and bikes along the narrow paths and they do not seem bothered by the crazy heat. Kobe runs from the car eager to play with his friends as though my little man feels time closing in on him as well.

Three wise men;

"I wake up each morning and am happy to be alive and healthy. I love my family. I love my country. People need to speak to each other and everything will be okay." These are the unsolicited words of a gas station attendant I meet for the first time this morning. He does not seem bothered by the monotonous job of filling gas tanks and washing car windows in the vicious sun. I leave my window down and continue to listen to this inspiring older man share his philosophy on happiness, shalom and life. I catch a glimpse of his aged grin from underneath his tattered baseball cap and I can't help but smile in his presence; I know that this simple man has the right ideas for people, Israel and the world full of complicated problems that start and escalate because people stop talking and stop smiling.

"My vision is a homeland for the Palestinians with territorial contiguity, a state where the inhabitants are proud to be part of the international community," the words of appointed Palestinian Prime Minister Sayad Fayad, formerly the Palestinian finance minister who has a PHD in economics from the University of Houston, worked at the World Bank and was raised in a West Bank village. "We are under occupation and the roadblock soldier has more power than a minister in my government. I am not asking anyone for an open check. I am saying that we are prepared and we are serious and just let us function. They see that you (Israelis) are continuing to build in the settlements and on the other hand they can't move freely in their own territories. This is pathological and it is no wonder that people are losing faith in the peace process."

"I shall be committed to nurture unceasingly those fine threads of fabric, which weave us together as a nation, when among us there are people with various opinions who fiercely fight for them. It must always be remembered that we are the sons and daughters of one Land of Israel. We do not have, and we are not looking for, another country." These words are from the new Israeli President, Shimon Peres' inaugural speech.

Israeli President Shimon Peres and Palestinians President Mahmoud Abbas were the two men who signed the Oslo Accord in Washington D.C. in 1994. Now as the Israeli President and the Palestinian President, I naively hope for another signature for shalom, but it can only succeed if the gas station attendants are also part of the process.

* * *

It is so bloody hot that I start physically to see heat floating in the air. Long lines of cars and buses queue to enter the parking lot to the kibbutz' water park each day filling the normally vacant road. The water park is full of giant slides and large pools—a summer oasis for Israelis and Kobe who begs daily to be taken there.

Eden's dance debut finally arrives. She performs as a French waitress in a ballet and then in a Lion King hip-hop dance dressed in an oversized lion costume. Eden moves naturally to the music and from the audience I can feel her pride and share her personal success. She made it all happen on her own this year; she was a seven-year old in a class full of ten-year old girls, not fluent in Hebrew and tagged as the foreigner yet she forged her way and once the music played and she started to move, she found her place with the girls who once did not give her the time of day. Tonight she seizes command of her performance and dances with great pleasure before an audience of thousands. As I watch all the performances, I imagine dance schools opening along the border of Israel and the West Bank and Gaza where small children and teenagers take dance classes together in peace centers and find a safe haven to express and share their feelings together through body movement and music. At the end of each session, thousands of parents; Jews, Muslims and Christians would sit together in a theater and watch their children share a stage and perform; within the magic of the arts, slowly these different people might shed their differences.

Sadly I know as my daughter and hundreds of young girls celebrate a years worth of dance study, the children of Gaza are exposed to a purely propagandist television show called The Pioneers of Tomorrow. The title of this week's show is 'Jews are Murderers'. Nahoul the bee is indignant that the Jews killed Farfour, his cousin the mouse, and he plans to continue on his path until he liberates Al-Aqsa and all of Palestine. During the show, a young Palestinian boy calls in and announces that he wants to be a journalist when he grows up and Nahoul enthusiastically tells him that this is very good, as it will allow him to show the killing of Farfour and little children by the Israelis. In the same piece, he encourages the small children to go and make jihad when they grow up. Dancing and singing?

Or Jihad? This should not be the question for children anywhere in the world.

* * *

Swift birds have arrived in Jerusalem's Old City making holy summer homes in the cracks of the sacred Western Wall along with pigeons, jackdaws and sparrows. Swift birds are remarkable; they remain airborne for ten months of the year eating and sleeping during periods of travel and then they come down for the remaining two months on their atrophied legs to nest in the Western Wall or in cliffs. These swift birds have been in flight for almost my entire tenure in the Holy Land and as they settle down, I prepare to leave.

Not far from the swift birds' assembly in the Old City, Palestinian President Mahmoud Abbas meets PM Ehud Olmert at his Jerusalem residence to discuss the release of two hundred and fifty prisoners and agree on a ban of unauthorized weapons in the West Bank. One hundred and eighty Fatah men on Israel's list of 'wanted men' agree to turn in weapons in exchange for the Israelis promise not to hunt them down. President Abbas calls on PM Olmert to continue humanitarian aid to Gaza where he is not the leader, but knows that hundreds of thousands of Palestinians are suffering under a Hamas regime. Due to terrorist threats, the Israelis have closed the Karni Crossing between Gaza and Israel stopping trade and commerce at this border, while at the open Rafah Crossing between Gaza and Egypt smugglers bring weapons into Gaza.

Hamas terrorists continue to send Qassam Rockets into Israel daily— today one rocket lands on a house in Sderot.

* * *

Cold watermelon and frozen popsicles are a brief respite from the punishing summer heat. The Mediterranean Seawater and the pool water are naturally quite warm and Eden ponders why there are no pool coolers and how much ice would be required to bring down the temperature of

233

the water. Yehuda works late and rarely wants dinner after traditionally long and leisurely lunch meetings; many evenings I take Eden and Kobe to the frigid malls where the cool air revives the appetite and the body.

PM Olmert is about to release hundreds of Palestinian prisoners who are all required to sign a letter that they will not deal in terror, but he has a few very vocal Knesset members who are opposed to this deal. The Knesset also opposes subsidizing the increase in bread costs for the poor, which results in a severe shortage of bread in the country. The intensity and quantity of the news in this country still makes me crazy, but time has calmed the storm of passion and once again, I understand how many Israelis can prescribe to, 'Al-ti-da-gee' and 'Ha kol yi-he-yay be-seder'.

* * *

A slender gray haired man with a long white beard does a free form handstand; his legs bent like lightening bolts out in different directions from his white diaper shorts. A few minutes later, this muscular and svelte Jewish Gandhi dark brown from the endless hours of sun is tossing a Frisbee with a partner. Admiring this gentleman I am reminded that I need to slow down again and focus. Life has sped me up and I feel as though I am on a whirlwind. I pack up the entire house, which is no simple feat. The apartment is not finished and the construction will have to proceed without us. In the meantime, I arrange to send all of our belongings to a storage facility on a nearby kibbutz to wait for the apartment to be completed.

* * *

Dov Airport is a small one-room building packed with boisterous Israelis on their way to Eilat. After checking in, a shuttle bus takes us to the very small airplane parked a short distance from the terminal building. We board the plane from the rear on a small set of accordion style stairs and slither through the narrow aisle to our cramped seats. The Arkia plane is like a shuttle bus; once the last passenger is aboard and the door is shut, the pilot taxies and takes off all in one motion. We rise over the sparkling

Mediterranean and then fly inland over Jerusalem and surrounding villages and cities in the vast arid desert lands. From the air, I can tell which developments are Jewish and which are Arab simply by the layout of the housing; the houses in Jewish areas are lined up in an orderly pattern, while the Arabs houses are scattered at random. I am sure we fly over Jewish settlements that continue to expand in Palestinian lands and fuel more anger and divisiveness in any peace plan for a two state solution. We pass the Dead Sea and then fly over the vast Negev Desert along the border with Jordan where the winds bounce the plane around. After fifty minutes, I spot Eilat's fancy hotels along the gulf of the Red Sea and the rows of houses that line the surrounding hillsides. As the plane touches down, we pass the bright wall of the Eilat BIG Shopping Center and I think of my husband who is in Spain for business. We step out of the very small plane and are literally hit by a force of shockingly intense dry heat.

We are staying at the Dan, one of the fancy hotels along the Bay of Eilat that I had spotted from the airplane's tiny window. The huge air-conditioned lobby is full of guests and outside by the giant pool there are hundreds of Israelis lounging and swimming. Eden and Kobe practically change into their bathing suits as we stand in line to check in, not wanting to miss a moment of sun and fun.

In the late afternoon, Noa, Jessie, Kobe, Eden and I arrive to the Ha-vat Ga-mal (Camel Ranch), nestled in the rolling desert hills above Eilat. In one corral on the hillside, a flock of proud camels congregates and in another enclosure, a ranch worker feeds a group of dark homely burros. At the center of the farm, we walk up a set of stairs to a narrow but high landing to mount the enormous creatures standing saddled and waiting for us comfortable in the oven hot air. Kobe and I mount the lead beauty, Gabriella and everyone else rides her own camel. Riding these desert monarchs is awesome and inspiring, even though they walk very slowly with an uncomfortable rhythm. I think about Yehuda who spent weeks riding a camel after the 6-Day War (1967) when his troop surveyed the Sinai desert territories they captured from Egypt, which with Jordan, Syria and Lebanon attacked their small nation. We make our way through the wadi (desert basin), which is the driest place in all of Israel receiving only seven centimeters of rainfall annually. As the sun disappears and the wadi becomes shaded, the temperature drops and the hills move from orange to midnight blue and then to chocolate brown. The leader, Etay is a skinny young man from Tel Aviv, who wears a Bedouin head wrap, loose clothing and sandals. Etay shares with us the story of how camels got their humps, he tells us that when G-d was giving all the animals their traits—the camel arrived late. G-d asked the camel to think hard about what she would like if he could still perform this one act. She thought for a bit and asked for the ability to live and move for long periods of time without needing to eat and drink. G-d gave the camel a hump where she would be able to store supplies. She was very pleased to receive her request; however, the other animals laughed and made fun of her hump, which caused her to run far off to the desert where it was peaceful and she would not be harassed—from this time on, she chose to stay in the desert.

The beautiful Acacia Trees scattered in the barren wadi remind me of the locale in the Lion King movie where the great stampede took place endangering the life of King Simba. Etay explains that camels eat the Acacia tree seeds, which are released and pollinated by their feces, and nourished by the water from flash floods. There is very little water in these parts as there are not many flash floods and this produces few Acacia trees. Jessie spots a brown desert fox that walks along the crevice of the rocky cliffs above where our pack travels. The thin and nimble fox moves quickly and disappears behind a mountain crevice a few seconds later. We return to the ranch sitting on Bedouin rugs under a large tent for our desert meal. Etay places chopped vegetables, cheeses and lebane on low flat tables in front of us and we watch him prepare the pita dough; first he mixes the flour, the salt and water in a metal bowl, then he gently kneads and spreads the dough on the round open ta-boon placed over a hot fire. Within minutes the soft doughy pita is cooked to perfection and we eat it with the cheeses and the lebane and drink small glasses of hot tea. I know it is a completely fabricated experience, but I love every minute; the warm dark night, the desert shadows, the fresh food and the female camels.

* * *

Excited Israelis surround the hotel's many buffet stations and fill their large plates with endless tempting and caloric free food. The breakfast is included in the room price and therefore this is a feast that all Israelis take seriously; they over eat and try everything. Waiters serving coffee and clearing plates dodge small children running in aisles already crowded by strollers and overflowing beach bags with a symphony of loud ringing cell phones in the background—all this commotion and it is not even nine in the morning. Kobe at five-years old fits in perfectly with the Israelis, his little voice releasing the word, "sle-kha" (excuse me) as he squeezes through the crowds for his Milkie (an Israeli chocolate pudding with whipped cream) and two pieces of cheese pizza. Eden, on the other hand, is intimidated by crowds and cannot navigate without my help. We sit outside in the morning heat to avoid the frigid air and boisterous Israelis but are quickly overtaken by the smokers' smoke.

We spend the entire morning at the vast swimming pool where Kobe wears floaties like the other small children and is thrilled by his autonomy; he and Eden swim round and round in the whirlpool and slide down the giant water slide. Quickly the water fills literally to the brim with Israelis on holiday pushing and screaming and enjoying the water and the heat. Noa and Jessie are nowhere to be found—asleep and avoiding us.

Late in the afternoon, Eden and I leave Kobe with the sleepy teens and take a cab to the Dolphinarium to swim with the dolphins in celebration of her upcoming 9th birthday. In our wet suits wearing masks and snorkels, we enter into the refreshing Red Sea to join beautiful gray marine mammals that swim by us, under us and around us—one by the name Sheba keeps coming over to Anat, our leader, for attention and to be caressed. Eden is in heaven and keeps squeezing my hand with delight; the high-pitched calls of the dolphins underwater are exhilarating. The wet suit keeps us afloat to enjoy our new friends and the large schools of multi-colored fish that swim around us. Along the sea floor, black and round sea cucumbers hang out, but seem not to move. Why do I think of my teenagers at the sight of the sea cucumbers? After the swim, Anat tells Eden the story of Sheba, the affectionate dolphin who kept swimming by us. She is the three-year old daughter of Nana, who now has Enzo, a male baby and only pays attention to him; this leaves Sheba feeling neglected and she is teased by the other dolphins. Anat feels terrible for her but knows that she cannot fix the situation and must let Sheba resolve it on her own, which over time will make her a stronger adult dolphin. I look at Eden who commenced this year feeling abandoned in a new environment and had to make it work more or less on her own; a personal success story she will carry throughout the rest of her life.

Back at the hotel, I stand on the balcony and look out at the Bay of Eilat. To the East, not many miles away, is the city of Aqaba with buildings mirroring Eilat on the Jordanian side of the Red Sea. In my fairytale brain, I wish I could walk through Aqaba eating Jordanian humus and pita and seeing and feeling the people. I would visit the market place where my imagination leads me to dream that I could discover the movie character Aladdin hiding. In the distant South I see the blue mountains of Egypt, another nation with whom we have a peace treaty and hence, can visit her beautiful Sinai beaches and ancient cities, but where the fear of suicide bombs and targeted attacks on Westerners and Israelis looms in the air. Once we fought bitterly with these nations and now we have peace treaties void of an amicable relationship between the people on both sides of the border, but they allow people to live their lives and not be pawns in war games. Unlike with the Palestinians, these territories were easier to define and their borders made cleaner separation possible. Further south of Jordan is Saudi Arabia, a nation Israel does not fight with, but which will not make public shalom with us.

That night, I walk with Eden and Kobe and mobs of enthusiastic and energetic Israelis along the dry and sizzling hot boardwalk packed with restaurants and retail stores tucked under hotels selling beachwear, Bedouin pants, sunglasses and toys; snack stands selling falafels, pizzas, sandwiches and icy flavored drinks; a giant ride throwing people in a ball up and down on huge bungee strings, smaller amusement park rides and stands of henna tattoo artists with large displays as well as Ethiopian women braiding little girls' hair. The heat may be oppressive but the excitement of the crowds is contagious. I hold the soft little hands of Eden and Kobe who want to dart out in all directions to experience and buy everything in sight.

Late at night, the noise of techno music enters through my sealed shut windows from the boardwalk that is still alive with Israelis enjoying the nighttime excitement. Eden and Kobe exhausted from a long day in the hot sun fall asleep quickly. I crawl into bed with my iPod and watch The Starter Wife, a new show I downloaded from iTunes. From my hotel bed in Eilat, I escape the perilous Middle East and enter the plastic world of a divorced Hollywood executive's wife in Malibu, California. Two different worlds and their inherent dangers are extreme, but I am in a land where this feels natural.

* * *

I finish a swim in the naturally heated pool and remain in my wet bathing suit while I clean out cupboards in the warm kitchen—the air-conditioning is not working again. Within minutes, the pool water on my body simply transforms into sweat. In one cabinet, I discover stacks of Kobe's art work; a years worth of white papers, formally folded khallah art bags crinkled and spotted with crumbs, portraying my Kobe's creations as they mark his transition from resisting artwork to drawing with bright and happy colors. I cannot bring myself to throw out my little Picasso's artwork. I have learned from the camp's website that Aaron far away in California has resumed his basketball career, he has a smile on his tan face and his six pack is back—a testament to what being awake and active during the day can do for a fourteen-year old boy in a loving structured environment away from his wicked mother.

I continue my work in the kitchen by attacking a set of drawers that remind me of yet another of my maternal weaknesses; hundreds of ketchup packs from Mc Donalds, other packets with Soy Sauce and Wasabi from Kyoto Sushi and plenty of chopsticks, napkins and forks from Giraffe Restaurant—"I did cook didn't I?" I ask myself. Slowly the house thins out—photo frames are gone, vases are packed up, artwork is wrapped up, unused toys donated to Wizo Center around the corner, catalogues and brochures are tossed, color and texture disappear, the loneliness of the creamy white castle returns.

That same afternoon, I walk through South Tel Aviv with my decorator, Alex, looking for apartment furnishings. South Tel Aviv usually bustles with people and energy, but this sizzling summer day people appear to be in hiding, the old narrow streets are empty, void of the commotion and customary cars and trucks blocking traffic to deliver packages. We start at a small shop selling knobs, handles and hooks and then walk down the street to Kastiel, a five-story boutique of beautiful hand crafted furniture, paintings by Israeli artists, unique home accessories and sculptures from Europe and Asia all exhibited in an ancient building with tiny stairwells. I finish my day at the large new furniture design center where I buy beds and mattresses for the new apartment.

* * *

Tisha B'Av (the ninth day of the Hebrew month of Av) is commemorated throughout the country; Orthodox Jews fast as they mourn the saddest day in Jewish history marking the destruction of the 1st Temple in 586 B.C.E. in Jerusalem and miraculously on the same date 656 years later when the 2nd Temple was destroyed in the same location. On this holiday, religious Jews do not greet friends and family behaving in the same manner as though sitting Shiva (the mourning period after the death of a family member). For secular Jews, the main reminder of this important date on the Jewish calendar is the closure this night of all food and entertainment establishments as dictated by law.

I place two copies of the new Harry Potter novel on the desk in Noa's room where she and Jessie are fast asleep. The books arrived at midnight in the Holy Land and they quickly work their magic—at the early hour of 12 noon I am startled to find the door to Noa's room open and inside with the air-conditioning blasting, the girls are reading the new novels.

While we have grown and changed as a family, my beloved Israel is afflicted with the same problems we encountered a year ago and which have plagued the Jewish state for many years. PM Ehud Olmert continues to speak with President Abbas of Fatah with no apparent progress; Former British Prime Minister Tony Blair spends time in the Holy Land trying to breathe energy into a peace plan; Israeli Jewish settlers in the West Bank continue to expand and build new settlements—just this week thousands of religious settlers marched to the illegal and abandoned settlement of Horesh with bricks in hand to build a temple for a second time; Jewish settlers fight with Palestinians from neighboring villages in the West Bank; Palestinians in the West Bank fight IDF soldiers at roadblocks with stones and fists; Hezbollah re-arms in Southern Lebanon; Hamas terrorists from Gaza send Qassam Rockets into Sderot and surrounding areas daily while digging tunnels through the desert to replenish weapons for more attacks; one Qassam arrives in Ashkelon, which is further away and proves that the terrorists can penetrate deeper into Israel; Iranian President Ahmadinejad continues his call for the destruction of the Jewish State and funds Hezbollah and Hamas to assist in these efforts while building nuclear weaponry; domestic stories of political corruption still make the news and a public sector strike commences—airports and railways are closed, as well as government offices, garbage collection, ports and postal services. Yehuda is in Mumbai and I hope he can get back to spend the last few days with the family before we depart for L.A.

$$* * *$$

Eden and I take a break from all the packing and stop to eat humus, falafel and pita at one of the warm outdoor restaurants along the marina's vibrant boardwalk filled with multitudes of summer visitors. The greatest indicator that summer is in full bloom is made evident by the return in mass of multi-bright colored Croc footwear. My daughter takes great pleasure in her food and I in her company and conversation listening intently as she imparts to me her delightfully naive nine-year old life's observations. Over her shoulder, I dubiously observe the Ethiopian security guard across the plaza as he checks people and their bags before granting them access from the parking lot. I still harbor the fear that the guard does not satisfactorily perform his duty and will let danger in, but the day is peaceful and glorious. Soaking in all the splendid summer activity here at the marina, it is almost inconceivable that bombs land and the threat of war looms. After we finish our Israeli feast, we pass a group dressed in bright orange life jackets preparing to go out to sea. We are tempted to put on a jacket ourselves and join them, but instead make our way hand in hand into the bright and shiny mall where we are welcomed by shockingly cold air. I admire how Eden finds exciting a meal of humus and pita, a sailboat full of strangers and crowds in a loud and hectic mall. I have cherished these last few weeks spending a great deal of time with Eden, my helicopter child, my hip-hop star and the child who I think had the roughest entry into Israel and made the greatest strides over the year.

* * *

I arrive to visit my khaver early and encounter gray clouds looming over the peaceful shore. The fresh morning air feels wonderful on my bare skin. The sounds of my breath and of the water unite serenading me as I walk slowly absorbing the salt air that tingles my tired body. Kobe was in my bed last night moving all over the place, his little body sensitive and aware that we are about to make another big change.

Yehuda slips back into Israel during a temporary ceasefire from the latest strikes to plague the nation. Eden works at Yehuda's office with his assistants Karen and Racheli who enjoy her company even though her constant conversation prevents them from their actual work. Kobe languishes with Gordon and his buddies at the kibbutz. Noa finished Harry Potter and has resumed her nocturnal life, coming out of her room late in the afternoon for coffee and fresh air. I visit Aaron daily on the camp's website and have concluded from the few photos he allows himself to be in that his re-entry has been a success. I spend many of my final hours in solitude, a theme I have become very comfortable with over the last year. My mind is finally free of clutter and I can think clearly once again. These days, I can actually remember and recite with clarity my thoughts, conversations and activities from the day before.

I have been married to an Israeli for eighteen years and have spent a great deal of time in Israel, but this year I bonded with the country. I traveled many territories of my gi-bor-ah and while it is not a large country, what it lacks in size, it makes up for in both quality and quantity—the characters, the ancient and modern attractions, the real and surreal rides and the divine refreshments make this country an adventurous and unforgettable destination. I appreciate even more the struggle to survive that runs through the veins of proud Israelis who daily put their lives on the line in many ways to honor and protect the country's existence. Even with the surrounding political corruption and hate, this is a nation that succeeds and smiles, an oasis, flourishing in a desert both literally and physically.

* * *

As the last grains of my sand clock slowly fall to the bottom half of the cylinder, I begin to make my rounds to say shalom and give my final hugs to my local friends. At the kikar, I buy the last schnitzel and say goodbye to Yigal, who asks when I will be back, but is more curious to know how I can leave such a wonderful country. I buy my ultimate overpriced pomelite and container of pomegranate seeds from Momy, and hear him call me "Mademoiselle Naftali" as he finishes a cigarette. I slice my last loaf of bread from Lechem Erez, one bread shop that is not affected by the bread strike and I purchase a few plastic Pokémon eggs from the machine in front of Gilgi's toy store to give Kobe on the airplane. Before I leave the kikar, I pay a final visit to my friend Oren at the pharmacy who reminds me that I did not play tennis this year. I concede the fact that I did not achieve all I had intended, but I accomplished a great many things. I have come to realize a year is actually a strikingly short amount of time and when carefully measured its brevity is daunting.

* * *

The evening air is warm and comfortable and streaks of orange and purple fill the sky as the sun begins its decent out in the Mediterranean. We walk along the beach still alive with activity in the early evening to celebrate Eden's 9th birthday at Yam Sheva restaurant with her friends, Katie from Australia, Jade from London and Eran from Israel. They walk ahead of us and independent Kobe brings up the rear. Where else in the world I tell myself could I walk from my house along the beautiful sandy beach to a fish restaurant built into the cliff so leisurely as though I am in my own backyard? Saba, Safta and Noa drive to the restaurant and join us for dinner. Eden and her friends giggle and speak in both Hebrew and English while they eat from plates full of schnitzel and fries. Currently when Noa is awake she is mad at me for making her leave Israel, but Saba and Safta as always are inebriated with love and happiness to be with their family. After the children finish eating, they walk down a few steps to the sand to play while we slowly savor our grilled fish and glasses of chilled Golan white wine. We walk home along the dark and cooler beach illuminated by the moon's shining path.

* * *

I stand in front of the kitchen sink imparting a few final words to my two remaining aquatic buddies, Dr Pepper and Mimi as they swim in their fish bowls. It is silly but I will actually miss my kitchen companions who have listened to me on many occasions offering unconditional support while fighting the odds and remaining alive. Shortly my friend Maya will pick them up and take them to live with her. The pots and pans, plates and silverware are all packed up and later in the day the cappuccino machine and water dispenser will be taken away leaving the kitchen bare.

I go to the office to pick up Eden, whom I discover eating lunch with her adult friends and speaking Hebrew. I stand outside the lunchroom and eavesdrop taking pleasure in her Hebrew fluency. Even Eden at the American School improved her Hebrew this year as she studied with her Hebrew teacher Nomi and spoke to her Safta.

I take a look around the office and admire the white walls decorated with photos of BIG Shopping Centers from all over Eretz Israel. For the last 4000 years, many great leaders have conquered Israel—why should my husband be any different? He arrived in this underdeveloped country at the age of six as a poor Iraqi immigrant, welcomed by spray to exterminate any reminders of the old country and to live in a tent on the sand dunes of Hadera. He was molded by a strong single mother in his early years on a socialistic kibbutz; herded sheep and cultivated the land;

and then he spent years jumping out of airplanes while fighting for his nation's survival. He escaped Israel for many adult years, returning as a modern day subjugator with his BIG Shopping Center's retail hold on the country from Eilat in the South to Nehariya in the North. My 21st Century Middle Eastern conquistador has worked longer hours this year than I expected—his burning passion and difficult labor evident daily in our lives

* * *

The air is hot and salty, but each step refreshes me. I am well aware that in a few days, I shall need to say shalom to my most faithful khaver which has seen me though the challenges with the children, the creamy white castle, the country and my life in general. This morning as I walk under the Mosque, I come face to face with the chief of the beach elders, a character whom I have observed leading the group partaking in lively breakfast feasts each morning on the yellow plastic furniture. A partner usually accompanies him, but today he walks alone with his golden retriever. When we meet today, he says, "Boker tov" and I reply, "Boker ya-fay" (Beautiful morning). He asks in Hebrew if he can join me and within twenty minutes this man has shared his life story, the joy the beach brings him each morning and the pride he feels to live in this amazing land. He finally asks my name and after I ask his. "Chaim" (pronounced kha-eem), he responds. His name strikes me as most profound and significant— Cha-im means 'Life', which Israelis celebrate, honor and respect with great passion and pride. I have met Chaim just in the nick of time. At Shablul Restaurant Chaim invites me to join the other for breakfast. It is not seven in the morning and my day oddly feels complete.

* * *

Tonight is Eden's true 9th birthday. We have been invited to have dinner at the home of Tariq, an associate of Yehuda's who resides with his family in the Arab village near to Tel Aviv. It is a bit odd to celebrate her birthday with strangers, but Eden started her merriment a few days earlier and plans to continue when she arrives to L.A. I have a feeling that this dinner will probably be the most memorable of all the celebratory events. Noa begrudgingly joins us after I promise we will be home early enough for her to go out with friends.

Tariq, his wife and four beautiful daughters roughly the ages of my children, warmly greet us at the door when we arrive. Tariq knows that we are leaving Israel in a couple of days and is all the happier that we took him up on his dinner invitation. He has just returned from the United States where he spent a month touring and promoting his work on Arab—Jewish dialogue. Tariq's wife is a successful businesswoman. I enter the house thinking there must be something different—they are Arabs and we are Jews. We have been conditioned to believe that we are different. As I look around, I pleasantly discover that an Arab house inside pretty much looks like a Jewish house. Their dining room table is beautifully covered in lace linens and china dishes and within minute, plates of food arrive served by the two older daughters. Tariq proudly shares that he has cooked many of the dishes—okay I find a difference, Yehuda never cooks dinner. The food is abundant and very good; I am prepared to fill my plate because I know if I don't it will be an insult to our hosts. While the children eat quietly, the adults speak as old friends meeting for a familiar meal and carrying on typical conversations about work, children, travel and daily life. Tariq asks Noa is she has liked living in Israel this year and for the first time this evening my daughter comes alive; her chocolate brown eyes shimmer as she quickly expresses her desire to stay in Israel. However, she cannot muster up any conversation with Tariq's oldest daughter who is her age. The little girls only speak Arabic, but for Kobe this is not a barrier and he happily leaves the table to watch television in Arabic and play in Arabic. Eden is glued to me. After dinner the older daughters clear the table—okay, I conceded this is another big difference, but again not racial or ethnic in nature.

After dinner we sit in one corner of the living room that in typical Middle Eastern style is lined with couches to comfortably accommodate a large group of guests. The daughters place platters filled with fruit and dessert on the one large coffee table followed by tea served in dainty glass cups that remind me of Aunt Shula. We continue to talk and there is no shortage of subjects. After awhile, Noa looks at me and rolls her eyes indicating that she is ready to leave. Yehuda and Tariq are embroiled in a deep conversation and as it comes to a lull, I suggest it is late and we need to get going. Tariq extricates Kobe from the upstairs. We leave and promise to meet again when we are back in Israel.

* * *

Today is my final goodbye ceremony with my dear khaver. I enjoy each step in the sand and savor each breath of fresh salty air with a smile as the gentle waves wash to shore. My final picture is perfect; the sky is a faded blue; a few lone surfers wade out in the powerless waves; a group of sailboats with white sails congregate in the distance; two motionless fishermen stand next to their poles staring out to sea; some beach regulars pass me; one lone silver pup tent graces the Northern beach; and patches of tempting shells and rocks are scattered on the sand. The beach of Herzelia Pituah is simply beautiful. I am thankful and appreciative that I have had this treasure to delight in as part of my unique journey this year. I walk up the stairs and half way up I turn around and look out to the sea and say, "Shalom khaver."

The moving company comes to take away the packed boxes containing all the remnants of this year that we will open one day with pleasure in the new apartment. I walk through the very hollow creamy white castle thinking about the stories that unfolded in the rooms, absorbing the life that existed here and find remarkable the passage of time and the impossibility to hold on to all that moves so fast and cannot be contained.

I sit with Achinoam and her husband Asher at lunch in a small outdoor restaurant just beyond the fields of the kibbutz and before the cliffs of the Mediterranean. Achinoam prepares to leave for a European tour. Asher, a pediatrician describes his new work on a medical Internet site. We talk about what it takes to pick up and move a whole family across the world for a year. It is hard work but it is exciting. I believe the rewards for my children will blossom over the years to come in many ways. We are all different people from those who arrived to the Holy Land a few days after the war one year ago. It is terribly hot and I can barely eat. While it is sad to leave the life I created here for my family this year, I am excited to return to L.A. I am thankful for this last lunch with my new friends in the fields of the kibbutz I watched over so carefully.

I pick up Kobe from the gan for the final time. Kobe gives Alona and Yamit big hugs, and a final bear hug to Gordon and tears well up in my eyes as his little body is affectionately enveloped in Gordon's big teddy bear body. Kobe has been at home on the kibbutz this year; I recognize that these fine people and the kibbutz have played a huge role in my child's growth. He gives Ayehli a big hug, and Ore and Ilad too. Eli gives Kobe a paper book he has drawn full of colorful imaginary creatures and Pokémon that Kobe holds tight; he loves and admires the artwork of his dear friend on the kibbutz. They lovingly hug one last time. Kobe and I walk hand in hand to the car and tears drip down my cheeks. Kobe is melancholy, but alive with pride and full of love. He knows in a way far beyond his years that he has accomplished so much and feels confident that he will always have a place with his friends on the kibbutz.

Eden and Kobe take a final swim in the naturally over-heated pool. They take final rides in the mirrored elevator that I have reminded them all year is not to be played on.

Safta and Saba spend the last few hours with us at the empty creamy white castle. Saba plays Pokémon with Kobe while Safta cries a great deal as she prepares for our departure. She thanks me over and over again for bringing the family to Israel this year. They have enjoyed the children immensely and will miss them tremendously. The children have been blessed to share this year with their grandparents, enjoying unconditional love, respect and lots of chicken and cheesecake.

I return to my original hope that my family would enjoy and benefit from this experience and I believe we all have, and we will continue to be surprised by what it brings. It is also safe to say, we all fell a little more in love with this nation over the year.

The creamy white castle is empty as we found it, but it is not sad anymore. Life was lived within its walls, stories were told in its rooms, and our family shared a unique year's adventure within its structure. I will miss this place as I carry the amazing journey with me back to Los Angeles. I do not say 'back home' because Israel is also 'home'.

New Years Evening 2009

We have returned to Israel for the winter holidays.

Many changes have transpired in our family; Noa joins us from Boston where she is a freshman in University; Aaron, a high school junior, has started to take his studies more seriously and is more present in our lives; Eden dances hip-hop and prepares for her Bat Mitzvah next summer in Jerusalem; and Kobe impresses us with his latest passions as a Lego technician and junior Laker team coach. The winter weather is mild and each day I visit my khaver for long walks and return in the afternoon to watch as Kobe and Eden surf the mild waves; Noa and Aaron have resumed their Israeli vacation life—awake at night and sleeping most of the day. I continue to question the affects of our year living in Israel; however, it is very apparent that the children's dual citizenships and rich backgrounds are very important in all of their lives. Yehuda's BIG Shopping Centers flourish; the most recent opening is a life style shopping center in the heart of Nazareth frequented by the local Arabs and Jews.

Tonight we are the guests of our Arab partners in the Nazareth BIG Shopping Center bringing in the New Year together at a dinner club full of celebratory Jews, Christians and Muslims. I am thrilled to be part of this merriment where the message of co-existence and mutual respect is vibrant as we ring in the new year and the new decade together; the party goers eat, drink, dance and embrace and count down the last 10 seconds of the year in unison and with great delight.

While I personally experience successful co-existence in Nazareth, I am cognizant that many of the same stories and themes still resonate in Israel and not enough significant progress has taken place over the last few years in the quest for a broader co-existence and shalom. The great Yitzhak Rabin said, "We must think differently, look at things in a different way. Peace requires a world of new concepts, new definitions," and this still rings true today. I have to believe that the collaboration of Jews, Muslims and Christians to create a shopping center where the Jewish and Muslim citizens of Israel eat, shop and congregate collectively is one part of the dynamic process as we venture forward on this difficult path. I remain an optimist in my personal journey and that of my giborah, equipped for whatever may come my way with the comforting expressions 'Al-ti-da-gee' and 'Ha kol yi-he-yay be-seder'.

* * *

Some names in this book have been changed to protect the identity of these people living in Israel.